VIRGINIA WOOLF AND
POSTMODERNISM

# Virginia Woolf

---

## & Postmodernism

### *Literature in Quest & Question of Itself*

incl. intrôd. *pref. &*

PAMELA L. CAUGHIE

xvii, 236
1991
0-252-06158-6

UNIVERSITY OF ILLINOIS PRESS
Urbana and Chicago

*This book is printed on acid-free paper.*

Library of Congress Cataloging-in-Publication Data

Caughie, Pamela L.
Virginia Woolf and postmodernism : literature in quest and
question of itself / Pamela L. Caughie.
p.  cm.
Includes bibliographical references and index.
ISBN 0-252-01763-3 (cl : alk. paper). — ISBN 0-252-06158-6 (pb : alk. paper)
1. Woolf, Virginia, 1882–1941—Criticism and interpretation.
2. Postmodernism (Literature)—Great Britain. 3. Postmodernism (Literature).
4. Feminism and literature. 5. Narration (Rhetoric). I. Title.
PR6045.O72Z567   1991
823'.912—dc20                                                    90-11174
                                                                    CIP

*To the Feminist Theory Group,*
*University of Virginia,*
*1984–86*

Is it better to be a coal-heaver or a nursemaid; is the charwoman who has brought up eight children of less value to the world than the barrister who has made a hundred thousand pounds? It is useless to ask such questions; for nobody can answer them. Not only do the comparative values of charwomen and lawyers rise and fall from decade to decade, but we have no rods with which to measure them even as they are at the moment.

—Virginia Woolf,
*A Room of One's Own*

Our clear and simple language-games are not preparatory studies for a future regularization of language. . . . [They] are rather set up as *objects of comparison* which are meant to throw light on the facts of our language by way not only of similarities, but also of dissimilarities. . . . we can avoid ineptness or emptiness in our assertions only by presenting the model as what it is, as an object of comparison—as, so to speak, a measuring-rod; not as a preconceived ideal to which reality *must* correspond.

—Ludwig Wittgenstein,
*Philosophical Investigations*

This may not answer the question, but one way of dealing with these problems . . . is to try to do both things at the same time, to occupy two places, both places. That is why deconstruction is often accused of being conservative and . . . not conservative. And both are true! We have to negotiate. . . . And what is the measure? You must check everyday what is the measure. . . . There is no general device.

—Jacques Derrida,
"Women in the Beehive"

# Contents

# Preface

Anyone writing on Virginia Woolf today should specify the reasons for doing so. Why Woolf? Why now? In this preface, I begin to answer these questions by explaining what this book is not and what it attempts to do. For more important than what this work tells us about Virginia Woolf and postmodernism is how it proceeds.

My purpose is *not* to claim Virginia Woolf as a postmodern writer, one who has been wrongly classified as a modernist and who is now to gain her rightful place in literary history. Nor do I merely sort out the distinguishing features of postmodern writing—loss of authorial control, metafictional remarks, contradictions, suspended endings—and note these in Woolf's novels. In fact, it is against these kinds of readings, ones that categorize texts or writers based on shared features, that this book has come into being.

What gave rise to this book were my responses to reading about Virginia Woolf and postmodernism in the early to mid-1980s. I felt dissatisfied with readings of Woolf that claimed to be new, even subversive, yet ultimately relied on assumptions about fiction they had hoped to dispel. Similarly, I was uncomfortable with broad applications of the postmodern label to the writings of Woolf and other modern novelists that merely singled out specific features in their works without also providing a new way of reading these writers. As a result, I wanted to explore the relations between Woolf's textual experiments and current theories of language and narrative, using her works to question the relations among modernism, postmodernism, and feminism in narrative discourse.

One problem facing feminist criticism today is a problem Woolf wrestled with in her own writings: how to resist and change the dominant tradition in literature, and in society, without establishing a new (alternative, oppositional, counter) tradition, which can become just as restrictive, repressive, authoritative. The answer, for Woolf and for feminist critics, lies not in reconciling, balancing, or choosing between two positions but in enacting, over and over again, certain ways of proceeding; not in arguing for any one position but in testing out the implications of many. Such a procedure characterizes postmodern discourse. It is my belief that in rethinking the assumptions and practices of a modernist literary tradition, Woolf raised many questions now informing our discussions of postmodernism. Because her writings, like much postmodern fiction, call attention to their narrative strategies and social contexts, they self-consciously reveal the way narrative conventions both respond to and engender certain kinds of social practices. Thus, postmodern assumptions about the function of art can provide a useful way of conceiving Woolf's feminist writing practice, enabling us to avoid the reductive generalizations that characterize arguments about different artistic traditions (such as male and female) that are seen to be opposing.

My argument is that neither feminism nor postmodernism should be defined only or always as *anti-, un-,* or *against* something else—not any longer, anyway. Such approaches have served their usefulness. Another way of proceeding is needed if we are to resist subsuming feminism and postmodernism under the models of discourse they have challenged, and if we are to attend to the implications of those challenges for literature and for society. My way of proceeding in the chapters that follow is to expand the contexts of my topic, Virginia Woolf and postmodernism, through a series of related explorations and thereby to enact a way of thinking about and responding to narrative discourse that considers different ways of relating things rather than the distinction between two things. In my readings of Woolf's novels, nonfiction, and criticism, I bring to the fore the aesthetic motives, narrative strategies, and the social and linguistic assumptions that can be said to manifest a postmodern strain in Woolf's writings in order to challenge some common assumptions about her works and about feminist criticism and postmodern novels. My aim is not to solve, but to expose and exploit the problem of defining feminism, the problem of theorizing postmodernism, the problem of reading Woolf.

Therefore, while this book takes shape within the framework of Woolf scholarship and attends almost solely to her writings, it is by no means simply another critical reading of Woolf but has, I hope, far-reaching implications for the study of twentieth-century narrative and for the practice of feminist criticism. Although I do take issue with a number of feminist readings of Woolf, most forcefully in my polemical introduction, my point is not to dismiss these readings; indeed, my own study shows my indebtedness to as well as my differences from such criticism. Instead, my point is to take the implications of feminist criticism further, into the very way we conceive and use narrative discourse. I certainly do not deny Woolf's feminism, but neither do I begin there and look for how feminism informed her writing. Rather, I begin with her writing and use it to question what can be said to be feminist. It is in carrying out this task that I find a postmodern aesthetics quite useful. If we attend to the stories postmodern writers tell us, we realize that there is no end goal toward which we are progressing, no common ground on which we can rest, no plot that liberates us or reveals hidden truths, no language we can use that does not already implicate us in a variety of symbolic systems and cultural institutions.

Postmodernism marks a change in aesthetic motivation. Where modernist literature sought to provide order in a fragmented world by opposing itself to social institutions and mass culture, postmodern writing assumes its implication in social systems in order to expose and exploit systems of cultural production. Instead of placing itself at the vanguard of culture, postmodern writing explores the relations between literary practices and social practices. What this change in motivation and social status means for our reading of fiction is the subject of this book. Drawing on Wittgenstein's linguistic philosophy, a philosophy informing postmodern discourse, I enact a method of reading that is more conducive to the claims we make for postmodern writing and for feminist criticism.

Whatever approach we use, however—modernist, feminist, postmodernist—what we find in Woolf's writings is not "there" prior to our readings but posited by and constructed in the very course of our readings. Thus, we must pay as much attention to our own motives, strategies, and contexts as to Virginia Woolf's.

I began this book in 1985, the year Toril Moi's *Sexual/Textual Politics* was published. On reading that book in 1986, I felt my own manuscript provided the kind of reading Moi calls for in her introduction—one that locates "the politics of Woolf's writing *precisely in her textual practice*" (16). By the time my manuscript was completed (in 1988) and accepted for publication (in 1989), several books on Woolf had appeared that seemed to shift the terms of debate as Moi had suggested by integrating "some of the theoretical advances of post-structuralist thought" (17). Thus, in my case, what began as a book intended to apply the theoretical insights of postmodernism to a reading of Woolf's texts has become, over time, a book as well about the change in criticism of Woolf that has taken shape over the past five years. In particular, my attempt to explore the political and aesthetic implications of Woolf's changing textual practice is also an attempt to explore the implications for criticism in general of the various ways in which Woolf's feminism has been inscribed in her writings and the various ways in which her textual practice has been described by her critics.

In undertaking this task, I adopt a functional approach to narrative rather than a thematic or stylistic approach, a practice that Moi calls *tex-*

*tual theory:* "the study of specific linguistic strategies in specific situations" (154, 155). A functional approach presents an alternative to what Robbe-Grillet calls that "leaky old boat—the academic opposition of form and content" (*For a New Novel* 42). Concerned with the consequences of language use, rather than the relation of form and content, this approach shifts our attention from how the textual strategies reveal or conceal the author's meaning to what functions they perform for their users in particular contexts. To demonstrate how a functional approach changes the kinds of questions we ask of a particular text and the kinds of conclusions we can reach, I focus my chapters on issues in Woolf criticism, not on individual works by Woolf, and begin by setting up the common approaches to these recurring topics, noting the problems they raise and offering another way of proceeding. Drawing on a postmodern aesthetics to reconceive the issues at hand, my readings apply a particular strategy based on particular assumptions to deal with particular problems. I do not claim my readings are more impartial than others, and thus truer to Woolf's *real* intent, only that they offer a more useful way of conceiving both her feminist project and a postmodern aesthetics.

And so, those looking here for an explanation of what postmodernism really is and what Virginia Woolf really believed will be disappointed. For my concern in *Virginia Woolf and Postmodernism* is less with what Woolf truly believed as a woman than with how she continually changed as a writer; less with what postmodern narrative strategies mean than with the significance of their use; less with answering questions commonly asked of Woolf's writing and postmodern novels than with discovering the assumptions about language, art, and life that give rise to them; less with revealing the right answers than with learning to ask the revealing questions.

In attempting to show the significance of Woolf's writings for the present moment in narrative and critical theory, and to show the usefulness of current theory for reading Woolf's writings, I do not want to neglect the personal motive behind my writing: the pleasure I continue to derive from reading Virginia Woolf. This book grew out of my delight in Woolf, my interest in language theory and postmodern novels, and my pragmatic commitment to feminism.

A word on the paperback cover. The suggestive parody of Andy Warhol's Marilyn Monroe seriograph capitalizes, of course, on one of the most famous images of postmodernism. I do so in order to call attention to the many images of Virginia Woolf that have proliferated over the past decade and to confront her commodification as she has become the canonical female modernist as well as the preeminent feminist writer. In typically postmodernist fashion, I resist synthesizing these multiple images in a vain effort to get at the "real" Virginia Woolf, and I challenge a concept of representation that would attempt to distinguish between spurious reproduction and authentic original. If Woolf has come to represent a variety of literary, critical, and political beliefs, it is precisely because she has no "true" nature. To acknowledge her status as a commodity in the academic marketplace and to affirm the multiple images that have been circulated by her critics is not to devalue Woolf as a woman or a writer. Rather, it is to reassess her status and significance as a writer in light of those very forces—theoretical, social, even economic—that have augmented the dissemination of these images. The parody and playfulness of the cover design, moreover, are as much elements of Woolf's writings as of postmodern texts.

A comment on my sources. A common assumption is that no one writing on women writers today from a poststructuralist perspective, as I do, can fail to draw on the writings of Luce Irigaray, Julia Kristeva, and Hélène Cixous, and that no one writing on postmodernism today can do so without relying on Brian McHale, Alice Jardine, and Fredric Jameson, among others. Although I have read these writers and draw on many of them, I do not accept this common assumption. To do so is to risk denying the specificity of a new work in the field and thereby to limit the things one can say. Filtering a different kind of approach through the accepted ones also risks straining off the telling anomalies and preserving, rather than scrutinizing, the common belief. A related tendency is to assume that if a critic draws on a specific insight or mode of questioning provided by a particular theorist or philosopher, she or he must buy into a whole system of beliefs that characterizes that body of thought. I do not share this assumption either, for subsuming a new critical work under the rubric of a familiar body of theory again limits the ability of that new work to challenge as well as extend the theoretical positions on which it draws. I do not say all this to assert the originality of my work. On the contrary, I say this to stress that a new work comes into being within the confluence of a number of theoretical positions and that, as readers, we would do better to attend to the consequences of bringing certain positions together than to assert the priority of those left out.

Having said this, I would like to acknowledge some of the people who have contributed to the making of this book. Like Virginia Woolf in her preface to *Orlando,* I feel the need to cite the many writers I have read, living and dead, whose works have shaped my thinking more than I could ever account for: Ludwig Wittgenstein, Ernst Cassirer, Thomas Kuhn, Barbara Herrnstein Smith, Richard Rorty; Barbara Johnson, Jane Gallop, Peggy Kamuf, and Naomi Schor (four women Catharine Stimpson has called "feminist postmodernists"); Michel Foucault, Roland Barthes, Jean-François Lyotard—but the list threatens to become too long and too tedious, and so I refer the reader to my notes.

I would also like to thank the many readers of this work, whether in its entirety or in its various stages, who have given me much valuable advice: Austin E. Quigley, whose teaching and writing on Wittgenstein have had a profound effect on my thinking about language and literature; Daniel Albright, whose knowledge of Woolf and modern fiction has greatly enhanced my own; Holly Laird and Renate Voris, whose understanding of feminist and poststructuralist theory has helped me clarify and refine my thinking; my colleagues, particularly Joyce Wexler, who read the *Flush* chapter in draft, and Paul Jay, who has counseled me on many issues; and those anonymous readers for this press who made helpful suggestions and, most importantly, gave this book their support. Like many other Woolf critics, I particularly owe thanks to Jane Marcus, and for far more than her comments on the *Orlando* and *Flush* material. However much we may disagree as critics, I know that if it hadn't been for Jane Marcus's work on Woolf, I would never have produced my own.

I am most grateful to Loyola University of Chicago for two research grants and a leave of absence that have enabled me to complete this manuscript; to Barbara Gusick for her help with indexing and proofreading; and to my editors at the University of Illinois Press, especially Ann Lowry and Theresa Sears, who have made my work easier by being so expert at their own. Finally, for his editorial assistance, friendship, and good humor, I express my deepest gratitude to my husband, Doug Petcher.

The *Orlando* material in chapter 2 was published separately in *Discontented Discourses: Feminism/Textual Intervention/Psychoanalysis,* edited by Marleen S. Barr and Richard Feldstein (University of Illinois Press, 1989). The *London Scene* material in chapter 4 was published as "Purpose and Play in Woolf's *London Scene* Essays," *Women's Studies* 16 (1989). My thanks to Gordon and Breach Science Publishers for permitting me to publish a revised version here. An earlier version of chapter 5, "*Flush* and the Literary Canon," appears in a special issue on "Redefining Marginality" in *Tulsa Studies in Women's Literature* 10 (Spring 1991). I would also like to acknowledge Professor Quentin Bell for his kind permission to quote from Virginia Woolf's *Flush* manuscripts. These manuscripts are held in the Henry W. and Albert A. Berg Collection at the New York Public Library. Like so many before me, I owe thanks to the late Lola Szladits, former curator of the Berg Collection, for providing this material to me.

# Abbreviations

| | |
|---|---|
| A | "'Anon' and 'The Reader': Virginia Woolf's Last Essays." Ed. Brenda Silver. *Twentieth-Century Literature* 25 (1979): 356–441. |
| AWD | *A Writer's Diary*. Ed. Leonard Woolf. New York: Harcourt Brace Jovanovich, 1953. |
| BA | *Between the Acts*. New York: Harcourt Brace Jovanovich, 1941. |
| BP | *Books and Portraits*. Ed. Mary Lyon. New York: Harcourt Brace Jovanovich, 1977. |
| CDB | *"The Captain's Deathbed" and Other Essays*. New York: Harcourt Brace Jovanovich, 1950. |
| CR | *The Common Reader: First Series*. 1925; rpt., New York: Harcourt Brace Jovanovich, 1953. |
| CW | *Contemporary Writers*. 1965; rpt., New York: Harcourt Brace Jovanovich, 1976. |
| Diary | *The Diary of Virginia Woolf*. 5 vols. Ed. Anne Oliver Bell. New York: Harcourt Brace Jovanovich, 1977–84. |
| DM | *"The Death of the Moth" and Other Essays*. 1942; rpt., New York: Harcourt Brace Jovanovich, 1974. |
| Essays | *The Essays of Virginia Woolf*. 6 vols. Ed. Andrew McNeillie. New York: Harcourt Brace Jovanovich, 1986– . |
| F | *Flush: A Biography*. 1933; rpt., San Diego: Harcourt Brace Jovanovich, 1983. |
| GR | *Granite and Rainbow*. San Diego: Harcourt Brace Jovanovich, 1958. |
| HH | *"A Haunted House" and Other Short Stories*. New York: Harcourt Brace Jovanovich, 1972. |
| JR | *"Jacob's Room" and "The Waves": Two Complete Novels*. New York: Harcourt Brace and World, 1923, 1931. |
| Letters | *The Letters of Virginia Woolf*. 6 vols. Ed. Nigel Nicolson and Joanne Trautmann. New York: Harcourt Brace Jovanovich, 1975–80. |
| LS | *The London Scene*. New York: Random House, 1975. |
| M | *"The Moment" and Other Essays*. New York: Harcourt Brace Jovanovich, 1948. |
| MB | *Moments of Being*. Ed. Jeanne Schulkind. St Albans: Triad/Panther, 1978. |
| MD | *Mrs. Dalloway*. 1925; rpt., New York: Harcourt Brace Jovanovich, 1953. |

MDP    *Mrs Dalloway's Party*. Ed. Stella McNichol. New York: Harcourt Brace Jovanovich, 1972.

MT    *Monday or Tuesday*. New York: Harcourt, Brace, 1921.

ND    *Night and Day*. 1919; rpt., London: Granada Publishing, 1981.

O    *Orlando: A Biography*. 1928; rpt., New York: Harcourt Brace Jovanovich, 1956.

R    *See* A.

RF    *Roger Fry: A Biography*. London: Hogarth Press, 1940.

ROO    *A Room of One's Own*. 1929; rpt., New York: Harcourt Brace Jovanovich, 1957.

SCR    *The Second Common Reader*. 1932; rpt., New York: Harcourt Brace Jovanovich, 1960.

TG    *Three Guineas*. 1938; rpt., Middlesex, U.K.: Penguin, 1978.

TP    *The Pargiters: The Novel-Essay Portion of "The Years."* Ed. Mitchell Leaska. New York: Harcourt Brace Jovanovich, 1977.

TTL    *To the Lighthouse*. 1927; rpt., New York: Harcourt Brace Jovanovich, 1955.

TW    *See* JR.

TY    *The Years*. 1937; rpt., London: Granada Publishing, 1979.

VO    *The Voyage Out*. 1920; rpt., New York: Harcourt Brace Jovanovich, 1948.

WW    *Women and Writing*. Ed. Michele Barrett. New York: Harcourt Brace Jovanovich, 1979.

# Introduction:
## *Taking Issue*

I must not settle into a figure.

—Virginia Woolf,
Diary, 1932

*Essence* is expressed by grammar.

—Ludwig Wittgenstein,
*Philosophical Investigations*

In or about December 1985, Virginia Woolf criticism changed. This book participates in and responds to that moment by providing a story of how we might read that change and how we might change our reading as a result.

Until the late 1970s, Virginia Woolf was typically considered an exemplar of a high modernist aesthetics. Criticism of the past decade has generally considered her an exemplar of a feminist writing practice. While both perspectives have their uses, each can be limiting, especially when we consider the change Woolf criticism underwent around 1985. In that year Toril Moi published *Sexual/Textual Politics,* an overview of Anglo-American and French feminisms that critiques, from the perspective of poststructuralism, the kinds of arguments that have characterized early feminist criticism of Woolf. According to Moi, Woolf's feminist critics rely on a realist aesthetics, with its belief in an autonomous self oppressed by a particular social order, whether they are promoting Woolf's presentation of women's experience or lamenting her flight from any direct attack on the social order. Thus, for these critics, "politics is a matter of the right content being represented in the correct realist form" (Moi 7). Moi argues that this shift from modernist to feminist readings of Woolf was really a step backward insofar as feminist critics adhered to the assumptions of a realist aesthetics against which modernism defined itself. As a result, feminist criticism of Woolf could not deal adequately with Woolf's textual innovations, and far from liberating her feminist textual politics, it actually perpetuated the humanist assumptions bound up with a patriarchal ideology. At the end of her introduction, Moi calls for a deconstructionist reading of Woolf, one that can provide a better understanding of the feminist politics at work in Woolf's modernist aesthetics.

Moi seeks to deconstruct the opposition between those modernist and feminist readings of Woolf that I mention above, as well as the implicit opposition between Woolf's aesthetics and her politics. Yet in doing so, Moi endorses another kind of opposition, that between two schools of feminist thought. These are commonly distinguished as the Anglo-American and French traditions, or the liberal-humanists and the deconstructive antihumanists, or the essentialists and the poststructuralists. Over the past few years, however, it has become evident that Moi's book is bound up with a broader transformation in literature and theory that we have come to call *postmodernism*. What has been described as a debate between opposing schools of feminism can now be seen as a change in the very way we conceive the relations between things. Thus, what is needed in Woolf criticism is a perspective that can free Woolf's writings from the cage of modernism and the camps of feminism without denying these relations in her texts. In this book, I provide one such perspective. By considering Woolf's works in the context of postmodern narrative and cultural theories, I want to change the way we conceive prose discourse so that we do not feel compelled to claim Woolf as spokesperson for any one group of writers. Virginia Woolf can enter into a variety of literary relations, for she has no essential nature.[1]

The change that has occurred in Woolf criticism, then, is not best thought of as a change from misguided modernist readings to authentic feminist ones, or from limiting feminist readings to liberating feminist ones. In fact, it is precisely this kind of story—a narrative of progressive enlightenment or a narrative of a radical break—that postmodernism forsakes. Change in Woolf criticism has not been that sudden or definite, yet change there has been, nevertheless. To deal with it, we need a critical account that is itself informed by changing concepts of narrative and criticism that have contributed to this moment in Woolf studies.[2] Such an account must be capable of dealing with the differences within Woolf's writings, as well as Woolf criticism, while resisting large claims for these differences, directing itself instead toward more localized narrative interests. For Virginia Woolf was not only concerned with modernist aesthetics and feminist politics; she was concerned as well with the nature and status of fiction itself.[3]

In the chapters that follow, I attempt to deal with the many changes and contradictions in Woolf's writings rather than search among them for the "essential Woolf." At the same time, I question our common classifications of her novels rather than assume that our classifications answer our questions. Consequently, my procedure is to challenge some of the common assumptions about Woolf's works that even her deconstructing feminist critics have accepted. I begin by taking on early feminist readings of Woolf as instances of the kind of critical practice I take issue with throughout. I end this introduction by briefly considering more recent feminist readings, not to show how far we have come, but to question how we can go on from here.

In *A Literature of Their Own* (1977), Elaine Showalter seeks to dispraise Virginia Woolf as "the mother of us all." She argues that Woolf was an unfit mother for women writers because her concept of an androgynous and anonymous art is a flight, not a liberation, from the dilemma of a polarized sexual existence. Several years later Jane Marcus's edited collections *New Feminist Essays on Virginia Woolf* (1981) and *Virginia Woolf: A Feminist Slant* (1983) take up the defense in the maternity suit, attempting to reaffirm Woolf's authority, which suffered from earlier prosecutions. Using militaristic language, Marcus portrays a very different Virginia Woolf: tough, committed, aggressive, even sneaky. Woolf is described as having "raided the patriarchy and trespassed on male territory, returning to share her spoils with other women: women's words, *the* feminine sentence, and finally the *appropriate* female form" (*New Feminist Essays* xiv; emphasis added). Important as these collections are in response to Showalter's reading of Woolf, Marcus overstates her defense by downplaying the doubts that inform much of Woolf's writing and by cataloging Woolf's spoils as unequivocal gains. But what is *the* feminine sentence, for surely Jane Austen's differs from Charlotte Brontë's, Dorothy Richardson's from Virginia Woolf's? What is the *appropriate* female form? Would Woolf have wanted to hand down to other women writers a characteristic, a prescribed, form or style? From the Angel in the House of Fiction that the contemporary woman novelist must kill (Showalter's portrait) to the mother she must honor (Marcus's), Virginia Woolf cannot escape our metaphors of her life and writing. It is precisely this problem that we must come to terms with.

In "Women and Fiction" (1929), Woolf does discuss the need for a female sentence; and in "Men and Women" (1920), she quotes (incorrectly) Hardy's Bathsheba—"I have the feelings of a woman, but I have only the language of men" (WW 67)—to urge new forms for women's literature.[4] In essays such as "On Not Knowing Greek" (1925) and through characters such as Bernard in *The Waves* (1931), Woolf expresses her desire for new words.[5] Certainly her experiments with subject matter, narrative voice, characterization, and rhythm have created new forms for narrative literature. But are we able to, and do we want to, define these forms apart from the functions they perform in Woolf's canon and in the history of the novel? Even if we could isolate and delineate the features of some appropriate form, would we want to present this as a "norm" for women's writing? What Woolf resists in her novels and essays is any attempt to *define* fiction by standards to which it conforms or from which it deviates. We can argue that women's novels diverge from patriarchal conventions *only to the extent that we accept those conventions that have been codified by patriarchal theorists*. Once we expose those conventions as arbitrary constructs, as a rigidifying of provisional and provincial responses to the novel, as so much feminist criticism has successfully done, then we make suspect the concept of *any* appropriate form. Woolf was more apt to expose concepts and conventions than to "raid" them.[6] She was more apt to affirm the tenuous and provisional status of literary forms than to replace one highly valued form with another. Which brings me to my main complaint against many feminist reinterpretations of Woolf: they often fail to change the terms of the debate.

First let me say that I applaud much of what early feminist criticism has done for Woolf criticism. Through historical research and manuscript studies, feminist critics have produced indispensable works on Woolf. Reconstituting her canon by their attention to such novels as *The Voyage Out* (1915), *Night and Day* (1919), *Orlando* (1928), and *The Years* (1937), as well as to the feminist essays *A Room of One's Own* (1929) and *Three Guineas* (1938), these critics have led us to reconsider Woolf's early portrait as an apolitical aesthete. In her introduction and her essay in *New Feminist Essays on Virginia Woolf,* Marcus provides a new perspective on Woolf by comparing her with Kafka, Brecht, and Benjamin. This is one of the most liberating functions of feminist criticism, for Woolf has too long been considered in terms of the modernism of Joyce, Eliot, Proust, Lawrence, Forster, and Conrad. Woolf herself felt the strain: "Lord—how tired I am of being caged with Aldous, Joyce and Lawrence!" (Letters 4:402).

Yet to see Woolf as important primarily in terms of female literary experience, as most feminist critics do, is potentially as limiting as to see her primarily in terms of the modernist literary movement, especially when such a view leads to claims like Marcus's that Woolf's writings exclude the male reader.[7] Just as I have trouble accepting Walter Pater as Woolf's "absent father" (the title metaphor of Perry Meisel's study of Woolf's criticism), so I have trouble accepting Woolf as the "absent mother" of women writers. I object equally to the questionable practice of influence tracing (which implies that certain writers naturally form a group prior to our grouping of them) and to the ethics of exalting a particular writer as a means of establishing some ultimate literary goal, some promised land of narrative. The "great author" syndrome leads to a "great tradition," whether a homogeneous tradition such as T. S. Eliot's or a linear tradition such as F. R. Leavis's. The concept of tradition as a "handing down" implies an ideal standard of values; it seeks out what is constant in literature; it defines the tradition by timeless features. But no author or literary tradition is of value in itself. Any tradition is a construct, defined by what it is compared with and contrasted to, and of value only in terms of a particular use to which we put it.

Woolf would not have wanted to submerge any work in the current of any one authority. She would have sympathized with Artaud's call for "no more masterpieces." However, many of Woolf's feminist critics, such as those I consider here, present her as the principal feminist craftsperson forging the appropriate feminine form, accepting literature as form rather than function, as polemic rather than extrapolation. In other words, many feminist critics end up accepting assumptions about Woolf's writing and about literature in general that they seem to want to denounce. Both modernist and feminist approaches to Woolf present us with restrictive readings, not because they separate her art and politics (as many feminist critics claim modernist readings do) or because they reconcile the two (as many feminist readings claim to do), but because they insist on the same problematic dichotomies. It is with these dichotomous approaches that I take issue.[8]

Critics who consider Woolf's works in terms of her historical position as a modernist see her as attempting to free the novel from the conventional forms prescribed by nineteenth-century writers and still adhered to by Edwardian materialists. Critics who consider Woolf's works in terms of her feminist politics see her as attempting to free the novel from the patriarchal forms established by mainstream male authors, and even unconventional ones such as D. H. Lawrence. According to one group, Woolf attacks the "conventional" character as archaic; according to the other group, she attacks the "egotistical self" as masculine. Both present her as exposing false forms of narrative, false forms of consciousness, false words, and false institutions to get at . . . well, it can never be adequately stated because it is always absent or silent or hidden or inexpressible in our tainted language, but it can best be intimated by the word *truth*. That is, in attacking what is false, Woolf uncovers what is essential or natural. Both approaches accept a necessary opposition between conventional and modern, masculine and feminine, appearance and reality, the external and the essence, as if each term were coherent and stable, as if the novel, the self, or the world could be so simply polarized. More importantly, both accept some stable and coherent "norm" for narrative, whether the conventional novel or the masculine form. By structuring their arguments in terms of oppositions, in terms of *us* and *them* (as in Marcus's militaristic language), these critics must choose sides. And here they run into trouble, because they end up ignoring much of what does not fit such neat dichotomies, or because they posit some tenuous synthesis of oppositions, or because they leave themselves no language with which to define what Woolf has discovered, and so they end up identifying Woolf's achievement with such nebulous terms as *absence, silence, emotion, void.*[9]

The problem with these similar approaches is not that they present Woolf as challenging previously established narrative forms, for she did, but that they see her as moving from the false to the true, the ineffectual to the effective, the limiting to the all-embracing, as if literature were evolving toward some *telos*. Moreover, this kind of reading accepts certain novelistic features or values as normative. It seeks an exhaustive form, though nothing in this world is exhaustive (except, perhaps, God and the Sunday *Times*). There is no progress or decline in the novel, for there is no fixed "core" against which to measure progress or decline. "We do not come to write better," Woolf says in "Modern Fiction"; "all that we can be said to do is to keep moving" (CR 150). When we run into trouble defining a female form or a new language, as Woolf did and as some feminists do, it does not mean that differences between women's and men's literature do not exist or are not important, only that they are not rigid oppositions or clearly defined contrasts. We need another way of talking about such differences.

I propose a twofold change in our approach to Virginia Woolf's writings. One is to think in terms of a dynamic model for narrative rather than a dualistic one, that is, in terms of possibilities, not fixed positions, in terms of functions, not appropriate forms. The other is to compare Woolf's experiments in fiction and criticism with a broader range of innovators and theorists in the novel, not just with other writers of her day or of her sex. Woolf's importance lies not in her having done in little what modernists like Joyce and Eliot did in large (Fussell 265), not in her having discovered an appropriate female form, but in her having enabled us to encounter a range of possibilities in the function of narrative literature and thus to reassess its status as art. Woolf adopted many different perspectives and narrative techniques in her fiction, but she did not single out certain ones as privileged or defining features. Her feminism should not be sought in her originating ideas or in her characteristic features but in the effects of her changing textual practice. Where many feminist critics begin by identifying Woolf's feminist beliefs and then look for the form they take in her writing, I see her feminism as *an effect of* her formal experiments. Rethinking the assumptions and practices of a humanistic and positivistic tradition in literature, Woolf raised many of the feminist and poststructuralist critical issues that have subsequently emerged as such. Her formal experiments resulted in what many have come to call a postmodern narrative practice, as well as in a feminist textual politics.[10]

I turn now to a discussion of selected feminist writings on Woolf to reconstruct the context in which my own readings have come about; in subsequent chapters I will place my readings in a more general tradition of Woolf criticism. If I focus here on feminist criticism, it is not because that is my target throughout but because feminist criticism has largely defined the course of Woolf studies in the 1980s, to the extent that earlier debates between modernist and feminist approaches have been reconceived (albeit misleadingly) as debates between two types of feminism. By learning to read this change differently, we will go a long way toward grasping the implications of postmodernism, not only for a reading of Woolf's texts, but for a feminist critical practice as well. Because my gesture throughout this book is to attend to the particular case rather than the general category, I want to forsake for the moment the convenient but suspect appellation "early feminist criticism" and focus here on specific essays included in Jane Marcus's two seminal editions of feminist criticism (*New Feminist Essays* and *Virginia Woolf: A Feminist Slant*), as well as on her latest collections (*Virginia Woolf and Bloomsbury* and *Virginia Woolf and the Languages of Patriarchy*).[11]

The fact that I focus on these four collections shows the importance of Jane Marcus's work to any discussion of Virginia Woolf. But my discussion shows as well how these works, invaluable though they are, have fostered a commonly accepted view of what feminist criticism of Woolf should be, a view that may have prevented us from finding other ways of talking about Woolf's feminism in light of new ways of conceiving narrative discourse. Thus, my purpose is not to dismiss as "wrong" or "inappropriate" the readings I take issue with, for according to a certain model of narrative, they certainly are appropriate. But they are not always so. It is not their feminist motives I question but their way of conceiving a feminist practice. When our motives as critics no longer suit our theory of narrative, when our actions contradict our claims, when our assumptions belie our aims, then our readings may no longer be very useful. By means of a discussion of several essays in Marcus's collections, I want to expose the constraining assumptions about language and narrative that encourage critics to classify Woolf's works definitively (as "modernist" or "feminist"), to trace an evolutionary development in Woolf's writings, and to sort out the features of a characteristic "Woolfian" or women's form. In taking issue with these critics and in considering Woolf's works in terms of postmodern motives and strategies, I do not intend to offer the right reading of Woolf; rather, I want to change the way we read Woolf so that we no longer feel compelled to argue for the right reading or to lapse into relativistic readings.

In *Orlando*, Woolf considers the problems that arise when one insists on right readings or appropriate forms. The narrator writes: "No passion is stronger in the breast of man than the desire to make others believe as he believes. . . . It is not love of truth, but desire to prevail" (149).[12] It is this desire that Woolf checks in her writings. When she criticizes the egotism of Lawrence, Joyce, and Eliot, she objects to more than their concern with self, their *male* ego. She objects to their desire to prevail, and to their certainty. Equivocation (as seen in such works as *Orlando* and *A Room of One's Own*) is for Woolf a stance against such certainty, a guard against the desire to prevail. It is for her a strategy to avoid prescribing an appropriate form or insisting on a particular metaphysical, mythical, or symbolic system. To explain away the equivocation in her writing in order to insist on her commitment to a particular position is, I argue, to nullify the very function of a feminist writing practice as Woolf came to conceive it. To write, Orlando must neither submit to the age nor insist on her "self" against the age, for "she was of it, yet remained herself" (266). Orlando, as a writer and as a woman, is both within the common language and apart from it. She need not submit to the tyranny of symbolic systems nor insist on another opposing system. Hers is not such a simple choice. As the novel makes evident, sexual identity, historical periods, and literary styles are all constructs. Each is structured like a language and as such has no fixed or natural relation to anything outside itself. We cannot discover the appropriate form or the true self or the innate differences between the sexes, for there is nothing stable to measure them against.

In other words, to think of language and writing as either true or false, authentic or inauthentic, is to assume they correspond to something else. Such thinking confuses truth with reference, thereby giving preference to only one function of language.[13] Reference-theory thinking leads us to believe we have gotten at the "true meaning" of a work when we have identified what its content is about (what it refers to) or what its form is like (what it corresponds to). It begs the question of what it means to talk about something apart from or prior to the language of the text. It begs the question of what it means to talk in terms of truth and falsity in a particular context rather than in terms of, say, rhetoric and style, or motives and import. Instead of discussing a literary work as true or false in terms of its form and content, it might be more useful to discuss its effectiveness in terms of its particular point. Woolf's novels explore how the novel functions. A new conception of how the novel functions does not necessarily prescribe a new form. There is no "correspondence" to be drawn.

Yet in reading Woolf's novels for "their meanings as well as their styles" (Marcus, *New Feminist Essays* xvi), for "the social criticism as well as the poetry" (5), for their "political vision" as well as their "experimental form" (Meyerowitz 238), many feminist critics, like the modernist critics they challenge, rely on such a split between form and content.[14] In separating meaning and style, these critics imply at once that earlier critics missed Woolf's political (feminist) content in their intent examination of her innovative (lyrical) form and that the content is somehow primary (the style always following "as well as"). Such a distinction leads to two responses: either these critics sort out the political comments from the obscuring stylistic context (as Beverly Ann Schlack does), or they reduce the complex stylistic form to the appropriate container for Woolf's political remarks (as Marcus does). That is, to present Woolf's writing as a prototype of feminist writing, they must conclude either that there is some necessary connection between form and content or that the one obscures the other. Either way this reasoning relies on the one-to-one correspondence theory of meaning that Wittgenstein and many postmodernists have confuted. Further, it assumes what Woolf herself challenged—that there is some "core of meaning" in a text—and accepts the very notion that feminist critics want to expose—that there is some fixed "norm" for language or literature. Most importantly, it risks downplaying the difference language makes by treating Woolf's prose as the vehicle for her ideas, as if language merely bears the burden of our thoughts, as if it has no significance, no history, of its own. As Wittgenstein points out in *The Blue and Brown Books,* the source of our confusion is that "a substantive makes us look for a thing that corresponds to it" (1). To separate form and content, to accept some norm for literature and reality, is to assume each term in the relation is stable and contained. The two can be separated only if we accept the work as a statement about some substantial world "out there," only if we see language as the dress of thought. Such thinking has generated the critical impasses that I examine throughout this book.

Setting up such dichotomous positions, for instance, leads Schlack to fall back into a "narrow" reading of Virginia Woolf's novels that she herself challenges. In the opening paragraph of her essay "Fathers in General," Schlack argues that failing to recognize the feminist perspective in Woolf's fiction is "to fall victim to *narrow* interpretive approaches . . . that make Woolf's politics and art mutually exclusive, fracturing the symbiotic, simultaneous connection she wanted from life and literature, private and public worlds" (52). Feminism is certainly an important component of Woolf's works, but her feminism may not lie where we look for it. To go through her fiction sorting out the feminist statements, as Schlack does, is to separate what Woolf and Schlack herself say cannot, or should not, be separated. Schlack's goal is "to have Woolf whole," yet she serves her up in parts, never clearly showing how feminism is reshaped aesthetically by the fiction and making Woolf uncomfortably like those she is supposed to be condemning. What Schlack notes as Woolf's putdown of Charles Tansley and politicians in *To the Lighthouse*—Lily's comment when she sees Tansley standing on a platform, "He was denouncing something: he was condemning somebody" (292)—seems to be the very action and tone Schlack imputes to Woolf. What is meant to be a revelation of symbiosis becomes an insistence on misleading oppositions. Indeed, Schlack may prove Woolf's observation in her essay "Women and Fiction" that when a writer protests or addresses a grievance, she splits the reader's focus (WW 47). We no longer read Woolf for the symbiotic connection of life and literature; instead, we look for the artist's potshots at the patriarchy.

The desire to uncover the most consistent feminist polemic in Woolf's canon neglects the many ambiguities and equivocations in her writings. For example, Jane Lilienfield, writing on *To the Lighthouse,* objects to what she identifies as the opposing views of Mrs. Ramsay. Whether critics see Mrs. Ramsey as the angel and ideal maternal figure or as the manipulator of her family and guests, they read the novel in the same way, says Lilienfield, as a portrait of the "eternal" union in marriage as structured by the patriarchal family. In contrast, Lilienfield argues that *To the Lighthouse* urges "new modes of human love and partnership" (149). This is a suggestive insight, but how does it affect our reading of the novel? Lilienfield reads Mrs. Ramsay's thoughts, feelings, and actions as an invective against the patriarchal marriage: she asserts that "the sequestered wife's unconscious anger at her position shapes her behaviour" (154). Mrs. Ramsay, then, embodies Woolf's personal attack on this kind of marriage, and thus Mrs. Ramsay's character is still read by Lilienfield in relation to the patriarchal marriage. Lilienfield's unambiguous opposition to this kind of marriage is projected onto Woolf, who in turn projects it onto Mrs. Ramsay. The anger we feel now at such marriages allows us to assume Woolf not only felt it but structured her character and novel in terms of it. Slighting other kinds of relations in the novel, Lilienfield herself downplays new modes of affiliation by insisting on oppositions.

Positing misleading oppositions can set up uncomfortable choices. This problem comes to the fore in Nora Eisenberg's essay on *Between the Acts* and "Anon." By seeing these works as envisioning an "old world" of the common life free of the conventional language, which is a masculine dominion, Eisenberg must attribute to this "ancient mother-world" a language "that is not quite language" (253). She ends up borrowing Bernard's phrase, a "little language," for this language of women and of the common life. The adjective "little" potentially trivializes women's specialty by opposing it to the "big" language of men, and Eisenberg thus comes to a dangerous precipice: equating women's realm with silence, emotion, and negation. She has found herself in such a position before when she commends Rachel in *The Voyage Out* for returning from her voyage into the world of words, to her "beloved sounds and silences," that is, to death and nothingness. But this is not a step Eisenberg wants to take, so she pulls back from the precipice by noting the danger as well as the attraction of this language of selflessness (254). If a woman can survive neither in the world of words nor in the realm of silence, then what is the alternative? Eisenberg sets up an opposition in which neither term is acceptable, and so the only recourse is to synthesize: all must learn both languages (255). In *Between the Acts,* Eisenberg says, Woolf presents this "new language" by supplementing the "failing language" (of males) with the "non-verbal forms" (of females), such as music, dance, and gestures (259). But in agreeing with Isa's insight that the words do not matter, that only the emotion counts (257), Eisenberg calls into question this new language. If words do not matter, if in the common life artist and audience are one, then what is to be gained by this synthesis? Why shouldn't artists throw out language (the words of men and patriarchal society) and replace it with emotion conveyed in nonverbal forms (the anonymous oneness of the common life)? Of course, since we have not yet achieved the old oneness, we must use words to communicate. But why should this new language be more liberating than the old? As Ionesco once noted, any established form of expression can also be a form of oppression (see Calinescu 119). And do we even want to agree with Isa that only emotion matters? When Woolf wrote her often naively accepted definition of the book as "emotion which you feel," she was not valorizing one component of the novel but responding to Lubbock's emphasis on form and refusing to concede emotion as ancillary to it.[15] Her definition has a particular use within its context. But in accepting it as a general definition, we are in danger, as was Woolf at times, of assuming we can get "beyond" or "beneath" conventional language to some "natural" form.

Setting up oppositions between types of readings, types of languages, or types of writing can bring to the fore assumptions, strategies, and values not previously noticed in Woolf's fiction, and to this extent, these readings have been productive. But what often happens is that we cannot get beyond the initial opposition.[16] Setting up a choice between two languages leads to such tenuous conclusions as Eisenberg's. It leads as well to such factious assertions as Sandra Gilbert's in "Woman's Sentence, Man's Sentencing." Establishing an opposition between the linguistic fantasies of male modernists and female modernists, Gilbert concludes that, "despite the apparently innovative rhetoric of the male avant-garde," the dialectic of the sexes and the male defensiveness it generates "obviously [leave] the woman as the only true exponent of the new" (222). The very conflation of terms should caution us against such exclusive choices: male/female, old/new, conventional/innovative, verbal/nonverbal, big/little, rhetoric/truth. The problem is not the critics' desire to note the differences between men's and women's use of language but the ways in which these critics frame their tasks and phrase their questions. It is not a matter of word choice—choosing between two languages—but of word consciousness—understanding what words do. It is not a matter of combining two languages but of learning to use language in more than one way. The combination of words, music, dance, and gestures that Eisenberg ends up describing as Woolf's new language is *drama*. In this sense, the emphasis in *Between the Acts* is on one particular use of language, not on a new language. An emphasis on performance directs our attention primarily to the production of the work, not to the world beyond or the self within.

This emphasis on performance informs Woolf's fiction and essays and can be detected most clearly in her concern with the reader. In her critical essays, which I discuss in chapter 6, Woolf is more interested in how a reader responds to and shapes a text than in elucidating an author's thematic statements or characterizing forms. Her fiction draws forth the reader's active involvement in the production and thereby calls attention to the text's construction. By these means Woolf discloses how the discourse is situated in relation to the reader as well as to past texts, and she reveals how different narrative strategies generate different thematic significances. Rather than setting up strict oppositions or tenuous syntheses—a characteristic strategy in Woolf criticism that I return to in the following chapters—we might do better to look at the contrasts Woolf explores in her fiction in terms of the *point* of her fictional and critical experiments.[17] It seems to me that one such point is to work against the tendency to codify conventions in literature and language use, so that certain elements become the defining features of a certain type of discourse, and against the tendency to accept certain features as givens, so that contingent relations come to be accepted as essential traits. What makes a novel like *The Years,* for example, appear to have no "center" of meaning and to lack closure is not Woolf's refusal to unify this work or her rejection of certain conventions but her adoption of a different motivating structure of thought from that of a differently ordered work, such as *Night and Day*.[18] Thus, Woolf's fiction forces us to consider how meanings are possible, how they are produced. It accepts "meaning" as multiple, neither universal nor relative, neither monolithic nor dualistic. In examining the ways our conceptions about literature and life affect each other, Woolf resists the rigid systematizing of conventions, making conventions disposable, in the sense of using them up, not doing away with them altogether.

Feminist criticism especially has acknowledged the importance of the reader in Woolf's works, but it is hard to reconcile an emphasis on the reader's role with an argument for a new form of fiction. For if we value the part played by the reader, we must accept a dynamic and provisional concept of the literary text. So often critics slip back into readings of Woolf that a performative emphasis would undermine, unearthing new meanings hitherto unseen beneath Woolf's textual surface. That is, they assume they have dug up the truth about Woolf. However useful, even necessary, such readings are in elucidating her feminist strategies, they go too far when, at the end of examining her response to particular conventions within a particular work, they leap beyond the immediate context to insist on some general, characteristic, authentic form for Woolf's, and for women's, writing.

For example, in her essay on *A Room of One's Own,* which concludes *Virginia Woolf and the Languages of Patriarchy,* Marcus elaborates a narrative strategy that she terms *sapphistry,* a "rhetorical seduction" of the woman reader, to explain how *A Room of One's Own* functions as an essay and how it exploits "classical rhetoric to subvert powerlessness" (169). Marcus's reading goes a long way toward accounting for the strategies and the effects of this particular work. But when she generalizes from *A Room of One's Own,* in this and other essays in the collection, in order to specify the traits of a female language, her argument is less convincing. As opposed to male discourse, Marcus says, women's writing is antiauthoritarian, unbounded, fluid, marked by repetition and interruption, an aesthetics of process rather than finished products. All this sounds familiar, and much like the claims for postmodern art, as Marcus realizes when she refers to Woolf's antiauthoritative narrative as "almost postmodern" (146). But of course, postmodern narratives are not exclusively written by women; indeed, some would say they are exclusively written by men. The question becomes, then, what is the nature of the relationship between women's narratives and postmodern novels? What is the point of terming such strategies *female, feminist,* or *postmodernist?* What function is our classification meant to perform, and what questions can it answer? Here we can see the limitations of relying on definitional properties to classify texts. Marcus assumes she has reached the end of her investigation by identifying these features as feminist; I claim she has only just begun.

These aesthetic standards, praised by feminist and postmodernist critics alike, are not the *property* of certain groups of writers, nor are they, as Alex Zwerdling points out, any more permanent than those aesthetic

standards they have displaced (34). Rather, they are the *effects* of a different way of conceiving art, one that calls into question the values of
permanency, continuity, and uniqueness—values on which many feminist
aesthetics would seem to rest. Whereas Marcus, Rachel Blau DuPlessis,
Marianne Hirsch, and others advance women's art as an aesthetics of process, I argue that an aesthetics of process (i.e., conceiving art in general
in terms of processes) enables us to stress the difference women's writings
make without the need to specify that difference in terms of an absolute
difference or, to borrow Andreas Huyssen's title phrase, a great divide.[19] It
is misleading, even potentially dangerous, to distinguish in general features
or values that are outmoded and authoritarian from those that are appropriate and liberating, for we cannot count on any one element functioning
the same way from one text to another, one context to another, one user
to another. An open ending could serve authoritarian purposes. The point
of Woolf's continually experimental form, like the point of postmodern
fictional strategies, is to resist the search for a totalizing, consistent reading
or for "a new and total culture" (DuPlessis, "For the Etruscans" 286).[20]

Unlike early postmodernist critics (such as Ihab Hassan and Susan Sontag) and early feminist critics (such as Marcus and DuPlessis), I do not
claim certain strategies—for example, contradictions, indeterminacy, discontinuity—as Woolf's own or use them to exalt the writings of women
and postmodernists over those of men and modernists. While these strategies do inform Woolf's writings, this is not because she wrote essentially
as a woman or prophetically as a postmodernist but because she changed
continually as a writer, testing out different conceptions of what art is,
and because contemporary fiction and theory have provided us with this
way of conceiving her practice and with another way of reading narrative
discourse. What all this means is not that we abandon feminist arguments
but that we change our tasks as feminist critics.

Within this context of feminist readings of Woolf, a postmodern perspective seemed useful in unraveling some difficulties prevalent in such
criticism: in particular, the critical impasse created by the necessity of
choosing between two alternatives and setting up definitive distinctions
between types of writing. I began to realize that whatever our theories of
narrative, when it comes to critical practice, we often mistake the referential as the primary use of language, the representational as the primary
function of narrative, the purposeful as the primary motive for writing.[21]
These functions are not in themselves erroneous, but our assumption of
their primacy in all circumstances is. What is so striking in postmodern
novels is the way they work to establish other motives for writing and other
uses of prose discourse, urging other modes of investigation. Noting simi-

larities between Woolf's writing and postmodernist writing, as Marcus has, I wanted to investigate how such a comparison might change our ways of reading Woolf. What gives rise to these assumptions and strategies in her works and how can we best deal with them? What are the implications of postmodern assumptions and strategies for criticism of the novel in general and for women's writing in particular? Why would we need or want to use the term *postmodern* at all? What does it mean to apply the term to Woolf's writings?

One thing it means is that I had to take issue with the consensus forming among many feminist critics of Woolf, a consensus produced by a shared method of investigation. In a recent article in *Critical Inquiry,* Catharine Stimpson refers to "feminist postmodernism" as one force that has disrupted the cultural consensus among feminists, that is, the assumption that one woman can speak on behalf of all women and the belief that women's writing can present a just and accurate representation of women's lives (228–29). Postmodernism, she argues, has raised questions about "the possibility of any reality beyond the discourse of representation" (229), about "the 'naturalness' of any sex differences" (234), and about the coherence and stability of any self and any text. Postmodernism cautions feminists against "both monolithic and dualistic thinking" (241). Although in the chapters that follow I question some common assumptions about postmodernism—in particular, the claim that there is no reality beyond textual representation and the tendency to emphasize postmodernism's disruptive quality over its reconstitutive quality—here I am most interested in Stimpson's response to the challenge of feminist postmodernism: rather than attack it for its emphasis on discontinuity or its reliance on male theory, rather than praise it for its particular textual conventions or its denial of all conventions, Stimpson notes the kinds of questions feminist postmodernism leads us to ask. Learning to rephrase our questions, and thus to attend to different ways of relating things, is the advantage I see in bringing Virginia Woolf and postmodernism together. The "and" in my main title is decidedly strategic.

As Linda Hutcheon notes, this "interrogating of the notion of consensus" is common to all challenges to humanistic thinking that we have come to term *postmodernist* (7). Such a challenge to humanist assumptions was launched, of course, by Moi's dissenting reading of Woolf. In this sense, then, I clearly partake here in the post-1985 moment of Woolf studies. Recent works on Woolf seek to expose, as Moi and I do, the inadequacies of early feminist responses to Woolf: namely, their reliance on a realist aesthetics, their narrow focus on gender oppositions, and their neglect of Woolf's modernist form in their insistence on her feminist content.[22] Drawing on the insights of poststructuralist theory, many recent critics deconstruct the opposition of aesthetics and politics that informs earlier readings of Woolf and focus instead on the relational, provisional, and historically contingent aspects of Woolf's writings. As a result, they show a greater tolerance for the ambiguities and contradictions within Woolf's canon.

But without the theoretical underpinnings of postmodernism, such readings fail to change our approach to narrative discourse as a result of this increased tolerance for differences. What often happens when we apply a new theory to familiar literature is that key concepts of that theory— such as ambiguity, contradictions, and provisionality—become the new features of, in this case, Woolf's writing in particular and women's writing in general.[23] However, unity, coherence, completeness, and originality are no more the traits of modernist or masculine writing than the absence of these qualities characterizes postmodern or feminine writing. Rather, they are the values created by a certain approach to literature based on certain critical motives and certain assumptions about the status and function of art. If so many critics are now talking in terms of disposable art, an aesthetics of process, and Woolf's provisional experiments, where they once talked in terms of essence, unity, harmony, and synthesis, the question is not what this change tells us about Woolf as a unique or representative figure but why we have come to talk in these terms and how such terms change our approach to reading literature. How can we read a text conceived as contradictory, self-reflexive, and multivalent without making such concepts into the new features of a highly valued form? While current work on Woolf provides us with an opportunity to reconceptualize problems in Woolf criticism and to reconceive our tasks as critics, it often falls prey to the assumption that it must argue for the *priority* of certain strategies in Woolf's texts rather than considering what it means to conceive her writing in these terms.[24] In arguing for the priority of certain strategies in women's writing, or in arguing for the uniqueness of Woolf's feminist critique, critics ground their *anti*modernist or *post*modernist arguments in a distinctively modernist reading practice.

Before we can begin to read Woolf's works from the perspective of postmodern writing, then, we must get straight what concepts of language and narrative we are working with and the consequences of these for our readings of the texts in question. To begin with a general definition of postmodern narrative devices, to identify isolated instances of these in Woolf's writings, and then to generalize on the relation between such narrative revolution and social revolution would not achieve anything essentially different from the correspondence theory of language and the representational theory of narrative that postmodern novels are seen as challenging. In their challenge to our faith in positivistic language, representational writing, and a substantial reality beyond the text, postmodern novels draw on poststructuralist conceptions of language and literature. It is not just that postmodern novels in particular enact a new theory of language presented in the writings of Saussure, Wittgenstein, Derrida, and others, as Alan Thiher argues, but that such a theory gives us a different way of conceiving the novel in general.[25] Instead of thinking of the novel as a substantive entity bearing some relation to the real, we can conceive of the novel as a transaction designed, in Kenneth Burke's words, to "do something" for the writer and the reader.[26] Such a conception changes the kinds of questions we ask. No longer do we question what a text means (what it refers to, what it is about) but how it functions and how it finds an audience. These are the questions motivating Woolf's study of narrative, "Phases of Fiction"; these are the questions motivating postmodern writing; and these are the questions motivating pragmatic thinking as well. The postmodern novel, I argue, is best approached from a pragmatic orientation, as presented, for example, in Wittgenstein's linguistic philosophy.[27]

Wittgenstein sees the problem of defining concepts (in this case, *postmodernism* or *women's writing*) as stemming from our "tendency to look for something in common to all the entities which we commonly subsume under a general term" (*Blue and Brown Books* 17). To avoid talking in terms of essence or common features, he employs the concepts of family resemblance and language games:

> We are inclined to think that there must be something in common to all games, say, and that this common property is the justification for applying the general term 'game' to the various games; whereas games form a *family* the members of which have family likenesses. . . . The idea of a general concept being a common property of its particular instances connects up with other primitive, too simple, ideas of the structure of language. It is comparable to the idea that *properties* are *ingredients* of the things which have the properties. . . . (17)

The problem of definition is a problem of grammar. The various questions, What is a novel? What is postmodernism? What is women's writing? actually involve different kinds of distinctions, but our grammar encourages us to equate them. The phrasing of our questions leads us to define these terms in the same way, seeking the thing each refers to or stands for and looking for the unifying element in all its applications (*Blue and Brown Books* 19). "I am saying," writes Wittgenstein, "that these phenomena have no one thing in common which makes us use the same word for all—but that they are *related* to one another in many different ways" (*Philosophical Investigations* #65). Both the polarity of our critical construct and our rhetorical commitment to oppositions encourage us to seek the necessary distinction between modernism and postmodernism, or between men's writing and women's writing, and, by implication, the essential unity of each. The pragmatist, however, changes our questions, asking about the *point* of the distinction and considering the relations between language and its users, not language and its referents. What motives and desires give rise to this distinction and how is it used and by whom? These are questions often taken for granted by those who look outside texts "subsumed under a general term" for evidence to justify a new category. When we ask the meaning of a word, Wittgenstein says, we are investigating "its use in the language" (*Philosophical Investigations* #43). Thus, we must pay more attention to the surface of language—not the surface in contrast to the significant depths, but the surface of expression itself: its grammar, its rhetoric, its contexts.

It has been Barbara Herrnstein Smith's work in narrative theory and literary value that has attended most rigorously to the consequences of this kind of thinking for literary criticism. Differences between types of literature, she argues, are not only historical and not simply formal but are based on the different motives, purposes, and contexts of different critical tasks. Since new sets of interests emerge continually in literary criticism, "there can be no ultimately basic set of relations among narratives, and thus also no 'natural' genres or 'essential' types" ("Narrative Versions" 222). Once we adopt an alternative to the correspondence theory of language, an alternative provided by Wittgenstein and certain pragmatists, such as Richard Rorty, we can approach narrative strategies not as representations of a certain set of conditions, such as women's lives or consumer society, but as functions of "multiple interacting conditions." Such an alternative concept of discourse, says Smith, would not only show why correspondence theories are untenable but would also move us beyond the poststructuralist denial of correspondence and its valorization of absences, contradictions, and ruptures (226). That is, it would show us how accepting the consequences of pragmatism, and postmodernism, changes the kinds of statements we can make about narrative discourse and literary value and the kinds of moves we can make as critics.

By using the term *postmodernism*, then, I do not mean to designate a repository of shared features but to demonstrate a shared way of behaving toward narratives based on shared assumptions about language use. For this reason, I place my readings of Woolf (chapters 1 through 6) before my general comments on postmodernism (Conclusion) to demonstrate a way of proceeding. To make the postmodern novel, not the modernist or the feminist, our point of reference for Woolf criticism is not just to isolate different textual elements, it is to assume a different critical stance as well. To situate Woolf in a postmodern context and to engage in the kinds of critical behavior relevant to postmodern narratives enables us to make the kinds of distinctions that are of more consequence for her "non-essentialist form of writing" (Moi, *Sexual/Textual Politics* 9). In particular, by attending to Woolf's playful discourse, her metafictional strategies, her fluctuating voices, and her changing narrative performances, I attempt to make subtle discriminations among the various motives informing her works and among the various functions her writings perform, calling into question the search for the essential criteria for understanding her writings and noting instead their "functional continuity." [28] My point is not just to show that certain characteristic features of modernist or postmodernist or feminist novels can function in different ways and enter into different relations with each other, producing different implications in different texts (though that is certainly one point I make), but also to show that our characteristic way of grouping texts by distinctive features can cause us to miss the telling differences and to mistake our critical categories for textual features. Shared traits such as playfulness, self-reflexiveness, contradictions, and indeterminacy, then, can best be approached as a set of related strategies for bringing out a potential function of narrative discourse and a possible way of responding to it.

In the chapters that follow, I read Woolf in terms of the writings of Kafka, Beckett, Robbe-Grillet, Sarraute, and others who, like Woolf, diverge from what we have come to characterize as modernist literature, enacting a series of readings that I feel are more in keeping with the claims we make for such "new" fiction. Whereas Marcus compares Woolf with Kafka, Brecht, Proust, and Benjamin based on their position *outside* the society—as Jews, homosexuals, Marxists, women, for whom language, literature, and culture belong to the "other," that is, the state or patriarchy— I look at their position *within* literary history (conceived as a palimpsest) and compare their fictional experiments in terms of what they were responding to within that history. That these responses are ideological and political as well as aesthetic I do not deny. But neither do I argue for the priority of ideological commitments or political arguments. On the contrary, *I argue that Woolf's experiments with narrative forms and functions engender certain ideological assumptions and political strategies, and thereby enable a feminist ideology to take shape.* Only in this way can we account for two apparently opposing values for Woolf: on the one hand, her commitment to and promotion of a feminist writing practice, and, on the other, her reluctance to prescribe such a practice and her resistance to the desire to prevail. In testing out possibilities in the novel form itself, Woolf tests out various theories of self, society, history, and language. She does not start with a theory to be expressed and then discover the appropriate form; rather, she articulates theories as they evolve from her fictional experiments.

In comparing Woolf with later writers, I do not mean to suggest that she was the "mother" of them all, a precursor of the *nouveau roman* or "postmodern" novel. And I do not want to imply that the novel is evolving toward some final or better form, or toward its own demise, a point I return to in the Conclusion. Rather, what I argue is that Woolf felt the strains in a changing literary scene as well as in a changing social and political climate, and that in working through some of the tensions in the novel form itself, she experimented with some of the same structures and concerns that characterize postmodern fiction. Thus, her writings can help us understand how a postmodern aesthetics or a feminist aesthetics comes about, not what it is in essence. By inquiring into the possibilities of novel writing, and by tracing the history and uses of prose in such works as *Orlando, A Room of One's Own,* "Phases of Fiction," and *The Second Common Reader,* Woolf exposes as contingent the classical, or patriarchal, forms that have been taken as essential or given. But in doing so, she does not delve beneath surface distinctions to some "truer" form; rather, she moves away from a set of defining features for the novel. Woolf recognized the "constructedness" of her own experiments, their provisional status. Her slogan was not the modernists' "Make it new" or the feminists' "Reject the old," for her sense of herself as participating in and creating anew a tradition while writing prevented her from valorizing the differentness or originality of her works. In fact, Woolf would have wanted no *one* slogan or manifesto, for that would link her with a particular movement with a defined goal and specified means of attaining it, a linear movement toward stasis. If Woolf valued anything in the artist it was her or his freedom to change. By accepting the provisional status of Woolf's art, we are better able to trace a variety of relations in her fiction and thereby keep her from settling into a "figure" (Diary 4:85).

In my readings of Woolf's texts, I discuss the structure of concerns and the shared strategies of postmodern writing *in terms of the particular problems in Woolf criticism that such a language can unravel*. I want to shed light on some functions of prose writing to which we are often blinded by our unacknowledged or unquestioned assumptions about language and to suggest where the difficulties arise that engender the problems. My purpose is to present a way of reading Woolf that does not rely on definitive distinctions, such as classical novel/modern novel, masculinist form/feminist form, modernism/postmodernism. Such categories, contrary to common assumptions of them, are not necessarily discrete, and certainly are not opposed. Rather, they are *constructed* to solve certain problems, and so they may be posited as distinct for certain purposes at certain times. Therefore, the generalizations we make about a category, such as a feminist narrative form or the postmodern novel, must be task-specific, holding only for the kinds of questions we are investigating by means of this category.

I do not argue, then, that "postmodernism" is the appropriate category for Virginia Woolf, only that her works are susceptible to analysis by means of this category and, further, that this category enables us to deal with certain contradictions in Woolf's works and with the problems critics face when they try to resolve or choose among them.

This brings me to my point in discussing feminist criticism and postmodernism together in this introduction. Many critics of feminist and postmodernist novels rely on the same assumptions about narrative discourse that ground the conventional or modernist novels from which these "radical" texts supposedly diverge. Whether the postmodern novel is seen as a radical break with or a logical extension of the modern novel, whether the feminist novel is seen as a revision or a rejection of the conventional novel, many critics accept such distinctions between old and new forms as obvious or given rather than as strategic. They accept a linear evolution of narrative form rather than considering the variety of ways in which this story of the modern/postmodern or conventional/feminist relation can be told. We have only to note the numerous histories of postmodernism and feminism now being offered to understand the multiplicity and instability of these terms.[29] What is often overlooked, however, is the fact that these histories are tracing certain *uses* of these terms, selecting their narrative elements from a variety of possibilities; they are not defining the thing itself. This knowledge does not prevent us from offering more valuable or rigorous definitions for these terms, but it does raise the question of why we are telling the story we are. The similarity among our claims for modernist, postmodernist, and feminist writing—for example, subverting outmoded conventions, critiquing the dominant culture, exposing false assumptions—is due less to the likeness of the texts in question than to the particular story we tell, a peculiarly modernist story in its emphasis on overcoming obstacles, eliminating falseness, defeating the opposition, winning new ground. A peculiarly postmodernist story might well focus on its own motives and its own methods in order to note what is at stake in the stories we tell and how we might tell them differently. From this perspective, there is no need to specify the right category for Virginia Woolf, only to attend to the kind of story we tell about her and the difference it makes.

Critics nonetheless continue to seek out *the* Virginia Woolf. The availability over the last ten years of Woolf's profuse personal writings, and feminist scholarship on these, has helped us understand the extent to which her writing changed, yet it has also given us the impression that we know the *real* Virginia Woolf. We are all fond of searching her personal writings for statements to support our readings of her fiction. Often, we offer these diary entries and letters as substantiating our claims for her fiction, as if her personal writings are somehow more authoritative than her fictional writings. Of course, when we find evidence for a certain reading in many writings, such evidence helps support that reading. But what makes us trust the writer revealed in the personal works more than the writer revealed in the fictional ones? However Woolf used her personal writings, we must remember that when we go to them, as when we go to her fiction and her essays, we do not approach them neutrally but with certain presuppositions. So when we pull out a line that seems, uncannily, to say what we have just said about her writing, we must remember that we were looking for such a line. As in biblical exegesis, we can find lines in Woolf's canon to support many different readings, for Woolf, like all of us, is at times contradictory.[30] When we fail to acknowledge this, we end up explaining away contradictions, smoothing out the wrinkles in her writing to reveal *the* pattern or the right map.[31]

To avoid the necessity of explaining away contradictions, of defining an appropriate form, and of reducing complexity to the process of choosing between two alternatives, we need to be ever vigilant in analyzing the relationship between our own critical activity and that which it opposes. We need to recognize that our own approaches reveal certain selections and comparisons of fictional elements rather than the appropriate form, the right map, or the definitive reading. We need to keep in mind that we are describing not Virginia Woolf's process or form itself but our own readings or metaphors that enable us to see that process or form. Much feminist criticism of Woolf risks one of two reductive conclusions: either it is in danger of keeping a masculine referential intact by defining feminist writing as against patriarchal writing, or it is in danger of asserting a feminine referential wherever it detects a masculine or patriarchal one. In opposing the stereotypes of male forms, much feminist criticism of Woolf risks setting up a counterstereotype of female forms. "The stereotype," Barthes tells us, "is the word repeated without any magic, any enthusiasm, *as though it were natural,* as though by some miracle this recurring word were adequate on each occasion for different reasons," or on different occasions for the same reasons (*Pleasure of the Text* 42; emphasis added). When certain feminist criticism sets itself up as the appropriate critical reading, it forces other feminists, like me, to take issue, albeit reluctantly. To avoid delineating a distinctive form for women's writing and then prescribing a social or literary order that can promote it, we can test out various possibilities, reading Woolf's works within a history of narrative literature that shapes and is shaped by them.

Reading Woolf in light of postmodernism must constantly be done in relation to a tradition of Woolf criticism, as I do in the chapters that follow, not just in relation to contemporary theory. Only in this way can we avoid the "before-her-time" argument, which would make Woolf into a prophetic figure, and instead (and more usefully) show how problems in Woolf criticism can be reconceptualized by drawing on the implications of postmodernism. Since postmodern writing contains within it the very practices and assumptions it seeks to challenge, a postmodern reading must, in Hutcheon's words, "call attention to both what is being contested and what is being offered as a critical response to that, and to do so in a self-aware way that admits its own provisionality" (13). This is my goal in reading Woolf's writing as an exploration and testing out of the possibilities of literature. Like much postmodern fiction, her literature is in quest and question of literature itself.[32]

Now, with the above caveat in mind, I will ever so cautiously offer an entry from Woolf's diary, not as proof of my point, but as a seemingly appropriate ending to this introduction: "I was led into trying to define my own particular search—not after morality, or beauty or reality—no; but after literature itself" (Diary 1:213–14).

## NOTES

1. I am certainly not the first to draw connections between Woolf and postmodern writers. As far back as the 1960s, Freedman in *The Lyrical Novel* (1963) and Levin in "What Was Modernism?" (1966) suggest connections between Woolf and the *nouveau roman*. Likewise, Richter in *Virginia Woolf: The Inward Voyage* (1970), Heath in *The Nouveau Roman* (1972), and Harper in *Between Language and Silence* (1982) briefly compare Woolf with Robbe-Grillet, Sarraute, and Beckett, respectively. More recently, Beja, in his introduction to *Critical Essays on Virginia Woolf* (1985) and West, in "Enigmas of Imagination: *Orlando* through the Looking Glass" (1986), argue that Woolf looks ahead to Barth, Nabokov, Borges, Calvino, Spark, and other writers of postmodernism; and Waugh includes a chapter on Woolf in *Feminine Fiction: Revisiting the Postmodern* (1989). But no one has yet undertaken what I would call a *postmodern reading*, attending to the implications of drawing such connections for narrative theory and criticism in general. To paraphrase Culler, when so many of yesterday's modernists are today's postmodernists, confusion arises over the differences between them (*On Deconstruction* 25). My approach to the differences between modernism and postmodernism, as well as to the differences within Woolf's canon, is a pragmatic one.

2. Like Woolf's assertion, "In or about December 1910, human character changed" ("Mr. Bennett and Mrs. Brown," CDB 96), my own date is admittedly arbitrary and provocative. The fact that I place Kamuf's article "Penelope at Work: Interruptions in *A Room of One's Own*" (1982) in the later stage of Woolf criticism and Marcus's collection *Virginia Woolf and Bloomsbury* (1987) in the earlier

stage does not disprove the general assertion of a profound change in relation to postmodern thought. It does, however, make salient the point Woolf's pronouncement raises: the need to interrogate our concepts of periodization and to make self-conscious our own motives for narrating historical change.

4. My point here is similar to Zwerdling's on Woolf, Hassan's on postmodernism ("Making Sense"), and Kristeva's on poststructuralist feminism (see Moi, *Kristeva Reader*). While neither denying the importance of nor neglecting the political, I do not grant politics *priority* in my reading of Woolf or in my account of the function of narrative discourse. The reason I do not will become clear later in this chapter.

4. Bathsheba's statement actually reads: "It is difficult for a woman to define her feelings in language which is chiefly made by men to express theirs" (327). The wording Woolf uses sends many feminist critics on a wild goose chase for a separate women's language that is often seen as opposed to men's. Their efforts seem to confirm Woolf's remark following her misquotation of Hardy: "From that dilemma arise infinite confusions and complications" (WW 67).

5. By the time she wrote "Craftsmanship" (1937), Woolf had changed from advocating a new language to advocating new uses of words. This is perhaps the difference Gilbert and Gubar see when they say Woolf's call for a "woman's sentence" is a *"fantasy"* that expresses her desire to change *"not woman's language but woman's relation to language"* ("Sexual Linguistics" 523). Yet there is no single relation between women and language and no change from the wrong relation to the right one. In *The Short Season between Two Silences,* Moore also argues that in "Craftsmanship" Woolf comes to see that words are associative, that they mean only in relations (104), though despite this insight, Moore still speaks of Woolf's quest for truth, as if there were a right relation.

6. I realize that Marcus's militaristic language and analogy are designed to jar us, for Woolf's pacifism and a feminist hostility to the military make this analogy glaring and provocative.

7. In *Virginia Woolf and the Languages of Patriarchy,* Marcus makes such assertions as if the value of Woolf's writings depended on their exclusive audience: "When do we realize," Marcus writes about *A Room of One's Own*, "that our inclusion in the 'we' of this narrative marks the exclusion of the male reader?" (172); and later, "What a radical novel *The Years* is, and no wonder men don't like it and women do" (50). A strength of Marcus's writing is that she makes her addressee clear, namely, women readers and feminist critics, just as Woolf makes her audience quite apparent in her two feminist essays, namely, college-educated women (*A Room of One's Own*) and the daughters of educated men (*Three Guineas*). But I hesitate to claim these writings as my own on the basis of these particular audiences. And I resist the implicit assumption that women read, as well as write, alike. In response to J. Hillis Miller's and Hartman's readings of a passage in *A Room of One's Own,* Marcus justifies her own very different reading by claiming every woman reader she knows reads the passage the way she does (*Languages of Patriarchy* 159). I do not find such consensus necessary, or even desirable; nor do I share Marcus's reading of this passage (see my p. 46).

8. It is this kind of thinking, relying as it does on an opposition between two

things, that characterizes modernism and is put into question by postmodernism. For related discussions, see, for example, Levenson's introduction to *A Genealogy of Modernism*, Lyotard's *Postmodern Condition* (sec. 4 and 5), Jardine's *Gynesis* (chap. 3), and Huyssen's *After the Great Divide* (182).

9. More recently, feminist critics, such as Marcus in the introduction to *Virginia Woolf and the Languages of Patriarchy*, substitute Kristeva's "semiotic" for these terms, thereby renaming the old dualisms without changing their approach to them, as Kristeva's writings encourage us to do. In *Virginia Woolf and the Problem of the Subject*, Minow-Pinkney gives us a more sophisticated, less reductive Kristevan reading of Woolf's novels, though her consistent use of the same semiotic/symbolic distinction makes her readings somewhat predictable.

10. My "broader" perspective on Woolf is by no means a denial of the feminist perspective but seeks to connect feminism with other reactions to this humanistic and positivistic tradition: namely, poststructuralism, postmodernism, and pragmatism. I stress the relations among these "isms" as a way of resisting the urge to polarize them (e.g., by seeing feminism at odds with postmodernism) or to conflate them (e.g., by seeing feminism and postmodernism as working toward the same ends).

11. This is an important point for my project. I take issue not with feminist criticism but with particular instances of feminist criticism. Throughout this book I challenge our generalizing habit of mind which often leads us to make sweeping claims for or against feminism or postmodernism based on isolated examples. Instead, I attend to particular examples of such writings and base my conclusions on the particular case at hand.

12. Although this passage uses the masculine pronoun, Orlando, now a woman, finds herself participating in such a struggle to prevail. Thus, contrary to some feminist claims, I would not argue from the words "breast of man" that this desire is essentially or characteristically masculine.

13. Quigley discusses the problem of giving preference to only one function of language in terms of Wittgenstein's language theory: "Wittgenstein demonstrates conclusively the inadequacy of attempts to view meaning as a single function of reference whether the reference is to external objects or internal concepts." Language, he continues, has no "single or central function" (*Pinter Problem* 37).

14. This tendency persists in some recent feminist criticism of postmodernism. For example, both Waugh and Kipnis complain that postmodernism is discussed and described by critics primarily in formal terms. I agree. But to downplay the formal experimentation by emphasizing instead the political commitment is to locate the politics elsewhere than in the writing. That is, to dismiss the formal for the political is to miss the insight postmodern writing provides; it no longer makes sense to draw such distinctions absolutely. As I argue, Woolf's formal experimentation enables her to express a mode of thinking, writing, and being conducive to new social arrangements. In other words, political readings of Woolf's works (whether Marcus's or Moi's) need not be seen as alternatives to narrowly formalist ones; instead, we can read Woolf's formal experiments as material practices, "short narratives" in Lyotard's sense, that enable her to test out various political positions.

15. By emphasizing emotion, Woolf seems to emphasize human motive over

end product as derived from a perceived design. For further discussion of her concept of literature, see chapter 6.

16. My remark may recall Baym's in "The Madwoman and Her Languages," especially since I go on to cite Gilbert's work. Attacking theory, Baym argues that "when you start with a theory of difference," as Gilbert and Gubar do, "you can't see anything but" (51). Yet the problem lies not in "a theory of difference" but in a concept of difference as opposition. While our points in respect to Gilbert's work are similar, our responses to feminist theory in general are not.

17. This is the strength of Zwerdling's *Virginia Woolf and the Real World*. We must look at Woolf's narrative techniques not in terms of general modernist or feminist projects, Zwerdling argues, but in terms of Woolf's "individual solutions to the problem at hand" (64). Noting that, for Woolf, narrative is a means to an end and that the ends of Woolf's novels are never the same, Zwerdling discusses each novel in terms of its particular point. What I add to Zwerdling's approach, I believe, is a theoretical perspective that enables us to analyze these changes in other than "individual" terms.

18. I discuss these two novels in detail in chapter 3.

19. This is what I mean when I say we need to take the implications of feminist criticism further in order to change the way we conceive of and respond to narrative discourse (see p. xii). Several writers present a similar view to the one I offer here, including Kristeva (*New French Feminisms* 165) and Johnson (*World of Difference* 164). Most recently, Messer-Davidow argues: "Some feminist critics mistakenly think that sex/gender traits characterize a creative process" (77). She also points out that the boundaries of an object of study are determined by our questions and by the problems we define, not by the intrinsic traits of the object of study (76). Her argument is similar to Smith's, which I cite later.

20. In "For the Etruscans," DuPlessis draws comparisons between women's writing and postmodern writing: "A list of the characteristics of postmodernism would be a list of the traits of women's writing" (286). She goes on to list shared traits as well as to caution that women's writing and postmodernism part company when the latter "becomes politically quietistic" or "devalues the female self" (287). But here is where relying on shared traits alone may not be very helpful, for as Jardine argues in *Gynesis*, postmodernism may make a certain kind of feminism (based on common features) no longer tenable. Jardine accounts for the similarities by claiming "woman" as a "new rhetorical space" created by postmodernism. I discuss Jardine's work further in the Conclusion.

21. See Lanham's *Literacy and the Survival of Humanism* for a discussion of the problems that arise from considering the purposeful, not the playful, as the primary motive for writing.

22. See, for example, Zwerdling's *Virginia Woolf and the Real World*, Minow-Pinkney's *Virginia Woolf and the Problem of the Subject*, Bowlby's *Virginia Woolf: Feminist Destinations*, and Waugh's *Feminine Fictions: Revisiting the Postmodern*.

23. This tendency is most evident in DuPlessis's *Writing beyond the Ending* and Hirsch's *Mother/Daughter Plot*, both of which contain sections devoted to Woolf.

24. For example, Waugh argues that women writers such as Woolf, because of their marginalized position in society, understood identity as constructed through power relations long before postmodern writers picked up this idea from post-

structuralist theorists (*Feminine Fictions* 3, 10). The implication is that feminism owes little to postmodernism and that we must keep feminism "pure" to maintain its authority. Like Marcus—who once acknowledged that she had learned much from Gayatri Spivak and Peggy Kamuf but she wished they would give up their reliance on male theorists—Waugh seems to think we can separate what we see from the theories that enable us to see it (Marcus, "Still Practice: A/Wrested Alphabet" 90).

25. Thiher's premise is that modern language theory since Saussure is "not only useful but often presupposed for an adequate reading of much contemporary fiction" (6).

26. Burke makes this observation in terms of a pragmatic approach to literature: "It assumes that a poem's structure is to be described most accurately by thinking always of the poem's function. It assumes that the poem is designed to 'do something' for the poet and his readers" (89). Burke makes another useful observation in connection with this pragmatic approach: that the differences among critical schools lie in the questions they ask.

27. Postmodern art, Lyotard writes, investigates "what makes it an art object and whether it will be able to find an audience" (75). He, Arac, Rorty, Hassan, and Fraser and Nicholson have all connected pragmatism with postmodernism. Thiher, McHale, and Lyotard also connect postmodern fiction with Wittgenstein's concept of language games.

28. I borrow this phrase from Hardy's reference to the barn on Bathsheba's farm (140). His comparison of the barn to a cathedral recalls Woolf's description of the barn at Pointz Hall in *Between the Acts,* and their points are similar: both stress continuity in change by noting the shared activity engaged in by members of a community to sustain a way of life. See my discussion of Woolf's last novel in chapter 1.

29. Examples of some recent books offering different histories and different definitions of postmodernism and feminism are: Huyssen's *After the Great Divide,* Hassan's *Postmodern Turn,* McHale's *Postmodernist Fiction,* Hutcheon's *Poetics of Postmodernism,* Jardine's *Gynesis,* Moi's *Sexual/Textual Politics,* and Ruthven's *Feminist Literary Studies.*

30. Bowlby comments as well on the error of assuming that Woolf's diaries are a more accurate account of experience than her fiction and on the relation between biblical exegesis and Woolf criticism (14, 136–37).

31. Marcus claims that by comparing Woolf to the men I have mentioned, she provides us with the "right map." By implication, the comparisons between Woolf and Forster or Lawrence give us the "wrong map," as if those comparisons are false and unrevealing.

32. The "literary act in quest and question of itself" is a line from Hassan's "POSTmodernISM." I read the article and borrowed the line as my subtitle long before I uncannily discovered Woolf's diary entry quoted at the end of this introduction.

# 1

## The Artist Figure in Woolf's Writings:
### *The Status and Function of Art*

They [the modernists] cannot tell stories because they do not believe
the stories are true.
                                        —Virginia Woolf,
                                           *The Common Reader*

Is telling stories telling lies?

                    —Patricia Waugh,
                       *Metafiction*

So many of Virginia Woolf's novels and essays portray an artist: Terence
Hewet (*The Voyage Out*), Ralph Denham and William Rodney (*Night and
Day*), Lily Briscoe and Augustus Carmichael (*To the Lighthouse*), Orlando
in that eponymous novel, Mary Carmichael (*A Room of One's Own*), Bernard and Neville (*The Waves*), Elizabeth Barrett Browning (*Flush*), and
Miss La Trobe (*Between the Acts*). Even those characters who are not osten-
sibly creative artists function as artist figures in their works: Rhoda (*The
Waves*), Sara (*The Years*), and Isa (*Between the Acts*) turn mundane events
and commonplace remarks into private poetry, and Mrs. Dalloway and
Mrs. Ramsay create transient works of art out of social occasions and personal relationships. Often Woolf's artist figures comment directly on their
difficulties in narrating the work we are reading: for example, the biographers of *Jacob's Room* and *Orlando* and the narrators of "An Unwritten
Novel" and "Mr. Bennett and Mrs. Brown." In fact, the first work Woolf
tried to publish was a fictitious review of a fictitious biography of a fictitious, and not very talented, writer named Miss Willatt (Gordon, "Our
Secret Life" 79). What are all these portraits of the artist about if not the
continual investigation of literature itself—its processes, its aims, its value?

And yet, a curious pattern emerges in these portraits. With the exception of Orlando and Augustus Carmichael, who eventually receive recognition for their poetry, and Mrs. Dalloway and Mrs. Ramsay, whose

parties finally come off, none of Woolf's fictional artists is confident, skill-ful, successful, or even very productive. Although Lily Briscoe may have her vision and La Trobe may produce her play, each questions the achieve-ment of her art, and so do many readers. If these works on the artist figure investigate art itself, why do so few of the artists create a consummate work of art or articulate a consistent theory of art? Why all these failed artists?

Of course, the question so often asked by Woolf's critics is a loaded one, for it rests on two assumptions: one, that Woolf is investigating the nature of art in terms of the art/life relation; and two, that frustration, doubt, and inconclusiveness express failure or despair. Both assumptions are bound up with a modernist aesthetics, one that informs much of our critical ter-minology and one that Woolf seems to question every bit as much as she does an aesthetics of realism. In this chapter, I explore the problems that a certain set of assumptions about modernist works have led to in criticism of Woolf's novels on the artist figure. In addition, I suggest an alternative approach that enables us to see how Woolf herself questions these mod-ernist assumptions that her critics often take for granted: in particular, the assumptions that the artist is a *special* and *self-sufficient* individual, that the artwork is *original* and *autonomous,* and that art is a means of providing *order* or revealing *truth.* Questioning such assumptions led Woolf to posit a different conception of the artist and a different model for narrative dis-course. To explore Woolf's changing notions, I focus in this chapter on the novels that directly explore the creative process—*To the Lighthouse* (1927), *The Waves* (1932), and *Between the Acts* (1941)—as well as Woolf's famous essay on the female writer, *A Room of One's Own* (1929). In these writings, the subject of many modernist works (the artist's work or theory) becomes a strategy of the texts themselves.[1] That is, what was once narrated—the doubts, difficulties, and resolutions of the artist—in novels such as Joyce's *Portrait of the Artist as a Young Man* or Woolf's "Unwritten Novel" or *The Voyage Out* becomes a structural principle of these works. Lily Briscoe, Bernard, and Miss La Trobe do not just produce works of art; in addi-tion, they produce—that is, narrate and interpret—the novels in which their art figures.[2] The artist's doubts and difficulties are not obstacles to be overcome, as they are for Stephen Dedalus; rather, they are motivating structures of the artwork.

A brief review of the commentaries on these novels soon makes appar-ent most critics' reliance on a modernist aesthetics. Most critical commen-taries present Woolf's artists as creating aesthetic harmony or unity out of the flux of experience (Mitchell Leaska on *To the Lighthouse,* Jean Guiguet on *The Waves,* James Naremore on *Between the Acts*); as exploring the rela-tion between art and life, the continual collapse of one into the other and the renewed effort to distinguish between them (Norman Friedman on *To the Lighthouse,* J. W. Graham on *The Waves,* B. H. Fussell on *Between the Acts*); as questing after the essence beneath or the truth beyond all surface manifestations and conventional forms (James Hafley on *To the Lighthouse,* Harvena Richter on *The Waves*); or, as finally doubting such essence or truth (Maria DiBattista on *Between the Acts*). Woolf's artists are seen as making "something perfect and lasting" (Pamela J. Transue paraphrasing *To the Lighthouse,* Guiguet on *The Waves*), as creating a new aesthetic form (Naremore on *The Waves,* Ann Y. Wilkinson on *Between the Acts*), or as fulfilling "the quest for artistic autonomy" (DiBattista on *The Waves*). The artists are seen as trying to free themselves from conventional forms to achieve an "unfettered mind" or to communicate a "private vision" (Transue and Leaska, respectively). Whether critics deputize Woolf's artists as exemplars of modernist or feminist writing, they assume the artist's desire is for freedom, originality, or truth.

All these commentaries rest on the assumption that Woolf and her artists are concerned with the nature of art's relation to life, where art and life are two realms of experience. They confuse Woolf's and her artists' continual and changing investigations of this relation with the quest for the right or essential relation, that is, with the quest for truth. But the fact that neither Woolf nor her artists ever quite net that "fin in the waste of waters" (the germinal image of *The Waves* and a commonly accepted metaphor for Woolf's artistic quest) need not be interpreted either as the failure of the quest for truth or as an affirmation of the quest itself. For truth may not lie where we look for it, whether at the end of the process or beneath the surface of the text.

As long as we accept authenticity, autonomy, permanence, and uniqueness as our aesthetic standards, and as long as we accept the relation of art to life (whether mental or material) as the defining relation of the novel, we will interpret a text that is fragmentary, contradictory, tenuous, or imitative either as a failed endeavor or as an accurate reflection of the chaos or banality of life itself. Such standards are not wrong, but they are not always appropriate. Our failure to acknowledge the norm against which we measure Woolf's and her artists' productions as failed communication, frustrated effort, or fragmented form encourages us to read all of these novels in the same way, as if Woolf and her artists were continually searching after the same thing: the nature of art or "life itself." It is this assumption we must question.

Woolf herself has questioned our common assumptions about the modern age and modernist literature in her last essay in *The Common Reader,* "How It Strikes a Contemporary" (1923). In a statement often cited as her own belief, Woolf expresses the prevailing opinion of her age: "It is," she declares in the voice of the critics, "an age of fragments" (CR 240). Such a remark gives credence to our common assumptions. "But," she cautions a page later, "it is just when opinions universally prevail and we have added lip service to their authority that we become sometimes most keenly conscious that we do not believe a word that we are saying" (241). In this essay, Woolf does not pay lip service to our common assumptions about modernist literature; rather, she reconsiders the basis for these assumptions. If the artist is seen as alienated and apart from society, if literature is seen as fragmented, pessimistic, or banal, it is not, Woolf suggests, because the age—or the self—is fragmented; that is, it is not because of what this art reflects. Rather, it is because the artists, as well as the critics, are intent on novelty and originality: "No age can have been more rich than ours in writers determined to give expression to the differences which separate them from the past and not to the resemblances which connect them with it" (242). Woolf does not argue for a return to the "common belief" that seems to inform literature of the past, nor does she argue against the expression of differences in the literature of the present. Instead, she considers the writers' motives for writing: to express their difference. And she emphasizes as well the need to place the present in relation to the past in order to understand both change and continuity in literature, and in order not to make the past into a norm against which to measure the present. That is, instead of accepting or denying the common belief, Woolf finds another way to proceed. And another way to proceed is what I am after here.

An alternative to discussing Woolf's novels on the artist in terms of the *nature* of art—the art/life, fact/fiction, or form/content relation—is to consider them in terms of the *status* and *function* of art. We can look at the textual relations themselves and the text/user relation. Increasingly in her novels on the artist figure, Woolf's concern is less with the reality beyond the rhetoric, as the fact/fiction dichotomy suggests, than with the rhetoric of reality. That is, her continual investigation of the artistic process is less concerned with what art is or what life is than with how life is narrated, less with the relation of narrative to the real (whether self or world) than with the narrative relations of and in the real.

Such a distinction between the what and the how or the process and the product is, of course, one that is often made between modernist and postmodernist texts: that is, modernist works are *about* consciousness or reality, while postmodernist texts are *about* writing and fiction.[3] But as my emphasis on *about* suggests, this change in the subject of the discourse merely shifts the concern with representation from outside the text (the world or mind) to inside it (writing itself). Such a view still relies on a correspondence theory of language, implying that if the text does not refer to what is "out there," then it must refer to what is "in here," as if literary language had nowhere else to go, as if its only function were to point.[4] To say, as so many critics do, that each of these novels is about its own process, about art itself or about women's writing, is not yet to say what kinds of narrative processes or artistic relations each explores.[5] Painting a picture, preparing a lecture, telling a story, and producing a play are analogous activities only in the most general sense. To subsume them under one category (e.g., texts about art) is to posit a similarity of structure and purpose where there is only a diversity of functions and motives.

The focus on the creative process over the product is not, then, the key distinction to be made between Woolf's modernist concerns and her postmodernist ones. In fact, the distinction works the other way. The consideration of these novels in terms of postmodern strategies and motives enables us to change the questions we ask about these texts and the functions we expect them to perform. Instead of asking what the text is about, we can ask how it comes about and what it brings about. Instead of expecting it to reveal truth, we can expect it to change behavior. As Woolf tests out the possibilities of narrative discourse, she questions its potential functions and the status of her own fiction. From private vision (Lily) to reader/listener response (Bernard) to public performance (La Trobe), Woolf enacts various aesthetic theories and exposes the partial and artificial nature of literary forms.

What the postmodern framework enables us to do, then, is not just to explore the writing process but to change our model for narrative discourse from one that relies on two terms to one that accounts for the changing aesthetic motives in Woolf's works. Exploring the process of textual construction itself, as Kafka does in "The Burrow," for example, reveals not only that as writers we create our own *Bau*—that structure of codes, conventions, desires, and beliefs both restricting and enabling—but also that in the process we create as well the enemy within, the very counterforce that pulls against our structure, disturbs our peace, and threatens our security. We can remain entrapped in our own constructs, digging our way ever further in, asserting ever more strongly the validity and necessity of our artistic structures, and producing in turn ever stronger doubts about their value and efficacy (the scenario presented in Kafka's story and in criticism of Woolf's works on the artist figure). Or, we can dig our way out, surface from the deep, to borrow Barbara Herrnstein Smith's metaphor, by conceiving of art and life not in terms of categorical distinctions but in terms of multiple and shifting relations among a variety of engendering motives and conditions.[6] Such a move does not liberate us from constructs or constraints but from the desperate activity of scuttling back and forth within one structure, one conception of language, one model of discourse. The artist's process includes her or his response to as well as production of the work, and Woolf's response to her own productions leads her to test out a variety of constructions rather than digging in the same burrow— or, a more apt metaphor for Woolf, fishing in the same waste of waters.

With Lily Briscoe in *To the Lighthouse,* Woolf created her first artist figure to tell the story of her own artwork as well as the story in which her artwork figures, and it is this narrative function of the artist that led Woolf to question some of the modernist assumptions with which she began.[7] The structure of Woolf's novel is the progression of Lily's painting: its inception in Lily's desire to paint Mrs. Ramsay (part 1); its dissolution following the death of Mrs. Ramsay (part 2); its renewal ten years later when Lily returns to the Ramsays' summer home (part 3); and its completion as the exhausted artist lays down her brush, declaring in the last line of the novel: "I have had my vision." As Patricia Waugh notes, *To the Lighthouse* is one of the earliest novels to stress "a sense of fictitiousness" (*Metafiction* 6), both the fictitious status of what it represents ("life itself") and the fictitious status of its own representations (the text itself). My two readings of "fictitiousness" recall, respectively, Erich Auerbach's modernist reading of *To the Lighthouse* as a "critique of representation" and J. Hillis Miller's deconstructive reading of the novel as an exploration of the act of creating the novel itself ("Rhythm of Creativity"). However, the involuted structure of this and the other novels on the artist figure suggests not just a reflexive relation of the framed artwork to the artwork of the frame but also a spiral relation. That is, it suggests both the way the subject matter of the novel turns in on and reflects its method and the way it winds out from and back to its method. In other words, it is not that the meaning of the novel is its method, or that the form and content are one and the same; rather, the subject matter of the novel is a function of the novel's discourse.[8] If *To the Lighthouse* is in quest of its own status as art, then in generalizing on this work we must remember that a particular kind of painting, and thus a particular kind of discourse, is at issue in this novel. As Lily explains to William Bankes in part 1, her painting makes "no attempt at likeness . . . the picture was not of them" (81). The painting, she continues, is a matter of *relations,* and it is these relations we must consider.

Throughout the novel, Woolf presents Lily's art as a matter of relating two things: the mass on the right of her canvas and the mass on the left; Mrs. Ramsay in the window and Mr. Ramsay in the boat; the shore on which she stands and the sea to which she looks. Early in the novel this relation is one of connection: "It was a question, [Lily] remembered, how to connect this mass on the right hand with that on the left. She might do it by bringing the line of the branch across so" (82–83). Most critics accept this connection between two things as the essence not only of this novel but of Woolf's art in general. "Throughout Mrs. Woolf's work," writes Naremore, "the chief problem for her and for her characters is to overcome the space between things, to attain an absolute unity with the world" (242). Certainly this line across the canvas that presages Lily's final brush stroke endorses such a reading. However, this is only one moment of Woolf's novel. By the time Lily completes her painting, the relation she seeks has changed from connecting two things to maintaining a balance between forces (TTL 287). As Lily nears the completion of her painting, she thinks: "One wanted . . . to be on a level with ordinary experience, to feel simply that's a chair, that's a table, and yet at the same time, It's a miracle, it's an ecstasy. The problem [of relations] might be solved after all" (299–300). The problem is solved, but neither by synthesizing two things nor by choosing between them. The problem is solved—or rather, removed—by a change in Lily's concerns: *the distinction to be made is no longer between two things but between different ways of relating things.* And what effects this change is Lily's function as narrator in part 3.

While Lily paints her picture in sections III–XIII of this third part, she moves back and forth between a loss of consciousness of outer things as she "tunnels" into the past, and a return to consciousness of external things as she looks out to sea. Both the memories Lily re-creates from the first part of the novel and the events she observes in the third part somehow function in the production of her art, and thus we must consider the role of memory and the function of the trip to the lighthouse. In her presentation of those memories, those boat scenes, and the relation between them, Woolf checks two modernist tendencies in Lily's art. One is the withdrawal from the public world of facts into the private world of vision to achieve some form of order. The other is the effort to synthesize the two to achieve some kind of harmony. I want to consider each of these tendencies in turn by looking at the way the memories and the boat trip are presented to us.

Critics often focus on the role memory plays in the production of Lily's painting as well as Woolf's novel. Clearly Woolf believed that memory is necessary to the creative act. She felt a special sympathy with Proust and shared his sense of the involuntary memory, the moment when habit relaxes and memories well up, merging past and present in one stream of time.[9] Yet Woolf's emphasis here is slightly different from Proust's. First, the memories do not enable Lily to express some hitherto unrealized experience, nor does the consciousness of the world around her disturb that vision, but the two together enable her to paint. Second, Lily's memories are not private but shared in that they activate the reader's memories. For example, when Lily hears a voice saying "women can't paint, women can't write," we have identified that voice long before Lily dips into her memory far enough to pull out the name Charles Tansley. This is a common strategy of Woolf's works on the artist figure. In the last chapter of *A Room of One's Own,* we encounter repetitions of events and phrases from the chapters before, and in the last section of *The Waves,* we share with Bernard memories of earlier scenes and images. A related experience is our remembering enough of English drama to catch parodies of Elizabethan, Restoration, and Victorian plays in La Trobe's pageant in *Between the Acts.* This reworking of earlier scenes implicates the reader in the narrative process, merging our memories with the artist's. We become aware of the person and the stories made up about the person, for the person does not exist outside those stories, yet failing to look at the person turns the imaginings in on the creator, allows one to accept one's own illusions as truth. This turning inward is the tendency toward subjectivism and aestheticism that Woolf evokes and disrupts in this novel.

Such disruption is dramatized in section IV when, at the moment of greatest intensity, Lily steps into the waters of annihilation in her frantic desire to bring back the dead Mrs. Ramsay. At that moment, Woolf breaks the spell with this scene:

> [Macalister's boy took one of the fish and cut a square out of its side to bait his hook with. The mutilated body (it was alive still) was thrown back into the sea]. (268)

This is life, "startling, unexpected, unknown" (268). The brackets, conventionally used to indicate an interruption, remind us of the reports of external events placed in brackets in "Time Passes" and presage the scenes where nature intrudes in the play of *Between the Acts.*[10] Who tells us this scene? If, as I will argue, Lily narrates the scenes in the boat, it seems unlikely that she narrates this action. This scene seems to be outside Lily's consciousness, disconnected from her, yet it brings her back to herself and to her surroundings. The very ambiguity of the perceiver and reporter of this scene, the startling break from Lily's consciousness, and the indifferent cruelty of the action make us feel the shock of life intruding on our illusion. This section functions not only thematically but also structurally. It keeps us from wading into the waters of annihilation by manifesting the structure of the text and by checking the consoling power of art. It reminds us that there *is* something beyond the text, but that something cannot be assimilated until it is made part of a sequence. In the placement of this section, Woolf makes us conscious of the process she has been investigating through Lily's painting, the moving back and forth from outer world to inner and of the virtual boundary between the two.

This losing consciousness of outer things and returning to it suggests the balance between fact and vision that Lily desires. But the language of these boat scenes indicates that what she looks at is also narrated, not merely observed. At the end of section III, Lily walks across the lawn and looks at the boats going out to sea: "there was one rather apart from the others. The sail was even now being hoisted. She *decided* that there in that very distant and entirely silent little boat Mr. Ramsay was sitting with Cam and James. Now they had got the sail up; now after a little flagging and hesitation the sails filled and, shrouded in profound silence, she watched the boat take its way with deliberation past the other boats out to sea" (TTL 241–42; emphasis added). Lily *selects* one boat and *decides* that this is the Ramsays'. The boat, the whole scene, is "shrouded in profound silence" until someone, here the artist, gives it shape by giving it some sequence ("Now they had got the sail up; now . . . the sails filled"). It is as if Lily narrates the boat scene given to us in the next section. Earlier that morning Lily had wondered how to make sense of the chaos of emotions, actions, and voices that filled the house after ten years' passage of time: "If only she could put them together, she felt, write them out in some sentence, then she would have got at the truth of things" (219). Mr. Ramsay's trip to the lighthouse seems to be that sequence.

Throughout section IV, the boat scene, Woolf employs the conditional "would be," at times suggesting the children's thoughts—"He would be impatient in a moment, James thought"—at others suggesting someone imagining the scene: "Now they would sail on for hours like this, and Mr. Ramsay would ask old Macalister a question—about the great storm last winter probably—and old Macalister would answer it, and they would puff their pipes together, and Macalister would take a tarry rope in his fingers, tying or untying some knot, and the boy would fish, and never say a word to any one" (244). If we are in the minds of the children in such passages, the choice of verbs would suggest their knowledge of their father's behavior on such boat trips; yet this is supposedly their first trip to the lighthouse.[11] *Would* calls attention to the *telling* of the boat scene; we are not watching *what* happens but *how* what happens could be narrated. Someone is creating all this, while we watch, and that someone seems to be Lily, who stands on the shore watching the little boat: "Yes, the breeze was freshening" (246). *Yes* evokes the presence of a perceiver, someone creating and confirming this vision, and links the various sections: "Yes, that is their boat, Lily Briscoe decided" (253). The words *now, would,* and *yes* evoke the perceiving and connecting mind.[12] The return to Lily on the shore in the next section (V) reminds us of the unreality of the scene in that boat, shrouded in silence, compared with Lily's actions on shore.

By means of Lily's function as narrator, Woolf stresses the reciprocal relation between life and art, how the creative process actualizes daily life. By calling attention to Lily's stories—of Mrs. Ramsay, of Paul and Minta, of Mr. Ramsay and the children—Woolf reveals that the nature of the relation between fact and vision, art and life, has changed. We are no longer concerned with *the* connection or *the* correspondence between two realms but with the connections we posit among a variety of elements selected from a range of possibilities. That is, we are no longer concerned with formal relations (as Lily is in part 1) but with narrative relations. Once we acknowledge this change in relations, we can better explain Lily's remark about the status of her artwork. Asking again the recurring question of this last part, "What does it mean?" Lily thinks of how Mr. Carmichael would presumably have answered: "nothing stays; all changes; but not words, not paint" (267). We can see why this attitude has brought Mr. Carmichael fame as a poet following World War I, for it validates the artist's activity in terms of its product, the thing that endures. When Lily thinks of her painting, however, she qualifies this view: "Yet it would be hung in the attics, she thought; it would be rolled up and flung under a sofa; yet even so, even of a picture like that, it was true. One might say, even of this scrawl, not of that actual picture, perhaps, but of what it attempted, that it 'remained for ever' . . ." (267).[13] Lily judges her art not in terms of how it differs from life but in terms of what it attempts; that is, in terms of its commitment to a form of behavior, not its devotion to a type of painting.

Woolf reiterates this point in *A Room of One's Own* when her narrator remarks that "good writers are good human beings" and that their writing is what matters, "and whether it matters for ages or only for hours, nobody can say" (110). Whether or not Lily's painting will be hung in an attic, whether or not women's writings will be canonized, whether or not La Trobe's play will be remembered matters less, Woolf implies, than the fact that these artists are creating. Their art is consumable, or disposable, not lapidary. Failing to note the change in relations that occurs in these texts, most critics accept these remarks at face value.[14] But a particular conception of art is at issue here. What makes these assertions more modest than the wholesale endorsement of any artistic activity by women is *the change in motive,* from the desire to connect two things and make a lasting product, to the desire to maintain a multiple perspective and participate in an ongoing activity. In essays like "Reading" and "Oxford Street Tide," Woolf contrasts "our" way (the present) with "their" way (the old) by attributing to past writers the desire to make something that will endure. Yet this same desire, as we have seen, can be detected in modernist writers of Woolf's day in contrast to postmodernist writers of our own. Thus, we can say, more precisely, that it is not old and new literature that Woolf distinguishes between, or male and female, but *different motives for writing.* Since literature is "attached ever so lightly perhaps, but still attached to life at all four corners" (ROO 43), and since life is constantly changing, literature must change continually as well. Because life is in part an effect of the artistic relations that shape it, the ongoing evolution of language provides a paradigm for reality.[15]

Woolf expresses this relation in the wavelike rhythm of Lily's painting. Lily feels urged forward and held back simultaneously. Her pauses and strokes form one process, so that the moments when the artist is not painting are just as essential as the strokes themselves. *Waves*, a noun, would seem to suggest a thing, a mountain of water with white foam curling at the top. Yet it actually signifies an action: the momentary lull after the break and before the next towering mound of water is part of the continual movement that is the wave. There is no definitive opposition between the fixed state and the duration. *Painting* reveals a similar lack of clear-cut distinctions: it refers to the marks on a canvas and to the process of marking that canvas. In this last section, Woolf explores the oscillating relations between the thing and the process that produces the thing. The aesthetic object consists not just of the marks on a canvas, or the words on a page, but of the pauses or spaces between them, the ongoing rhythmic process in which they take on meaning. Without such pauses, we could not see the strokes; without spaces, the words would run together; without looking out to sea now and then, the vision would overwhelm.

This wavelike rhythm is, of course, the movement of *The Waves* as well. In a diary entry Woolf writes, "I say I am writing The Waves to a rhythm not to a plot" (Diary 3:316), though plot is not eliminated altogether. This wavelike movement also characterizes other works on the artist figure: in the pattern of digression and return that structures *A Room of One's Own,* in the oscillation between dark and light in the cab scene of *Orlando,* in the catchwords of *Between the Acts,* "unity and dispersal." Even the rhythm of repeated phrases in one novel recurs in the phrases of another: "Which is happiness . . . which pain" in *The Waves* echoes "Which was truth and which was illusion" in *A Room of One's Own,* and the narrator's continual action of "looking out of the window" in *A Room of One's Own* mimics Lily's looking out to sea in *To the Lighthouse.* The similar patterning implies likeness while the words stress difference; the rhythmic variation implies both continuity and change. This movement is what keeps our fictions from hardening into some permanent form. Even those moments when all seems to come together into a unified whole, as when Mrs. Ramsay says, "Life stand still here," even those moments disintegrate as we grasp them: the dinner scene breaks up and becomes the past as we look at it; Lily's vision becomes the past as she has it; and La Trobe's audience disperses just as they have converged. Even as Lily, in her intense desire to touch that empty center, cries out, "Mrs. Ramsay, Mrs. Ramsay," for one moment stepping into the "waters of annihilation" (269), even then Lily must return to external things. But we have seen through Lily's dual function as artist and narrator, as the one who observes and the one who organizes those boat scenes, that these external things are not the reality with which the illusion must be compared. The reality is itself a construct, a plurality of stories others have created.[16] The silent world pulling against the expression, the objective world breaking into the vision, keeps the question "What does it mean?" from being answered.

And so the final brush stroke signifies the artist's commitment to a certain behavior, not the answer to a general question—What is the value of art? What is the nature of women's art? What does it all mean? The dramatic gesture with which Lily completes her painting recalls the initial brush stroke. Early in the novel Woolf stresses the inception of the work, the courage of the artist to commit herself to the project before her, for the first strokes of the artist, like the first words of the novelist, eliminate other possibilities and both inscribe and fill in the space to be enclosed. After that gap of ten years, Lily, in part 3, stands empty before her canvas: "Where to begin?—that was the question[,] at what point to make the first mark? One line placed on the canvas committed her to innumerable risks, to frequent and irrevocable decisions. . . . Still the risk must be run; the mark made" (235). Similarly, the last stroke of the painting claims attention: "With a sudden intensity, as if she saw it clear for a second, she drew a line there, in the centre. It was done; it was finished. Yes, she thought, laying down her brush in extreme fatigue, I have had my vision" (310).

Already, with the last stroke of the brush, with the last words of the novel, the vision is past, receding as the harmony of the dinner scene recedes, as the wave recedes, for the vision must be perpetually remade, the relations must be forever reestablished. This line is not the union of two kinds of experience but the affirmation of one possible form of activity, a gesture that implies not so much the completion of the act as its exhaustion, the crossing out of the current enterprise and the crossing over to a new one.[17]

The implications of this change in aesthetic motives, from connecting two things to exploring different relations, can best be seen in Woolf's next two, and closely related, works on the artist figure: *Orlando* and *A Room of One's Own*. Since I discuss *Orlando* at some length in the next chapter, I focus here on Woolf's essay. *A Room of One's Own* takes the form of a lecture, or rather, the story of how the lecturer came to the opinion she holds on the topic of women and fiction: "a woman must have money and a room of her own if she is to write fiction; and that, as you will see, leaves the great problem of the true nature of woman and the true nature of fiction unsolved" (4). The problem of the "true nature," like the problem of the relation of art to life, remains unsolved because Woolf's essay, as we will see, investigates ever-shifting relations. More so than in *To the Lighthouse,* Woolf's method of constructing *A Room of One's Own* is highly self-conscious. She exaggerates diction ("On the further bank the willows wept in perpetual lamentation, their hair about their shoulders" [5]); she employs metafictional comments ("As I have said already that it was an October day, I dare not forfeit your respect and imperil the fair name of fiction by changing the season . . ." [16]); and she tells stories within her stories (the story of Mary Seton's mother; the story of William Shakespeare's sister).[18] However, of most importance for our concerns here is her use of the fluctuating narrative persona and the changing interrogative approaches. Both strategies illuminate her conception of the artist and the artwork and demonstrate the point of her essay, which she states in the first paragraph: "—one cannot hope to tell the truth. One can only show how one came to hold whatever opinion one does hold. One can only give one's audience the chance of drawing their own conclusions as they observe the limitations, the prejudices, the idiosyncrasies of the speaker. Fiction here is likely to contain more truth than fact" (4). This is not to say that there is no truth, only fiction (a belief often naively attributed to postmodernism), but that the truth to be "found out or made up," as Woolf says, is an effect of the fictional strategies. That last sentence can be read in two ways: fiction is likely to contain more truth than it contains fact (with its implicit opposition of truth and fact), or fiction is likely to contain more truth than fact contains (with its implicit opposition of fiction and fact). The penultimate sentence of that paragraph complicates things further: "Lies will flow from my lips, but there may perhaps be some truth mixed up with them" (4). As we will see, however, this "radical requestioning of the status of *fiction* and (intrinsically) of *truth*" that Alice Jardine associates with postmodern fiction and feminist theory (*Gynesis* 59) requires a different kind of procedure and attention to different kinds of concerns. Rather than distinguish between two things (e.g., fact and fiction), we need to ask the point of any distinction we make.

Truth through fiction, truth through lies—the avowed intentions of this essay would seem disturbing, and indeed they are for many modernist writers and for many Woolf critics. In "How It Strikes a Contemporary," Woolf says of modernist writers: "they cannot tell stories because they do not believe the stories are true" (CR 244). Fiction lies because it is no longer grounded in a common belief that informed, so they believe, literature of the past. For the moderns, this lack of belief in their stories leads to despair of something lost. For Woolf, as for the women writers of *A Room of One's Own,* this lack of belief leads to affirmation of something gained. Theirs is not the loss of a common ground to our stories but the realization that the common ground is shifting, unstable, slippery. What foments

Woolf's realization are the stories she tells, in this essay and in *Orlando,* of the emergence of the woman writer—which did not destroy the common ground but did explode the myth that the common ground was ever a solid foundation. Many modernists responded to the perceived loss of a common ground by turning inward to their own experiences (as Woolf argues in "The Leaning Tower") or by forging a new order, some metaphysical or mythical system that can ground belief. Woolf responded to the exploded myth of a common ground by adapting her aesthetic model, making it more flexible and responsive to change.

As the narrating "I" tries to explain how she came to her conclusion about the money and the room and to discover the conditions "most propitious to the act of creation" (ROO 52), she undertakes various approaches: introspection (chap. 1), theory (chap. 2), historical reconstruction (chap. 3), literary history (chap. 4), textual analysis (chap. 5). In each chapter the narrator draws various contrasts between women and men: men are prosperous and women are poor (chap. 1); men draw conclusions and women draw pictures (chap. 2); men desire fame and women desire anonymity (chap. 3); the values of women are not the values of men (chap. 4); a woman's sentence is not a man's (chap. 5). After so many such contrasts, the "I" writes in chapter 6 what will be the opening sentence of her lecture: "it is fatal for anyone who writes to think of their sex" (108). Yet it seems as if the narrator has thought of little else! We are faced with an apparent contradiction. Elaine Showalter accepts this assertion at face value and concludes, quoting from Woolf's review of American fiction, that for Woolf "consciousness of self, of race, of sex, of civilization . . . [has] nothing to do with art" ("American Fiction"; *Literature of Their Own* 289). But surely Woolf was conscious of her gender when she wrote *Orlando* and *A Room of One's Own.* Surely she was conscious of British civilization when she wrote *Between the Acts.* Gender mattered to Woolf, as did history and facts. The problem is our tendency to see these things in terms of stable oppositions (male/female, past/present, fact/fiction) and to fix labels on things. When the narrator in *A Room of One's Own* considers the "comparative values" of women and men, charwoman and barrister, she cannot draw a conclusion because the measuring rods, as she calls them, change, just as they change in Woolf's essay. As the "I" remarks, "it is notoriously difficult to fix labels of merit in such a way that they do not come off" (110). Sexual differences have everything to do with art; it is just that sexual differences in writing are provisional and contingent. Woolf objects not to gender distinctions but to a certain way of thinking about gender distinctions: "this pitting of sex against sex, of quality against quality" (110), this thinking in terms of "two parties" and "opposing faction[s]" (62). The way out of these oppositions has been demonstrated in *A Room of One's Own:* to see the artist as a composite figure, not an empirical being; to consider the text in terms of the task it undertakes as well as the truth it reveals; and to adopt various methods, not to codify or prescribe the right method.[19]

For this reason we must reconsider some common assessments of this essay. Nigel Nicolson, in a spring 1986 lecture at the University of Virginia, claimed *A Room of One's Own* is a "false argument" because it is not logical. John Burt agrees that the essay is not logical and is not, finally, an argument because its two main arguments clash: Woolf expresses faith in progress and despair of it, he says; she reaffirms the values of the past and deprecates them (192–97). Unlike Nicolson, though, Burt finds this central contradiction "honest," not weak. The arguments cannot be reconciled, he claims, for *A Room of One's Own* is not an argument but a portrayal of how the mind attempts to come to terms with its world (197). Certainly Woolf has told us that her work is such a portrayal. But she has also told us something about this mind she portrays: that the "I" who narrates this work "is only a convenient term for somebody who has no real being" (ROO 4). As the "I" tells us this story, it fluctuates; in an aside, the narrator says, "call me Mary Beton, Mary Seton, Mary Carmichael or by any name you please—it is not a matter of any importance" (5).[20] It is not the mind's method we explore but the storyteller's. And this particular storyteller is a woman. But that woman, the "I," is as much a fiction as is the text, for the "I" is implicated in its own stories. That is, as both narrator and character, the "I" is a construction of its own fictions. While the composite "I" functions to undercut the authority of the traditionally male lecturer, it also undercuts the authority of this specifically female author; or rather, it does not *undercut* authority but *relocates* it: not the empirical author but the fictional construct ("somebody with no real being") has the last word. Truth and authority are fictions. In other words, the name is of no importance here, not because Woolf is tracing the process of all minds or all women, but because she is testing out the implications of the concepts of art and self developed in her previous novels, *To the Lighthouse* and *Orlando*.

If "I" were an empirical being with a name, then contradictions would be legion in *A Room of One's Own*. Since the "I" changes, however, and since there is no common ground to these stories (on the contrary, "truth is only to be had by laying together many varieties of error" [109]), what appear to be contradictions may well indicate a change in mind, or at least in method. But we may not have to choose between argument and inquiry, as Burt does, for the argument is an effect of its discourse, not a "nugget of pure truth [wrapped] up between the pages" (ROO 3). Just as Mr. A's argument for the self-sufficient individual is an effect of his barlike narrative "I" that casts its shadow over all he writes (103), just as Professor Von X reaches his conclusion about the inferiority of women by isolating certain pieces of information about women from their historical and social contexts (31–32), so the narrator of *A Room of One's Own* makes her argument against categorical distinctions by means of her fluctuating "I" and changing method that keep our distinctions context-bound and task-specific.[21]

Thus, what Elaine Showalter, Patricia Spacks, Diane Gillespie, and other feminist critics see as *interfering* with Woolf's argument actually *makes* her argument. Woolf's continually experimenting form that Gillespie regrets (145), her evasiveness that Spacks laments (14), and her "elusive" strategies, which deny "any earnest or subversive intention," that Showalter dismisses (283) must be seen in relation to the point of the essay and the consequence of the aesthetics Woolf is demonstrating. If truth lay outside of or existed prior to the story, then the method would indeed be distracting. If the world and the writer were stable and self-contained, then such a playful and elusive argument would be suspect. Yet by paying attention to her narrative, not reading through it as Showalter suggests, we soon see that Woolf's argument is not, as these critics would have it, for distinguishing between male and female writing, for establishing a countertradition in literature, or for determining the right relation between women's writing and man's world. Rather, the changeable "I" and flexible approach suggest that the truth we seek is not single but multiple, not subjective but intersubjective. What is "honest" about Woolf's method is its very self-consciousness.

If the narrator's peroration ("Do not dream of influencing other people. . . . Think of things in themselves" [115]) sounds a bit like Walter Pater's prescriptive remark (a poet should see the object in itself as it really is), the remark of the "I" differs in that the "I" is not an individual "I": "I am talking of the common life which is the real life and not of the little separate lives which we live as individuals" (ROO 117). Of course, such an emphasis on the writer as part of some common life, as a component of tradition ("the experience of the mass is behind the single voice" [69]), recalls Eliot's "Tradition and the Individual Talent," but with this difference: Woolf tells a different story of tradition by rewriting our familiar history.[22] For if Woolf believes in the necessity of fictions, those sustaining illusions of our lives, if she recognizes that fiction works in and out of our daily lives (ROO 4), if she sees that how we write is tied up with how we live (48) and how we live with what we read (80), then whose stories get told makes all the difference.[23] Woolf tells stories of women writers to make a difference, to change literature, to change tradition; but it does not follow that the difference she makes is woman's realm or that she replaces one tradition with another, one literary form with another.

Thus, when Alex Zwerdling comments that Woolf has been largely responsible for "the currently fashionable way of thinking about women's writing as an independent tradition" (226), we might do well to consider the different implications of this way of thinking. Certainly Woolf discussed women writers in relation to other women writers more than in relation to the men of their day, and she considered the writings of the obscure as well as the famous, thereby helping to shape a women's tradition. Clearly this way of assessing women's writing offers useful insights and strategic advantages for feminist criticism. And admittedly, this way of thinking may well be behind Woolf's outburst quoted in the Introduction—"Lord—how tired I am of being caged with Aldous, Joyce and Lawrence!"—here considered as men, not modernists. But however much Woolf's critical method has helped shape a feminist critical practice, it does not establish two traditions, or two standards, as Zwerdling implies. He notes, for example, that Woolf assessed women's works "not against some absolute standard of greatness . . . but against the psychological and material forces at work in their lives" (226). I agree, but unless we also adopt a new way of thinking about and evaluating *all* art, not just women's art, we risk setting up two sex-based standards for art, and we risk assessing women's art (because it is rooted in the everyday, because it is the art that perishes) as unsuccessful, insignificant, or disposable. This danger can be seen in Zwerdling's reading of *Between the Acts:* without allowing for Woolf's changing concept of the artist, Zwerdling must conclude that La Trobe's alienation from her audience (as a woman, a lesbian, a foreigner) is a "symptom of the artist's increasing insignificance" in the face of war and the collapse of Woolf's belief in human perfectibility (321). The danger here (not one Zwerdling necessarily succumbs to but one his reading allows for) is seeing the woman, the lesbian, the foreigner, or the feminist writer as insignificant because alienated, because unable to unify her audience, or her culture, in a common belief. This is to assume that Woolf's desire was for unity; it is to read Woolf's female artists *against* a dominant male tradition, whether they are thereby forgotten or martyred. But seeking out and acknowledging the doubts and difficulties of the creative process and the instabilities of literary tradition, as Woolf does in *Between the Acts,* enables differences to emerge and enables us to question their effects, without establishing another tradition. What the woman artist needs, I argue, is not freedom from a male tradition but freedom to change our very concept of tradition, whether patriarchal or matriarchal.[24]

We have trouble reaching a conclusion about *A Room of One's Own* if we see Woolf's goal either as creating a countertradition of female works or as adding women's works to the established tradition. Woolf has done neither. Rather, the point of the essay is to introduce into the concept of tradition the concept of change, of instability. Thinking of the literary tradition as homogeneous and authoritative leads the modernist writers discussed in "How It Strikes" and some women writers discussed in *A Room of One's Own* to assert their difference from the past and to adopt the language of liberation, transcendence, and novelty. Yet if modernist or women writers break out of traditional forms, what matters, Woolf's narrator says, is the point and the situation of such change: "Mary [Carmichael] is tampering with the expected sequence. First she broke the sentence; now she has broken the sequence. Very well, she has every right to do both these things if she does them not for the sake of breaking, but for the sake of creating. Which of the two it is I cannot be sure until she has faced herself with a situation" (85). As the narrator has done, and as Miss La Trobe will do, the woman writer must break the sequence as a way of effecting change; however, she must also expose the sequence as a way of measuring and evaluating change. Too much emphasis on difference produces fragmentation or cacophony and fosters the illusion that the artist is transcending obstacles and achieving freedom. Too much emphasis on sameness neglects the multiplicity and instability of any age, or either sex, and fosters the acceptance of the prevailing opinion, or a common belief.

In this essay, Woolf adopts a comparative rather than a correspondence model for discourse, a cooperative rather than a competitive model: "For books," the narrator says, "continue each other, in spite of our habit of judging them separately" (84). Reiterating this point in "The Leaning Tower" (1940), Woolf employs the analogy of a family resemblance among books: "Books descend from books as families descend from families. . . . They resemble their parents, as human children resemble their parents; yet they differ as children differ, and revolt as children revolt" (M 130). Of course, this analogy brings to mind Wittgenstein's family resemblance model for language (*Philosophical Investigations* #67), and Woolf's point here is similar to Wittgenstein's: both argue for continuity in our books or our words without specifying a common core of shared features. Asking what is the essence of language games, Wittgenstein writes: "I am saying that these phenomena have no one thing in common . . . but that they are *related* to one another in many different ways" (#65). Different kinds of relations have been our concern here. But there is a further comparison to be made: Woolf enacts a theory of art as Wittgenstein enacts a theory of language; neither one reduces the theory to rules (#68). And the reason they do not is that neither believes in empirical stability.[25]

Woolf demonstrates this lack of empirical stability, which prevents us from drawing definitive distinctions between two things, through her narrator and her narrator's double perspective: one needs "to think poetically and prosaically at one and the same moment, thus keeping in touch with fact . . . but not losing sight of fiction either" (ROO 46). The one is no more true than the other, and in this text, at least, there is no point to distinguishing finally between them. It is the way of relating things that matters, and the writer's function is to differentiate the undifferentiated mass of common life by making some sequence, telling some story. Looking out the window, the "I" creates another scene:

> At this moment, as so often happens in London, there was a complete lull and suspension of traffic. Nothing came down the street; nobody passed. A single leaf detached itself from the plane tree at the end of the street, and in that pause and suspension fell. Somehow it was like a signal falling, a signal pointing to a force in things which one had overlooked. It seemed to point to a river, which flowed past, invisibly, round the corner, down the street, and took people and eddied them along, as the stream at Oxbridge had taken the undergraduate in his boat and the dead leaves. Now it was bringing from one side of the street to the other diagonally a girl in patent leather boots, and then a young man in a maroon overcoat; it was also bringing a taxi-cab; and it brought all three together at a point directly beneath my window; where the taxi stopped; and the girl and the young man stopped; and they got into the taxi; and then the cab glided off as if it were swept on by the current elsewhere.
>
> The sight was ordinary enough; what was strange was the rhythmical order with which my imagination had invested it. . . . (100)

This is not the mind of the individual artist, as the nonempirical "I" makes clear; nor is it the mind of a culture, as the three Marys make clear, for that would imply something constant in the culture, as if it were univocal. Rather, this is the cohesive principle in literature, one that is figured in the poet Orlando; it is the mind of the writer who thinks back through her ancestors, mothers as well as fathers (ROO 107). It is not the personal or the impersonal element but the interpersonal relation, a relation brought out in Woolf's next work on the artist figure.

The early drafts of *The Waves* contain a narrative "I" that functions as a controlling, enduring presence: "I am the force that arranges. I am the thing in which all this exists. Certainly without me it would perish. I can give it order" (quoted in Blain 120). By the final version of the novel, though, this "I" has become the shifting pronoun identified with each of the six speakers: Bernard, Neville, Susan, Rhoda, Louis, and Jinny. Picking up on a suggestion in Woolf's diary (AWD 140), J. W. Graham argues that Woolf dropped the original "I" because it became too "arty" (107). But what could be more arty than the opening speeches of the novel:

> "I see a ring," said Bernard, "hanging above me. It quivers and hangs in a loop of light."
> "I see a slab of pale yellow," said Susan, "spreading away until it meets a purple stripe."
> "I hear a sound," said Rhoda, "cheep, chirp; cheep, chirp; going up and down." (TW 180)

It is this very artiness that Woolf emphasizes, and it is the failure to attend to the effects of this "highly artful style" (Naremore 159) that has led critics to read *The Waves* as continuing, even completing, the quest of *To the Lighthouse:* that is, the search for the "essence" of consciousness and for an art form capable of expressing a "timeless unity."[26]

Granted, the common readings of *The Waves* in terms of the narrative concerns often identified in *To the Lighthouse* are reinforced by the many similarities between these two novels.[27] And the language of this novel not only encourages the common conclusion that it is about the emergence of a single consciousness but also reinforces the sense that we are witnessing the mind's "soliloquy in solitude" (Woolf's phrase in "The Narrow Bridge of Art" [GR 19])—in particular, the consistency of the style from speaker to speaker; the repetition with slight variations of images and events; the use of the "pure present" tense that Graham discusses ("I see a ring"); and the sense of what Nathalie Sarraute calls *sous-conversation,* the profusion of images, memories, and impulses that "jostle" one another on the "threshold of consciousness" (*Age of Suspicion* 105). However, if this novel is about consciousness and art, it is not necessarily about the essence, permanence, or unity of these things, and the reason it is not can be located in the artificial style, which critics try to reconcile with what they see as Woolf's theme of a pure presence beneath all surface manifestations.

What I argue here is that the thematic concerns—for example, the formation of identity, the emergence of consciousness—come out of the structural concerns of the novel: the desire for new narrative relations freed from the egotistical self of Joyce or Richardson and able to convey the simultaneity of life through the sequence of fiction. What makes the language and style of this novel so highly self-conscious are the changes Woolf makes from the other works under consideration here: the change from narrative "I" to dramatic personae and from a visual artist who can create in solitude to a verbal artist who requires a reader/listener. Rather than generalizing about the relation of art to consciousness or identity, it would be more useful to look at the kind of art and the concept of identity presented in *The Waves.* Both, as we will see, have much to do with the artiness of this novel.

"Bernard says there is always a story," Neville tells us. "I am a story. Louis is a story" (TW 200). Whereas in *To the Lighthouse* the use of a visual artist looking at Mrs. Ramsay or looking out to sea brings to mind Berkeley's proposition, that to be is to be perceived, in *The Waves* the use of a narrative artist telling stories of his and others' lives amends this concept of the self: To be, Woolf seems to say, is to be narrated. As in Beckett's trilogy, speaking or narrating guarantees existence.[28] Both the speeches the characters recite and the stories Bernard tells evoke the presence of an audience. As Bernard says, "The truth is that I need the stimulus of other people. Alone over my dead fire, I tend to see the thin places in my own stories" (230). An audience is as necessary for his identity as for his stories: "Thus my character is in part made of the stimulus which other people provide" (267).

Bernard begins his last speech by summoning up a listener: "Now to sum up. . . . Now to explain to you the meaning of my life" (341). The scene is set: Bernard and his silent interlocutor in a restaurant. Addressing his companion, Bernard compares telling the story of his life to turning the pages of a book, linking identity and story. Those pages are the ones we have turned over in this novel as well as the ones Bernard's nurse turned over in his picture book, teaching him his world with his words: "That's a cow. That's a book" (342). If this were the only language Bernard had learned, the language of reference, then we could read this novel as being about identity: This is Bernard. This is the essential self. And indeed, this is the language many critics have learned. For example, Harvena Richter sees the composite "I" as six aspects of a common identity (120–21), and James Naremore explains Woolf's artful language in this novel as an expression of her "misgivings about the ego and about the words which are its *signs*" (189; emphasis added). However, in addition to the language of reference, Bernard has learned another language, the language of narrative: "But in order to make you understand, to give you my life, I must tell you a story—and there are so many, and so many— . . . and none of them are true" (341). Which Bernard we know depends on which story he tells, that is, which selections he makes and which combinations he forms from the recurring images and motifs of this text. The story depends as well on which role he assumes from the many roles he has played in the earlier sections, for this last section, an oral annotated summary of the first eight sections of the novel, like each of the preceding sections, "has given the arrangement another shake" (365).

This sense the novel gives us that all parts of the text are present at once, endlessly reshuffled like the permutations we get in a Beckett or a Robbe-Grillet novel, is an effect of the consistent, stylized language conjoined with the changing, individuated speakers. When in this last section

Bernard adopts his earlier role as the biographer of himself in order to tell his story, the resumption of a previous role and the "biographic style" thus resumed convey the sense of things happening simultaneously and things happening sequentially. Further, this sense fosters the notion that the self or the artwork does not exist prior to or beneath the discourse but in its various versions.[29] Even in that famous "world without a self" passage where Bernard, like Wallace Stevens's persona in "The Snowman," tries to describe a world divested of self and story, the language and texture of that speech remain unchanged from the others, suggesting we never enter that silent world, or we have been there all along.[30] This is not Maurice Blanchot's "I" as empty space but "I" as fictional space. This passage is not the silent core of the text but yet another arrangement of its elements. Silence is not other than language but one function of discourse, and Bernard's questions about how to communicate a world existing apart from language or a self existing apart from others are not the key questions in terms of the structural concerns of this novel. As this text has already shown us, we cannot know the world apart from our present awareness of it as manifested in our verbal acts. This is the reason for the dramatic soliloquies and the pure present tense. We cannot form a self apart from the stories we tell and the stimulus from others they call forth. Instead, the important questions raised by Bernard's speech concern the aesthetics shaped in Woolf's earlier novels and enacted in this one: *What kinds of narrative relations are possible once we have relinquished the concepts of a central self, a stable world, and an individual artist? Where are we to ground the multiform artwork if not in the artist or in the world?*

In dropping the narrative "I" for the six speakers, Woolf intimates an answer by making it difficult to locate a controlling consciousness or an authorial presence. Although in the recurring reference to the lady writing in the garden of Elvedon, the lady writer is presumably the author, she seems to be a creation of the characters she creates. This garden scene is presented as if it were another of Bernard's stories. The author, it seems, is as much a construction of the story as are her characters, yet the author is threatening. Bernard and Susan must flee this scene, for to disturb the author would mean death. If she ceases to write, they cease to exist, like the dreamer in Jorge Luis Borges's "Circular Ruins" who dies when he realizes he has been dreamed by another.[31] The author in *The Waves* does exert some control, but she does not necessarily have the first word. Still, we seem to be in little danger, or hope, of locating the author. After all, where *is* Elvedon? And whose story is this?

In this metafictional scene, the author plays a part in her own story, much as the other characters, particularly Bernard, play certain roles in the stories they tell. The self-conscious and arty style calls attention to this role playing. In one scene, for example, Bernard writes a letter to his girlfriend in which he *feigns* sincerity, *poses* as casual, and *affects* naturalness (TW 228–29). The whole letter, like the novel itself, presents a kind of "rehearsed natural spontaneity."[32] Woolf no more than Bernard gives the reader a sense of the writer's "true" identity. Instead, both writers call attention to the stylized, the posing, the artificial dimension of self and art. Woolf's concern in this novel is with artifice, not essence.

This dramatic and arty style gives us some insight, then, into the questions raised by *The Waves*. By means of the word-play and the role playing, Woolf reinforces Bernard's comment in the last section: "Life is not susceptible perhaps to the treatment we give it when we try to tell it" (362). Life is not *like* the stories we tell. There is always something left out of our arbitrary designs, as Bernard says. To compare lives with stories, as Woolf has done throughout this and other novels, and yet to constantly remind us that life is not a fiction, as Woolf does here, is not to say there is something beyond or beneath our fictions, some pure consciousness or eternal presence that cannot be captured in words. Rather, it is to call into question the correspondence of art to life. Bernard's stories are not true because the question of true or false no longer pertains in this text; and the six speakers do not represent the surface manifestations of some deep consciousness because the relation of surface to depth no longer pertains either. For Woolf's concern is not the relation of art to life but the relation of art to audience.

It is in the use of art by its audience that we must locate its meaning and value, not in some correspondence between art and life, whether subjective or objective. If the artwork consists of its various arrangements, as the self consists of its various roles, and if these versions are all potentially present at once, though enacted in sequence, then we must attend to the choices made on any one occasion for any one purpose by any one user. The contradictory readings of *The Waves*—that the novel is Woolf's "ultimate synthesis" and that the novel generates doubt of its own art—accept the relation of art to life as the defining relation of the novel. The center of vision that Woolf relinquishes in this novel, though, is the belief that art has a center of vision, that it can reveal some truth or effect some "ultimate synthesis." Once we relinquish the belief that we can ground art in some stable center, then, as Bernard says, "All is experiment and adventure" (256). The artwork changes, not just because the world is unstable or the self is unstable, but because the world, the self, and the artwork are *dramatic,* formed in relationship to others and staged in the theater of language.

The critical preoccupation with the relation of art to life neglects the relation of art to its users and thus fosters the illusion that art is a subjective experience. The emphasis on artifice, arrangements, and audience undermines the belief that art is autonomous and sustains the belief that it is interactive. In this dramatic novel, what Woolf called her play-poem, we see an increasing emphasis on the public and interpersonal status of the artwork. In Woolf's final novel on the artist figure, the posthumous *Between the Acts,* the fictional audience as well as the reading audience play an active role in the artist's production. These two works together bring the domain of narrative close to the domain of theater.[33]

Woolf's last novel, not surprisingly, is often read as the "final stage" in her "eternal quest" for that right relation between opposed things (Guiguet 323). Avrom Fleishman reads it as evidence of Woolf's "faith in the collective imagination of mankind to create a harmonious consciousness . . . a vital culture" (quoted in Zwerdling 354). *Between the Acts,* Stephen Fox says, attempts to combine all Woolf's former themes as well as to resolve all her old difficulties over inner and outer life and the gap between them (468). If this were so, then perhaps, as Mrs. Manresa says of La Trobe's dramatic review of English history from its beginnings to the present, we might say of *Between the Acts:* "Ambitious, ain't it?" (82). Such an ambitious undertaking could only result in the failure and despair that many critics sense in this novel.[34] Although Lily doubts her painting and Bernard doubts his stories, here the artist's doubt seems to pervade the very texture of the novel. As James Naremore writes, in defending *Between the Acts* against charges of formlessness: "In other words, what Leavis and Friedman have taken to be the absence of structure is in fact a conscious faulting of structure, a questioning of the power of 'significant form' that runs deeper than Lily Briscoe's feeling that her vision is past or Bernard's criticism of words and compacted shapes—deeper because the criticism is embodied in the very form of the work as in no other novel by Virginia Woolf" (236). It is interesting to note how our conception of the form of the novel determines our reading. Naremore, who argues for a conscious faulting of structure in this novel, sees the opening scene set in the evening as a conscious breaking of the symmetry of a one-day structure (236). By contrast, Howard Harper, concerned with the dramatic unity of the novel, sees symmetry in the evening-to-evening movement of the text (285–86). How we read "the very form of the work" depends, of course, on what we compare it to and on what we see as Woolf's point in the novel. What others see as a despair of art and a faulting of structure, or an affirmation of art through some unifying vision, I see as a testing out of the postmodern implications evident throughout Woolf's works on the artist figure. Looked at from the postmodern perspective, this structure suggests not the failure of art or its unifying role but a means of assuring its survival.

The structure of *Between the Acts* is very much like the structure of La Trobe's play. Both consist of scraps of verse, bits of conversation, half-finished sentences, forgotten lines, and words dispersed by the wind. They contain disjointed scenes and some bad writing, as well as some effective lyrical passages. The audience of the play, and the readers of the novel, are united through the widely remembered patriotic songs, folk songs, nursery rhymes, classical pieces, literary works, historical events, and cultural symbols that inform both texts. In this sense, both novel and play present the kind of literary and cultural collage we get in much postmodern fiction, such as Barthelme's *Snow White* or Acker's "plagiarized" novels. The gaps in the play, for example, the breakdown of the gramophone and the intervals between acts, bring to the fore the numerous gaps in the novel itself (over thirty blank spaces between scenes). Since the novel was unrevised at the time of Woolf's death, we may wonder which, if any, of those breaks were meant to be there, just as the audience wonders whether or not those moments when Albert, the village idiot, breaks onto the stage are meant to be part of La Trobe's script. The final scene of the novel dramatizes these interrelationships. As La Trobe departs Pointz Hall, she crosses the terrace outside the room where Giles and Isa sit and imagines a scene of two figures at midnight. Later, at what seems the hour of Giles and Isa's moment alone, the artist, sitting in a pub, creates her next play: "She heard the first words" (212). The scene La Trobe envisions seems to be the final scene of the novel:

> Isa let her sewing drop. The great hooded chairs had become enormous. And Giles too. And Isa too against the window. The window was all sky without colour. The house had lost its shelter. It was night before roads were made, or houses. It was the night that dwellers in caves had watched from some high place among rocks.
> Then the curtain rose. They spoke. (219)

The effects of this involuted structure—that is, the way the play works in and out of the novel and the layering effect such similar structuring produces—reminds us that neither the novel nor the play is a discrete literary event. La Trobe's play, a review of English literary history, cannot be evaluated apart from both the texts and contexts it evokes and reconstructs. Those contexts are not always delimitable, though. In one scene, for example, we watch a play within La Trobe's play as the actors represent the audience of the Globe Theatre and watch the parody of an Elizabethan play. As we read we are reminded of our situation in relation to this novel: Virginia Woolf creates characters who play characters created by La Trobe, who recreates characters from earlier dramas (Congreve's, for instance), who are themselves parodies of historical figures, and these figures are characters in another text, the text of English history. There seems to be no end to this chain of creations, unless it is in the prehistoric mud that covered England before human life appeared, the fertile mud from which La Trobe creates anew at the end (212). While the fragmented conversations, the interrupted scenes, and the abrupt endings of the play and the novel suggest an uneasiness about the future and the efficacy of literature, the continuity provided by the chorus and the music, by the familiar scenes and sayings, by the landscape of Pointz Hall, and by the annual occurrence of this pageant assure us that this creative process has been functioning for a long, long time and will continue to function into the postwar era. Literature, as this structure implies, is not evolving toward any final form or toward its demise; rather, literature is evolving from other literature.[35]

Here we can see, then, the consequences of Woolf's concern with making art responsive to change and with seeing it in relation to others as they are enacted in La Trobe's collaborative and heteronomous production. In no other work of Woolf's artists does the audience play such an important part. Its members provide the stage, the props, and the money. They provide the stimulus and the occasion. And they provide the final scene of the play as they are caught in the mirrors of the actors. Of course, this relation between the artist and the audience is far from serene. The audience is caught by the artist's noose (122, 180), yet the artist must give way to the demands of the audience: "Writing this skimble-skamble stuff in her cottage, she had agreed to cut the play here; a slave to her audience—to Mrs. Sands' grumble—about tea; about dinner—she had gashed the scene here" (94). Lily fears an audience; Bernard woos an audience; La Trobe withstands her audience. More than any other artwork we have considered, La Trobe's play reveals the extent to which art depends on its audience and on various contingencies, such as unpredictable weather, teatime, limited budgets, and world war.

*Between the Acts,* even in its title, does not just account for those contingencies and interruptions that so enrage La Trobe, it gives them preference. Those numerous breaks many critics see as a sign of discontinuity and a faulting of structure actually enable the acts to be continually renewed. If the purpose of the artwork were to produce harmony and unity among its elements and its audience, then certainly such breaks would be disturbing. But Woolf's humor and exaggeration in presenting such an attitude in this work undermine such readings. For example, in response to the interruption for tea cited above, La Trobe behaves rather extremely: "Curse! Blast! Damn 'em! Miss La Trobe in her rage stubbed her toe against a root" (94). The response of Lucy, the religious one, also raises questions about the value of harmony. During an interval, Lucy caresses her cross and reflects on the play: "Sheep, cows, grass, trees, ourselves—all are one.

If discordant, producing harmony—if not to us, to a gigantic ear attached to a gigantic head. And thus . . . we reach the conclusion that *all* is harmony, could we hear it" (175). Whether that "gigantic ear" is Lucy's God or some universal aesthetic value, in either case it is a bit absurd.[36] Even in her own writing, Woolf calls into question such harmony by calling attention to her transitions: "Then suddenly, as the illusion petered out, the cows took up the burden. . . . The cows annihilated the gap; bridged the distance; filled the emptiness and continued the emotion" (140–41). If Woolf took her text quite seriously, we would read such intrusions of nature as evidence of the pattern behind the cotton wool of daily life. Such transitions, however, are not only contrived, they are contrived to look contrived.

If we read this novel with unity as our standard, then we will interpret the many strategies used to frustrate our unifying impulse as a despair of or a threat to such harmony. But if we read it with a sense of the various relations that make up the artistic event, then we will look for the effect of such disruptive strategies. As Austin Quigley notes, what is presumed to be a device used to frustrate our desire for unity and understanding may be the "thematic consequence" of a text that treats "truth and reality as negotiable concepts" (*Pinter Problem* 71).

It seems, then, that art has many functions. One is to create unity, to bridge gaps, to weave scraps and fragments of history and daily life into a pattern (the function we see, for example, at the end of *A Room of One's Own*). Another is to arouse doubts about such patterns, to raise questions about the order of things, the power of illusions, and the function of art. And the various functions of art depend on its users. The problem of interpretation, then, does not lie in the discontinuity or the exaggeration of the text but in the expectations and the responses of its readers. What frustrates the audience of La Trobe's play is not the interruptions (for those are there in response to the audience's demands) or the exaggerations (for the audience is willing to observe the conventions and consider the artist's means). What frustrates them is their desire "to leave the theatre knowing exactly what was meant" (BA 164) in a play where nothing is concluded and no one takes responsibility. The futility of such a response is brought out in Mr. Streatfield's hesitant and trite exegesis (191–92). The only definite conclusion he can reach is the amount the pageant has grossed. If we try to summarize what *Between the Acts* is about, we are likely to be about as articulate and illuminating as Mr. Streatfield is, for the point of the novel is not to make some statement about the present condition of art or its future fate. To see this June day in 1939, poised on the brink of war and distracted by the movies, the motor bus, and the newspaper, as offering impoverished material to the artist is to give preference to certain kinds of material and certain kinds of criteria. However, if we cannot predict the future, it might be best not to limit the artist's materials. The significance of La Trobe's play and Woolf's novel is to be found in their effects on their audiences. The point of each production is to change our responses to art and to show how the production of art changes in response to different audiences and different occasions. Their art does not tell us what the world is or should be like; rather, it changes our behavior in the world by changing our relations to the various discourses that construct it. These texts make us self-conscious of the different ways we use literature, whether for the sake of profits, for the sake of pleasure, or for the sake of tradition. Their art, like La Trobe's final scene, brings us back to ourselves.

Throughout the play the spotlight is on the audience's responses as much as the artist's script or the actor's performance. "Our part," Bart says, "is to be the audience. And a very important part too" (58). The audience asks numerous questions: "Was it, or was it not, the play?" (76); "What's it all about?" (79); "What idea lay behind, eh?" (97); "Was it an old play? Was it a new play?" (109); "Do *you* understand the meaning?" (197). They discuss the performance and hum its tunes during the intervals. And in the last scene they must confront themselves not only in the mirrors held up to them by the actors but in La Trobe's "ten mins. of present time" (179). This is an uncomfortable moment for the audience, like those silent intervals in Beckett's drama and the silence of a Cage composition, for the empty stage or the silent hall makes us painfully aware of our own reactions, and by their very absence the conventions we rely on are brought to our attention. At this point in La Trobe's play, a voice from the bushes, "a megaphonic, anonymous, loud-speaking affirmation," enjoins the audience to "break the rhythm and forget the rhyme. And calmly consider ourselves. Ourselves" (186–87). The voice, like the play itself, is the great leveler, linking universal events (a pilot dropping a bomb) with local ones (a bungalow spoiling a view) and implicating us all in the perpetuation of literature and culture. At the end, the artist refuses to come out of the bushes, leaving the audience unsure of whom to thank and whom to make responsible, but also leaving them with a sense of the commonality of the artist and the complicity of the audience.

In this sense *Between the Acts* might be usefully compared with a novel like Italo Calvino's *If on a Winter's Night a Traveler*. The repetitive, self-reflexive, *mise-en-abyme* structure of these texts could suggest the exhaustion of literature and the artist's loss of faith in the efficacy of art, as so many critics of both novels conclude. Yet those very devices that frustrate our reading can be understood as the "thematic consequences" of texts that make error, uncertainty, frustration, and discontinuity elements of, not obstacles to, reading. As Joann Cannon writes of Calvino's novel:

"This violation of the text is a necessary part of reading," for otherwise reading is mere transcription (106). By dramatizing the audience in their novels and by insisting that the artists must capture their readers (whether in La Trobe's net or Calvino's traps), both Woolf and Calvino force us to consider our own needs and desires as readers and to accept our responsibility as well. The survival of art, then, is affirmed and assured in the very process of reading these texts.

It is not that La Trobe or postmodern writers "abandon authorial control" to the reader, as Judith Johnston suggests of Woolf's novel (264), for La Trobe, like Beckett, Cage, or Calvino, creates those silent scenes and evokes the audience's discomfort. It is not a question of control or no control but the effect of the control. What do we attend to? The effect of Woolf's novel as well as La Trobe's play is to adapt narrative performance to external contingencies and to focus on responses to art. *Between the Acts,* like Calvino's *If on a Winter's Night a Traveler* or Nathalie Sarraute's *The Golden Fruits,* consists largely of the fictional audience's responses to the fictional work that is its subject. And as in Sarraute's novel, the verdict on La Trobe's play is doubtful: "I thought it brilliantly clever. . . . Oh my dear, I thought it utter bosh" (BA 197). Woolf's novel, too, evokes conflicting responses: Northrop Frye seems to think it brilliantly clever; F. R. Leavis thinks it utter bosh.

Seen from the perspective of postmodern art, the mood of Woolf's last novel is not one of despair but one of affirmation. What Jean Guiguet, Alex Zwerdling, and others see as doubt and disillusionment in the narrative is merely the text's refusal to be lured by its own voice, to harden into "significant form," to take itself too seriously. A refusal to take oneself too seriously may be a kind of defense when facing the threat of an ending or of an impending war, but it can also be a way of avoiding setting up oneself or one's art as an authority or model. As she looked to the future of literature, Woolf did not lose confidence in the creative act, but she did fear losing the reader who is a necessary part of that act. In her diary entries of this time, Woolf worries about the war taking away any public for which to write. In the summer of 1940, she writes that in war there is "no public to echo back" (AWD 326); and in the fragment of her last essay, "The Reader," she says that the importance of the reader "can be gauged by the fact that when his attention is distracted, in times of public crisis, the writer exclaims: I can write no more" (R 428). Her works on the artist figure concentrate on creating that audience, on teaching us how to create the literature of the future, which will be a collaborative act. This last novel in particular raises questions about who will occupy the position of reader/listener/audience. In the face of an uncertain future, or an unstable tradition, it may be best not to limit the audience for art or to take that audience for granted. Woolf's changing concept of art raises questions about who can produce art and who can receive it. However, it does more than expand the range of those included as artists and audiences (a liberally democratic gesture); indeed, it changes the relations between artist and audience: the artist (e.g., La Trobe) no longer represents her kind (women, lesbians, feminists) or transcends her time (a universal presence). Woolf's artist is no longer a spokesperson for a culture or a constituency, for Woolf's concept of art is no longer unifying and her concept of culture is no longer one of consensus. The cacophonies of Woolf's novel and La Trobe's play may well be the sounds of a unified and univocal audience dispersing.

Through her recurrent focus on the artist, then, Woolf foregrounds various relations potential in narrative discourse and tests out various possibilities for its use. In doing so she both projects and prepares for a new reading audience. This process is most clearly evident in La Trobe's art: she cuts and rearranges her script to suit the desires and the needs of an audience both familiar and new—familiar in that they gather for this pageant every year, new in that "they" are never the same.

## NOTES

1. Rose makes a similar observation when she claims one of Woolf's achievements as a novelist is making the tenuousness of the self (a modernist theme) the basis of her literary method (156).

2. My focus on self-conscious art leads me to single out these particular artist figures for a discussion of Woolf's changing views of art. For a different discussion of artist figures in Woolf, see Rigney's essay on Clarissa Dalloway, Mrs. Ramsay, and Jinny; Abel's essay on Cam as artist figure; and Hirsch's discussion of *A Room of One's Own* and *To the Lighthouse*.

3. See, for example, Waugh, *Metafiction* 102. Also, McHale's basic argument in *Postmodernist Fiction* is that modernist texts are about epistemology (perception, mind), while postmodernist texts are about ontology (worlds in creation).

4. Quigley (*Pinter Problem* chaps. 1 and 2) and Smith ("Narrative Versions") discuss the problems created by a naive acceptance of the correspondence theory of language: that is, the assumptions that a sequence of elements in the text represents a corresponding set of conditions in the world and that the problem of interpretation lies in the gap between these things. Both writers counter these assumptions by focusing on the functions and contexts of any language act.

5. Many critics comment on how these novels reflect their own processes. For example, Miller argues that the various forms of creativity in *To the Lighthouse* (Lily's painting, Carmichael's poetry, Mrs. Ramsay's party) are analogous and symbolize the act of creativity represented by the novel itself ("Rhythm of Creativity"). Abel remarks that this self-reflexive novel represents "its own narrative ambiva-

lence" (" 'Cam the Wicked' " 171), and she goes on to point out that the novel is concerned with "different models of textuality" (172). See also Daiches (*Virginia Woolf*), Leaska, and Cohn on *To the Lighthouse;* Naremore and DiBattista (*Major Novels*) on *The Waves;* and Sears ("Theater of War"), Rose, and Fussell on *Between the Acts.* More recently, Waugh has warned against "a critical tendency to interpret the political, philosophical and broader human concerns of [Woolf's] novels in terms of self-reflexive aesthetic artifice," a tendency she attributes to a *modernist* perspective (*Feminine Fictions* 89).

6. What Smith refers to as "surfacing from the deep" in the last chapter of *On the Margins of Discourse*—that is, a conceptual model for narrative discourse that recognizes dynamic and multiple relations rather than relying on some correspondence between surface and depth—is similar to the distinction Sarraute makes between modernists like Proust—who try to reach "the ultimate deep where lie truth, the real universe, our most authentic impressions"—and postmodernists like herself—who know that there is no ultimate deep, that "our authentic impressions" are successive layers of discourse and not some fundamental ground of it (*Age of Suspicion* 59–60).

7. Spivak notes Lily's narrative function as the timekeeper of the novel (315). Although Leaska, Hartman, and Naremore all connect Lily with the narrator of the traditional novel (as opposed to the modernist narrator of "Time Passes" or Mrs. Ramsay's "wedge-shaped core of darkness" passage), their concern with drawing distinctions between two kinds of narratives prevents them from following up on the implications of Lily's narrative function for Woolf's conception of fiction.

8. Quigley notes that content is a function of structure, not something to be separated from it or equated with it (*Pinter Problem* 20). The term *involuted* is often used in criticism of postmodern fiction to refer to the way a text turns in on itself, even to the point of disappearing, but it can also refer to the spiral curve evoked here to suggest the ever-renewed and ever-changing relation between the act of perceiving the world and the act of inscribing it.

9. The function of memory in Proust's work is sensitively and insightfully described by Beckett in *Proust.* This extended essay, as Daniel Albright has suggested to me, is useful in discerning affinities between Beckett and Woolf as well as between Woolf and Proust. On the role of memory in this novel, see, for example, Richter and also Naremore.

10. Cohn draws these connections as well. See also Hirsch's discussion of this passage in terms of the reader's response (115).

11. *Would* suggests not only that this boat trip has occurred before but that it has occurred several times before. *Would* marks the *iterative* in narrative, a repeated event presented only once. Here, however, the narrative time (iterative) conflicts with the story time (this is their first trip), making the sequence clearly a function of the narration.

12. Of course, this perceiving and connecting mind suggests a modernist belief in the organizing consciousness that brings order to the phenomenal world. But unlike James and Conrad, Woolf does not insist on a separation of the perceiving consciousness and the objective world, nor, like Ford, on their collapse (cf. Levenson 116). The emphasis here and in *A Room of One's Own* on the artist at work, on

the artwork in progress, calls into question the stability and authority of any order that may obtain.

13. Waugh also contrasts Carmichael's modernist conception of art with Lily's more provisional conception (*Feminine Fictions* 99).

14. Harper argues that it is not the painting that matters but the artist's "experience in creating it," in "discovering the authentic expression of her own deepest feelings" (158). Naremore says that the artwork is "an 'attempt at something,' and that something is what survives" (149). Hirsch remarks that the "process of writing . . . not the product" is the basis for Lily's and Woolf's aesthetics (115).

15. Moore makes a similar observation, namely, that Woolf's conception of reality "finds its model in the way language changes. For language is in a continuous evolution, transforming its conventional forms to express new emotions, while simultaneously pointing back to the older forms" (*Short Season* 104).

16. Kristeva makes a similar point in her reading of the ending of Beckett's *Molloy,* which both asserts and denies that it is midnight and raining: "However, the negative form [reality] is neither more real nor more true than the positive form [writing]; both are discourses that mutually presuppose each other" (*La révolution du langue poétique* 352, quoted in Jardine, *Gynesis* 60).

17. My reading of *To the Lighthouse* might usefully be compared with Hirsch's reading (108–16). Hirsch argues that "Lily's solution to what art should be and her completion of the painting" depend on her rejection of the aesthetic criteria of harmony, balance, order, and permanence (112–13). Thus, the end of the novel does not resolve the tensions between two forces but maintains them, and Lily's line can be said to connect the masses on the right and left of her canvas as well as to acknowledge their disconnection (114). Yet where Hirsch, like DuPlessis, discusses such writing by women in terms of "the aesthetic of 'both/and'" (115), I argue for a pragmatic approach that emphasizes multiple and changing relations. Compare also Froula's explanation of Woolf's continual experimentation and Lily's disposable art ("Rewriting Genesis" 216).

18. These are, of course, common strategies of postmodern fiction, strategies I discuss further in chapter 2.

19. The change that Woolf presents here, from oppositional distinctions to operative ones, brings to mind Lyotard's analysis of postmodern thought: the "type of oppositional thinking [that opposes two kinds of knowledge] is out of step with the most vital modes of postmodern knowledge" (14).

20. For an understanding of the cultural and historical importance of the three Marys, see Marcus's essay "Sapphistry: Narration as Lesbian Seduction in *A Room of One's Own*" (*Languages of Patriarchy* 163–87).

21. Kamuf reads this essay as "turning away from the historical preoccupation with the subject, closing the book on the 'I'" ("Penelope at Work" 11). Jardine sees this turning away as one intersection of postmodernism and feminism (*Gynesis* 58).

22. Woolf, like Eliot, stresses the point that "books are the outcome of many years of thinking in common" (ROO 68). Unlike Eliot's tradition, though, Woolf's is not traceable; rather, it is more a weblike structure with many gaps, overlappings, and loose ends. A metaphoric contrast might help to make this distinction clear. Eliot's tradition is a restricted club. Certain artists are admitted by meeting certain

criteria that affirm the value and assure the survival of the club. Woolf's tradition is a cab, a public conveyance that can transport all kinds of people to all kinds of places following all kinds of routes. Some riders leave behind obvious signs of their occupancy—a twisted glove, a half-smoked cigar, a whiff of perfume—while others leave no ostensible sign of themselves.

23. Tompkins, in her introduction to *Reader-Response Criticism,* writes: "When discourse is responsible for reality and not merely a reflection of it, then whose discourse prevails makes all the difference" (xxv). Schweickart makes an observation similar to Woolf's point in *A Room of One's Own:* "For feminists, the question of *how* we read is inextricably linked with the question of *what* we read" (40).

24. I do not deny Zwerdling's insight that Woolf probed the process of socialization that discouraged women from taking their work seriously (222–23). But to avoid the dilemma thereby created for feminists—either insisting on sex-based standards for women's art or showing how women's art satisfies the same standards as men's—I argue that Woolf used this insight to change not just women's psychology but the artists' and audiences' psychology as well.

25. I am indebted to Austin Quigley for this understanding of Wittgenstein's model.

26. The terms are Naremore's, but this kind of reading informs DiBattista's, Harper's, Transue's, and Richter's commentaries, among others.

27. As Hafley was the first to note, *The Waves* seems to originate in the language of "Time Passes" (*Glass Roof*). Both *The Waves* and *To the Lighthouse* include an uncommunicative and prepossessing individual whom almost everyone, especially the artist figure, tries to grasp: Mrs. Ramsay and Percival. Both novels, in their last sections, are narrated by the artist figure who connects all the sections and who makes us aware of the aesthetics the novels disclose. Also, Bernard's "world without a self" passage recalls Lily's "waters of annihilation" passage, although Lily nearly loses herself in the illusion she has created while Bernard nearly loses himself as he ceases to create illusions. Woolf herself connects the inception of *The Waves* with the conclusion of *To the Lighthouse* in a diary entry dated February 7, 1931, that records the end of *The Waves* (Diary 4:10).

28. The comparison is not an idle one, for *The Waves,* like Beckett's trilogy, gives us the sense that all parts are present at once, in ever-changing combinations, as well as the sense that the novel is progressing. In the earlier sections, Bernard assumes the role of his own biographer and, like Molloy, speculates on his future self (see, e.g., TW 199). In the last section, he resumes that role in order to present his earlier self with a story, much as Moran seems to create Molloy.

29. Smith makes the point that the narrative exists in all its versions, not in some "deep structure" ("Narrative Versions" 218–19). The significance of this kind of thinking for concepts of identity, whether personal or national, was made clear by Smith in a paper presented at the Liberal Arts Education conference (Duke University and the University of North Carolina–Chapel Hill, September 1988). Smith criticized E. D. Hirsch's concept of a "national culture" by pointing out that such a culture exists only in its ethnic, racial, regional, and class differences, not in some common element that transcends these particularities.

30. Bernard's desire to see not his own consciousness reflected in the land but

the land stripped of his consciousness and his fictions is presented in terms of a winter scene: "No sound broke the silence of the wintry landscape" (TW 374). *The Waves* contains many other passages that recall Stevens's poems. In an earlier section, Bernard describes Jinny: "She made the willow dance, but not with illusion; for she saw nothing that was not there" (351). And in the Hampton Court dinner scene, Bernard compares himself to a snowman (332). Such passages suggest the romantic modernist side of Woolf and of Stevens, namely, the Shelleyan desire to express the inexpressible and to find a new language. But they also serve as reminders of the "supreme fiction" of our imaginative constructions. As in *To the Lighthouse,* Woolf both evokes this Shelleyan desire and resists it in *The Waves.*

31. In reference to the device of introducing into the text the writing of the text, McHale writes: "this reconstruction of the act of writing depends upon *what has been written*—on the text we read. In this sense, the writing itself is 'more real' that the act of writing that presumably gave rise to it" (198). In *Comedy and the Woman Writer,* Little comments on the characters fleeing their author in this passage from *The Waves* (81).

32. Lanham uses this phrase to describe the effect of artificial naturalness produced by postmodern art, which presents a dramatic conception of self and world (20–23).

33. Sarraute discusses the fiction of Dostoyevski and Kafka as a fabric of relationships without any center. This conception of fiction, she says, moves the action from "inside" (i.e., the analysis of character) to "outside" (i.e., the interactions among characters). In particular, it moves the novel close to the domain of theater (59–82 passim).

34. Because of the unresolved confusion of the real and the fictive, Guiguet says, *Between the Acts* reveals a "deep disillusionment, akin to despair": "Never had Virginia Woolf expressed her pessimism so categorically" (327). Fussell concurs with this reading, claiming *Between the Acts* displays "the failures of art in man's endless struggle with meaning" (266). Zwerdling reads this novel as an expression of Woolf's despair of ever improving human relations (305). Though many feminist readings have reassessed Woolf's mood in *Between the Acts,* they do so by stressing her political argument, not her aesthetic motives, as I do here (e.g., see Johnston 253–77).

35. I use "literature" here in the broadest sense, not in the sense of "great books" as distinct from popular culture.

36. Zwerdling shares this reading of Lucy's unifying vision (313–14) and also points to the juxtaposition of the beautiful and the sordid in the novel as well as the play (315). And we both question readings of this novel that stress its coherence and synthesizing power. But what leads Zwerdling to such conclusions is his assumption that the discontinuity of the novel, the jazz rhythm, the interruptions all *threaten* the unity, continuity, and permanency of art—a reading every bit as dependent on modernist assumptions as the unifying reading he opposes.

# 2

## Characters and Narrators:
### *The Lonely Mind and Mrs. Brown*

The first thing is that the novel should seem to be true. It cannot seem true if the characters do not seem to be real.[1]

—Arnold Bennett,
"Is the Novel Decaying?"

Odd, that they [the *Times*] shd. praise my characters when I meant to have none.

—Virginia Woolf,
Diary, 1931

Allen McLaurin's *Virginia Woolf: The Echoes Enslaved,* exemplifies an all-too-common way of talking about Woolf's characters. Although McLaurin rightly points out that Woolf's artist figures "cannot be pinned down to certain fixed traits" because "they are open to all sorts of influences and possibilities" (169), he then gives us the "distinctive traits" of Woolf's artists: "androgeneity, and the division of the self" (169). In doing so, McLaurin fails to draw a connection between the artists' openness to possibilities and the kinds of art they produce, and the kinds of art that produce them. Once we accept that the artist changes in response to a variety of influences, then such an understanding has consequences for the way we talk about the components of the artwork—in this case, the novel. Characterization is, of course, one such component, and clearly we can no longer define characters apart from their contexts. As I argue in this chapter, the "androgeneity" and instability McLaurin notes in Woolf's artists might be better thought of not as *traits* of a certain character type but as *effects* of a certain approach to characterization.

For years readers like McLaurin have been commenting on how much Woolf's characters differ from those of nineteenth-century novels and of modern stream-of-consciousness novels. Often they feel compelled to propose new terminology for *character*—for example, personality, figure, caricature—because the conventional notion of character, at least after *The Voyage Out* (1915) and *Night and Day* (1919), no longer fits Woolf's fiction. But to change the terminology is to assume that the conventional concept of character is normative in fiction. The assumption that a character is a unique, discrete being at the center of the novel's action is one Woolf herself rejected in her debate with Arnold Bennett. Most critics point to "Mr. Bennett and Mrs. Brown," in which Woolf challenges Bennett's conception of character, to show that she was redefining character as "life itself." Yet what the essay does is examine not what character is but how character functions, how character is used by writer and reader, how writer and reader respond to character. In pursuing Mrs. Brown, Woolf does not seek a new *type* of character; after all, Mrs. Brown is in many ways like a Bennett character. Rather, Woolf explores the means of expressing character in fiction.

With this understanding, we can correct Woolf's remark from her diary entry on *The Waves* cited above (Diary 4:47). By claiming she meant to have no characters, Woolf seems to acquiesce in Arnold Bennett's criticism of her novels as well as much criticism of the "new novel." In his essay "New Novel, New Man," Robbe-Grillet writes: "We are told: 'You do not create characters hence you are not writing true novels.' . . . But we, on the contrary, who are accused of being theoreticians, we do not know what a novel, a true novel, should be" (135). Similarly, Woolf avoids saying what a novel or a character should be and instead explores how each functions. Although she claims she intended to write a novel without characters, as Flaubert desired to write a novel without a subject, what she actually does in her fiction is explore the ways characters come into being, not create a new kind of character or abolish character altogether. That is, her desire is not to do away with the convention of the character; rather, her desire is to underscore the conventional in order to make "a common text [her] own."[2] Woolf does not abandon character in a novel like *The Waves* (1931) or *Jacob's Room* (1922); on the contrary, she makes character so highly self-conscious that the concept itself becomes more important, not less. And so, she could dare to agree with Bennett that character is of supreme importance to the novel.[3]

When Woolf wrote in her diary, shortly after the publication of *Jacob's Room,* that hers was an age in which "character is dissipated into shreds" (Diary 2:248), she was not, at that time, expressing her own view of character, as both Geoffrey Hartman and Morris Beja (*Critical Essays*) imply. Despite her apparent agreement with Arnold Bennett in the first version of "Mr. Bennett and Mrs. Brown," in this diary entry a month later she presents this opinion as the "old argument," the "post-Dostoevsky argument" of the reviewers and critics, such as Bennett, who decry "modern"

characters, such as Jacob. By accepting some norm for character in fiction, these critics see modern characters as failing to measure up. Woolf
could have argued with Bennett by refusing to concede that character is
central to the novel, as the new novelists like Robbe-Grillet and Sarraute
seem to do when they argue against androcentric conceptions of the novel
and essentialist concepts of the individual.[4] But by accepting Bennett's
premise, Woolf exposes his limiting and essentializing view of character.
She changes not the *terms* of the debate but its *import:* what matters is
what character does in the novel, not what character is in the world. She
neither dissipates nor rejects character; rather, she foregrounds character
by exploring its ontological and formal status. Foregrounding ontological
issues, Brian McHale argues, marks a "change of dominant" from modernist to postmodernist fiction (10).

One way Woolf foregrounds character is by making the narrative perspective opaque, not transparent, something we look at, not through.
Most critics attend to the unobtrusive and subtly modulating narrators in
Woolf's fiction. Because her narrative perspective merges with her characters' perspectives, and because the aim of such a multipersonal method is
seen as unity (as in Erich Auerbach's reading of *To the Lighthouse*), Woolf is
said to posit some kind of universal mind in her fiction, that is, the "lonely
mind" she meant to embody in *The Waves*. Hartman's conclusion is typical:
"there is only one fully developed character in Mrs. Woolf's novels, and
that is the completely expressive or androgynous mind" (75).

Such interpretations rest on two dubious assumptions. First, they assume that Woolf's narrators are unobtrusive. Yet what is striking about
her narrators is just how obtrusive they are. Second, such interpretations
assume that the dissolution of character-narrator boundaries represents
some authorial metaphysical theory that preexists and finds expression in
the narrative method. Yet Woolf's characters and narrators do not present
a consistent theory of self and world. Instead, they make us self-conscious
of theorizing about self and world by making the narrative strategies self-
conscious. Before we can consider new ways of reading (whether the novel,
the self, or the world), our habitual relationships to the narrative must
be revealed and disturbed so that the primacy of a discursive strategy is
made apparent. In *Jacob's Room, Mrs. Dalloway,* and *Orlando,* Woolf calls
attention to the artificial nature of literary forms and to the tenuousness
of literary language. These novels from the 1920s, the only novels besides
*Flush* that are named after their central characters, raise most noticeably
the issue of characterization and its related issue of narrative perspective.
Through her use of characters and narrators in these novels, Woolf draws
attention to narrative strategies and thus to the ways in which characters
and, by implication, notions of identity are produced.

An example from *Jacob's Room* illustrates this point. Consider the scene in the penultimate chapter, where we stand with Mrs. Pascoe in her garden: "Shading her eyes with her hand Mrs. Pascoe stood in her cabbage-garden looking out to sea. Two steamers and a sailing-ship crossed each other; passed each other; and in the bay the gulls kept alighting on a log, rising high, returning again to the log, while some rode in upon the waves and stood on the rim of the water until the moon blanched all to whiteness" (175). Here the narrator seems to modulate unobtrusively into Mrs. Pascoe's perspective. We seem to look through Mrs. Pascoe's eyes at the steamers and the sailing ship, at the gulls on the log and the gulls on the waves, at the reflection of the moon on the water, only to be told in the next sentence that "Mrs. Pascoe had gone indoors long ago." This revelation is abrupt and disturbing. We can connect it with those recurring references to what was "unseen by anyone" and conclude that we are in some universal mind.[5] But the immediate impact of this passage is to startle us into noticing the narrative perspective, to make us conscious of what is usually muted in narratives. It gives us a rather uncomfortable feeling to find we are not in the consciousness we thought we were in. It is as if we have found ourselves commenting on a painting to the woman next to us only to find that she has moved on. We become self-conscious. Such a narrative strategy does not make us *despair*, but it does make us *discriminate*. That is, it makes us aware of our habit of willingly assuming certain narrative points of view; it makes us reconsider our relation to the narrative perspective and the relation of the narrative perspective to the thematic concerns. Such scenes play with narrative strategies and make us self-conscious of the ways we attach meanings to things.

We miss this point, however, when we persist in talking about Woolf's characters and narrators in the same terms. Commentaries on *Jacob's Room*, for example, are remarkably consistent. They cite the same passages, isolate the same themes, and rely on similar descriptive phrases. Critics comment on the novel's fragmentary structure, its lack of plot and stable character, and its multiple narrative points of view. Disagreement emerges, though, when attempts are made to account for these features. Some critics take a modernist perspective and attribute these traits to Woolf's attempt to free the novel from its conventional form (e.g., Jean Guiguet); others take a feminist perspective and attribute them to Woolf's attempt to free the novel from "authoritative masculine voices" (e.g., Virginia Blain). To E. M. Forster, Jacob is a solid character (*Virginia Woolf* 14); to Leonard Woolf, he is a ghost (Diary 2:186). For Bernard Blackstone the novel is about the nature of reality; for S. P. Rosenbaum it is about the nature of consciousness. Jean Love claims Woolf intrudes too much in those

"essayistic passages" that present the author's theories; Barry Morgenstern takes such critics to task for attributing this narrative voice to Woolf
herself. Whether the critics voice a consensus of opinion or seemingly opposing beliefs, they approach *Jacob's Room* in a largely conventional way,
all the while labeling it Woolf's first experimental, and thus unconventional, novel. They infer her theories from the narrator's generalizations
while admitting that narrator is unstable and uncertain. They interpret
Jacob's character from his actions and thoughts while conceding that Jacob
is never fully or consistently realized. It seems we go straight ahead in-
terpreting as we always have, while defensively asserting (not to be taken
in, mind you) that such interpretation is never adequate. We seem to be
caught in a contradiction.

This contradiction has to do with what happens to characterization in
the novel. Jacob as a character is in danger of becoming lost within a multiplicity of details. He is refracted through a myriad of isolated objects—his
chair, his shoes, his room, his bucket, his books—and through the numerous perspectives of and on people associated, however remotely, with him.[6]
Without a consistent point of view and a stable focus on him, Jacob can be
neither a traditional character presented through his actions in the world
nor a modern character presented through "the atoms as they fall" ("Modern Fiction," CR 155). One might be tempted, then, to claim Jacob as a
postmodern character in that postmodern novels often seem to abolish the
individual subject. Often their characters' names degenerate into letters
or sounds—Kafka's K., Robbe-Grillet's A, Beckett's Mag, Pynchon's V.—
or are omitted altogether, as in Sarraute's novels, or flaunt their fictional
status, as do Barthelme's Snow White and Acker's Don Quixote. "What is
obsolescent in today's novel," says Roland Barthes, "is not the novelistic, it
is the character; what can no longer be written is the Proper Name" (*S/Z*
95). But Jacob *has* a proper name: Jacob Allen Flanders. Indeed, *Flanders*
seems to take him from the extreme of metonymic displacement to the
extreme of metaphoric substitution by allegorizing him.[7] When it comes
to deciding what Jacob *is,* it would seem that, in the words of Jacob's narrator, "the problem is insoluble" (JR 82)—if, that is, we agree we have
a problem. If we assume characters can only be defined by traits, or that
they represent discrete individuals, then we do indeed have a problem.
However, if we look at character as a function of the text, as one of several
relations in the narrative, then the problem is capable of resolution.

Like the mark on the wall in one of the stories that engendered this
novel (AWD 22), Jacob is that spot around which the various images,
scenes, statements, and memories cohere. Like Mrs. Brown, Jacob is what
we seek, "all the while having for centre, for magnet, a young man alone
in his room" (JR 95). As the organizing principle of the novel, Jacob is a
structural element, not just a thematic representation. In this sense he does

seem to illustrate the postmodern concept of character as Patricia Waugh presents it: "the anti-mimetic idea that 'characters' cannot be understood through comparisons with 'real people'"; "'characters' . . . dissolve into the categorizations of grammar" (*Feminine Fictions* 3, 7). Yet Woolf's method of presentation suggests a different point to her investigation of character, the point readers like Waugh and McLaurin may neglect. When McLaurin says that proper names in this novel "have reference, but no meaning" (167) because what they refer to constantly changes, and when Waugh laments the postmodern dissolution of character (as Bennett lamented the modern dissolution of character), they assume that conventional characters acquire meaning in only one way—that is, in terms of their correspondence to something else. Instead of accepting such an assumption, Woolf tests out various narrative possibilities that allow for different conceptions of self and world. Her fiction works on the assumption that narrative activity precedes any understanding of self and world. Thus, Woolf seems to ask: What effect does the so-called dissolution of character or decentering of the subject have on the possibilities of the novel as a genre as well as on our possible conceptions of self and world? When I say we must consider Woolf's *point,* I do not mean her intention, that is, some preconceived meaning to be expressed through the text, for that assumes literary language is a transparent medium of some purposeful communication, which is not the postmodern view of language I explore here. Rather, by "point" I mean how Woolf's works function within a larger context of narrative discourse, including the writer's and the reader's motives which compel them to enter into this text—that is, their various motives and purposes for playing this particular language game.

So what's the point? In its title, *Jacob's Room,* and in its movement of digression from and return to Jacob, this novel calls attention to the notion of *centers* in narratives: the center of attention (main character), the center of vision (point of view), and the center of meaning (theme). If the first two are unstable and shifting, then we must ask what happens to the third.

In being made up before our eyes, aging but not growing, Jacob discloses the juncture of Woolf's notions of narrative and self. From the multiplicity of perspectives in this novel—the almost desperate sense of needing just one more view—and from the text's adjectival insistence—the piling up of descriptive phrases as if despairing of closure—*Jacob's Room* reveals, in Avrom Fleishman's words, that "every inclusion marks an exclusion" (54). Fleishman's point states the obvious: that every narrative selects and arranges items from a range of possibilities. What makes Woolf's narrative strike us as postmodern is that it hyperbolizes the obvious. It exploits the narrative necessity that "one must choose" and connects it with the privations of the self: "But no—we must choose. Never was there a harsher necessity! or one which entails greater pain, more certain disaster; for wherever I seat myself, I die in exile" (JR 69). This necessity of choosing, this sense that we cannot experience all perspectives at once, compels many critics to focus thematically on the reiteration of gloom in *Jacob's Room*. Yet the inclusion of so many obscure characters and trivial objects in this text, and the exaggeration on the level of syntax and diction in this passage and others, should caution us about taking the narrator too seriously. The narrator frequently mocks her own method and mimics her own style. For example, she draws attention to the odd conjoining of adjectives in the many descriptions of Jacob—"savage" and "pedantic," "awkward" but "distinguished"—by exclaiming over Bonamy's own flagrant modifiers (e.g., "sublime," "barbaric," "obscure"): "What superlatives! What adjectives! How acquit Bonamy of sentimentality of the grossest sort" (164). Such parodic statements should serve to keep us from reading through the stylistic surface to the thematic significance. The necessity that we must choose a limited and limiting perspective would be a sad one only if we believed in some ideal of wholeness or unity, for either character or self.[8] However, in this novel, as in so many postmodern novels, we come to see that such choice is ineluctable. Since the text, like the self, is never complete, each scene we have of Jacob is partial and provisional. By calling attention to this fact—"For example, take this scene" (JR 125)—Woolf calls into question the selection in the act of selecting and reminds us that Jacob and *Jacob's Room* could have been the locus of another equally virtual and equally suspect set of experiences, impressions, and traits. Jacob may be a text whose pages we turn, but he is certainly no closed book.

Woolf's comparisons of characters and texts bring to the fore the status of the character as a convention in narrative. In *Jacob's Room* characters are described as "rude illustrations, pictures in a book whose pages we turn over and over as if we should at last find what we look for" (97).[9] As in *Orlando*, this comparison between reading others and reading books reveals that the essence of a character, like the ending of a novel, is a conventional expectation, a learned response that lures us on to seek something that does not in actuality exist (O 294)—that is, it does not exist outside its rhetorical conventions. What we find is what we seek: "What do we seek through millions of pages? Still hopefully turning the pages—oh, here is Jacob's room" (JR 97). The syntax presents Jacob's room and *Jacob's Room* as both the answer to the question and a distraction from it. Whether Jacob's room is what we seek or what we find, whether it is the space that Jacob encloses (the *room* in Woolf's fiction, critics tell us, often represents the *self*) or the space that encloses him (his society or culture or novel) is not the issue. The point is the textual and contextual relationship between the self and the world, between the character and the narrative, between the desire and the expression.

This relationship is foregrounded by the narrative voice. What is most salient and disconcerting in *Jacob's Room* is the pervasive uncertainty on the narrative level itself. The narrative voice questions, doubts, and speculates (45); asserts then denies (95); affirms then contradicts (79). The narrator points out the biases of her own point of view, "granted ten years' seniority and a difference of sex" (94), as well as the limitations of every other point of view (71–72). The narrative voice fluctuates from "we" to "I" to "one" to "you" in a confusion of pronouns like those in a Sarraute novel. Many paragraphs begin with what seems to be the narrator's generalization— "For he had grown to be a man, and was about to be immersed in things" —only to end with a character's view that undercuts the generalization —"as indeed the chambermaid, emptying his basin upstairs, fingering his keys, studs, pencils, and bottles of tabloids strewn on the dressing-table, was aware" (139).[10] Here the chambermaid stands in for the narrator, as Mrs. Norman does earlier in the novel (30–31; see Bowlby 106), where elsewhere the narrator stands in for a character. As her reference to her difference in age and sex signals, the narrator becomes a character in her own story, much as Fowles's narrator does in *The French Lieutenant's Woman*, thereby disturbing ontological boundaries. It's no wonder we have trouble defining Jacob, for we cannot find a stable place to stand.

This narrative uncertainty is usually interpreted as Woolf's belief that we can never know another being because all experience is relative and subjective. But this reading overlooks Woolf's emphasis on the observer's *situatedness,* both the narrator's and characters' in relation to Jacob and the reader's in relation to the narrative. Knowledge of another is not relative to each individual but to certain perspectives and relationships. As does *The Voyage Out,* with its recurring distant views of the land from sea and the sea from land, *Jacob's Room* stresses narrative perspective itself. We cannot take for granted what constantly changes. The perspective keeps shifting from metaphoric longshots (Cambridge as a glow seen from the sea) to metonymic close-ups (the skull left behind on the beach), from what a character sees to what a character "should have seen" (17), to what one "would have seen" if anyone had been there (13), to what one could not possibly have seen, such as Seabrook six feet under (16). Such conditional views elude us as they are called forth, much as Jacob does.

We must look to the narrative perspective, then, in our attempt to understand Jacob as a character. Jacob changes shape, not because the modern (or postmodern) self is unstable, and not because the modern (or postmodern) character is unreal, but because the narrator changes roles. Sometimes she addresses us as an Austen narrator would: "Elizabeth Flanders . . . was, of course, a widow in her prime" (15). Sometimes she sounds like a biographer: "Jacob Flanders, therefore, went up to Cambridge in October, 1906" (29). Sometimes she speaks to us directly like Thackeray's narrator in *Vanity Fair:* "Let us consider letters" (92). And sometimes she withdraws from the fictional world, as Flaubert's impersonal narrator does, focusing on a commonplace object that in its singularity taunts us with potential significance (Charles Bovary's hat or Jacob's crab). These different narrative voices evoke different kinds of reality; Austen's world is not Flaubert's. They make us aware that Jacob and *Jacob's Room* derive significance from a heterogeneous tradition of narrative discourse. They disclose the narrative authority as contingent. And they make us aware of the status of the character as a verbal artifice, alterable according to narrative flow.

It is now possible to state more clearly the problem critics face. While accepting *Jacob's Room* as representing a new *form* (experimental or modernist) and as embodying new *content* (a new theory of identity), they neglect its *function* for the reader. Whether critics rely on conventional terminology (plot, protagonist, theme) or modernist (significant form, fragmented narrative, time shifts), their similar approaches to the novel encourage them to set up misleading contrasts: plot or no plot, solid character or dissipated one, novel of consciousness or novel of reality. Most critics agree that *Jacob's Room* is not *about* Jacob (e.g., John Mepham, Avrom Fleishman), but in defining Jacob as a void (Jean Guiguet) or an absence (Robert Kiely), they displace the focus of the text, its referent. They say *Jacob's Room* is about Jacob's room, that is, his society, culture, or "living space," or about consciousness, or about writing, specifically, the writer's struggle to bring a character into existence. Such readings rely on the language of representation; they work for a referential reality but not for a rhetorical reality. For this novel, though, we need new questions, ones that ask not whether or not the novel has a plot but what it does with plotting, not whether or not it has a central character but what it does with characterization. We need to ask not what *Jacob's Room* is about (what it is saying on behalf of the author) but what it brings about (what it is doing on behalf of the reader). What does it tell us about the relations between narrative and self and world? As seen in the "narrative trick" discussed earlier, *Jacob's Room* exposes the dangers in an unself-conscious acceptance of certain narrative strategies. Put another way, Woolf's strategies show us the danger of attributing too much authority to the narrator and not enough to the narrative, a response Henry James has cautioned against in his prefaces. Virginia Woolf, like an irritating daughter, nearly parodies James's suggestion by acting enthusiastically upon it.

The uncertainty, instability, even deceptiveness on the narrative level tell us little about Jacob or the narrator or the author as personalities. But these strategies tell us much about narratives and readers. Such strategies do not undercut the conventional character but undermine our conventional readings. Contradiction, in defying our interpretive grids, brings them to the fore. Paradox, as "a rhetorical device used to attract attention" (*Handbook to Literature*), italicizes the rhetoric, not just the theme. Flagrant repetition, by highlighting the narrative elements as parts in a composition, shows that these elements derive their significance from their context, not from their correspondence to a world apart. Thus *Jacob's Room,* much like a postmodern novel, insists on its narrative strategies. That is, Woolf highlights the often concealed devices of narrative: "But then concealment by itself distracts the mind from the print and the sound" (79). This reads like a line from one of Kenneth Burke's "Flowerishes" or from a John Cage lecture. Woolf's novel, like so much postmodern art, *attracts* the mind to "the print and the sound"—which may be what David Daiches means when he says *Jacob's Room* is a book written for the sake of the style (*Virginia Woolf* 61). But Daiches implies that such attention to style is justified only in the service of a new form. To read Woolf's novels looking for the new form, though, or to read *Jacob's Room* looking for the new character, is one way of reading narratives. Those who subscribe to this method progress through Woolf's novels the way Sandra Wentworth Williams progresses through life: "[swinging] across the whole space of her life like an acrobat from bar to bar" (161). That is, readers often search among Woolf's novels for the distinctive style, characteristic themes, or familiar subjects, reading her different novels as if they were parts of a whole, swinging across the space of her canon, groping for the next bar in the series. Yet in revealing a variety of narrative and reading strategies, in taking us down the "chasms in the continuity of our ways" (96), *Jacob's Room* cautions us against such a reading and indeed against any one reading approach. This novel does not dissipate characters; it liberates readers.

It is because Woolf tests out various narrative perspectives in *Jacob's Room* that Jacob's function as a character becomes our concern. It is because we must pursue Jacob through shifting viewpoints that we become aware of what is usually overlooked in narratives. As in a Beckett, Robbe-Grillet, or Sarraute novel, actions usually passed over are exaggerated: "Mrs. Pascoe stood at the gate looking after them; stood at the gate till the trap was round the corner; stood at the gate, looking now to the right, now to the left; then went back to her cottage" (55). Inaction becomes significant action when it is our only focus. It is not that complete, unambiguous communication is impossible or that language is inadequate for our needs (two common interpretations of Woolf's theme in this novel). Rather, unambiguous communication is *one kind* of communication, and *one function* of language is inadequate for all our needs. For communication to occur, therefore, we must pay attention to expression itself. The narrator in *Jacob's Room* performs a phatic function, in Roman Jakobson's sense of this term.[11] It keeps us in touch with textuality itself, keeps the channels of communication open before us and to us. Joan Bennett finds this method of characterization "crude" because "the writer obtrudes herself" and "by doing so she disturbs the illusion" (25). However, the important question is what effect disturbing the illusion has on our reading of this novel. To read through the narrative surface of the text to some generalization beneath is to accept unself-consciously one possible function of narrative as "given" or "normative." It is to make narrative strategies "innocent." It is to set ourselves up for the narrative trick and for the critical contradiction.

When we come, then, upon an often quoted passage like "all history backs our pane of glass" (49), we should be wary of reading it as a statement of the author's metaphysical theory. In the context of this novel, the passage could suggest not that history is a complex of forces determining character and event (a common interpretation) but that history is a narrative capable of intervening to change those forces that appear to determine character. Such generalizations in Woolf's novels are rarely unambiguous, though. Often they are followed by "but," indicating an exception and marking context. To accept such generalizations as Woolf's views is to give preference to the objective, detached point of view in narrative over the contingent, limited, and partial point of view of the situated observer. No matter how serious the generalization in *Jacob's Room*, the narrative calls it into question, mocks it, or undercuts it, even as it insists upon it. The point is not to dismiss the implications of such generalizations but to consider the consequences of such thinking.

For example, in chapter 12 of *Jacob's Room* the narrator presents a devastating argument against the "character-mongers," those who try to sum people up by listing their traits: "For however long these gossips sit, and however they stuff out their victims' characters till they are swollen and tender as the livers of geese exposed to a hot fire, they never come to a decision" (154–55). If the character-mongers are wrong, then "we are driven back to see what the other side means" (155). Those on the other side see character drawing as a frivolous art. They say individuals are not autonomous beings but driven and shaped by an "unseizable force" that the novelists never grasp in their characterizations. This seems to be the all-history-backs-our-pane-of-glass argument; the paragraph presenting this view describes the death of "blocks of tin soldiers" falling "like fragments of broken match-stick [*sic*]" (155, 156). We seem to be suspended between equally untenable views, while the text shows signs of adhering to both. On the one hand, we seem to have the novelist's art pitted against historical forces, and we might expect the narrator to defend the former. On the other hand, we seem to have the Arnold Bennett view of character, where characters are individualized, versus the lonely-mind idea, where individuals are components of a larger whole, and we expect the narrator to support the latter. But we do not face a choice here. It is precisely because the narrative presents such different views and tests out the consequences of relying on one view over another that we have such conflicting opinions on Jacob as a character and on the theme of this novel. The meaning is not relative to individual readers but contingent on changing narrative strategies. Woolf forces us to confront the profound implications of seemingly innocent narrative choices.

A similar problem of reading emerges in *Mrs. Dalloway*. Both it and *Jacob's Room* reveal the problems we run into when we accept certain conceptions of characters and narrators as normative. At first *Mrs. Dalloway* would seem to be a far cry from *Jacob's Room* in its characterization and narrative method. Surely Mrs. Dalloway could never be described as an absence or a void, as Jacob is. And while *Jacob's Room* makes narration conspicuous, *Mrs. Dalloway* seems to make it discreet. Or so most critics would seem to believe, for their readings focus on the modulating narrative voice, on the continuous narrative flow, and on the subtle transitions in *Mrs. Dalloway*. These devices, most critics conclude, demonstrate Woolf's belief in one mass mind (Harvena Richter), a luminous halo of consciousness that transcends individual minds (Howard Harper), a watery world in which identity is muted and self blends with what is outside it (James Naremore). These readings—shared by Jean Guiguet, David Daiches, James Hafley, and others—accept Woolf's original intention, as she reveals it in the introduction to the Modern Library Edition of this novel: to present Septimus as the insane view of life, Clarissa as the sane. That is, these critics accept Woolf's claims for results; they assume that what she says is what she does. *Mrs. Dalloway*, Maria DiBattista argues, is the first novel to present Woolf's "philosophy of anonymity" in that "the creative mind consciously absents itself from the work" (*Woolf's Major Novels* 63). And so, despite their differences, *Mrs. Dalloway* and *Jacob's Room* are often read in terms of the same thematic concern: the expression of a unifying vision of life.[12]

However, these readings of *Mrs. Dalloway*, as Harper admits and Naremore implies, do not account for those places in which the narrator is clearly distinguished from the characters, as when the narrator observes what no one notices (a common occurrence in *Jacob's Room*), suggests motives for characters' actions, satirizes characters, and inveighs against Proportion and Conversion. Nor do they account for those strained transitions, which Naremore calls "arty" and others call "contrived," such as the little girl in the park who links Peter Walsh and Rezia. In other words, these readings do not account for the "exceptions" that make up a significant portion of the novel and that undermine its seamless quality. The fact that Sir William Bradshaw's sense of proportion, Miss Kilman's religious belief, Peter's possessive love, Lady Bruton's social conscience, and Clarissa's party all present a unified vision of experience should caution us against employing the term *unity* too loosely, against celebrating it as a value in itself, and against positing a single unity where there are only different ways of effecting unity.

The problem, again, comes from setting up two options. For example, Naremore observes that the narrator hovers between traditional omniscience, where the narrator is removed from the character's mind, and modern interior monologue, where the mental processes are presented as if unmediated by a narrative consciousness (92–102 passim). Richter shares this reading and concludes that we get the illusion of penetrating into subjectivity rather than the actual presentation (52). What we encounter, though, are not two kinds of narration but the narrative strategies involved in connecting those detached and those intimate perspectives. The narrative draws the reader's attention to the mediation of scenes and thoughts. Blurring distinctions between characters and between characters and narrator, Woolf makes the source of a thought doubtful, thereby inhibiting our tendency to seek the author's view in the characters or in the narrator. This attenuation of the text-author, as well as the text-world, connection frustrates our attempt to draw one-to-one correspondences or to see the meaning of the text as that to which a statement or action refers. J. Hillis Miller recognizes this narrative emphasis when he says that *Mrs. Dalloway* is an exploration of narration, which he equates with what Woolf called her "tunnelling process" (*Fiction and Repetition* 182). However, valorizing unity leads Miller, Naremore, and Richter to elide the narrative focus and insist on the thematic: all minds are joined beneath surface distinctions in some universal mind. As in *Jacob's Room*, though, Woolf refuses to subordinate the narrative strategies of *Mrs. Dalloway* to the thematic statement.

Attention to narration is effected by Clarissa herself. Just as the narrator merges with characters yet remains, for the most part, detached, so Clarissa participates in scenes even as she stands apart from them. She shares Woolf's artist figure's dual perspective of being both within a scene (creating) and without (observing): "She sliced like a knife through everything; at the same time was outside, looking on" (MD 11). At her party Clarissa is not only its organizing center but an observer of its organization. This notion of intimacy-yet-detachment parallels the narrative strategy. The act of perceiving is stressed by means of those observers in the street and by the "arty" and "contrived" transitions. These adjectives, so often used pejoratively to describe Woolf's transitions in this novel, emphasize that the art by which these scenes are created is brought to the fore, while the critics who use them imply that such art should be kept in the background, for contrivance disrupts unity.

If we attend to the didactic narrator as well as the modulating one, the fragmented structure as well as the continuous flow, and the narrative leaps as well as the subtle transitions, we find that what *Mrs. Dalloway* reveals is not some metaphysical unity but how unity is perceived and contrived. It is not Woolf's intentions that are divided but the reader's attention. We are aware at once of some kind of narrative unity and of the process of constructing such unity. Rather than Naremore's and Richter's watery world where all blends, *Mrs. Dalloway*, like *Jacob's Room*, highlights the selection and arrangement of elements in a composition. We are aware of things existing side by side and of the associations that can link them. The obtrusive transitions provide a network of relations. Miller observes that the network of solid objects—such as the airplane and the car—reveals that we are all unified in our responses, however different, to the "same" world. But Woolf, though she conveys the sense of a shared world and a communal response to it, also calls attention to its constructedness as a symbolic structure, as well as to our tendency to take our own value of unity as a quality of the world or of consciousness. The text questions the world as given (the "same" world), seeing it instead as a construct. Unity, then, is not a theme but one relation in the novel.[13]

The world of *Mrs. Dalloway* is aleatoric rather than unified; it does not unite us in some absolute *beyond* the moment but immerses us *in* the moment: "What a lark! What a plunge!" (3). The imposition of some perceived unity on a multiple, fluctuating world seems to be what Woolf points toward but does not supply. Those characters who promote unity as a social or moral value do not all walk in the "same" world. Those who respond to the airplane by straining to make out some message and by turning it into a symbol are the sane (Mr. Bentley) and the insane (Septimus) alike. Those rhetorical devices of unity—metaphor, symbol, personification, substitution—are strained and heightened by the narrative: for example, in the personification of St. Margaret's clock as a hostess receiving her guests (74), in the self-consciously "arty" language of Clarissa's and Peter's first meeting (66), in Elizabeth's complaint that people compare her to natural things, which they then do (204–5, 287, 294),[14] in the abundant bird imagery signaling itself in the flight of wings in Clarissa's drapes that for her "unify" the party (256, 258), and even in Clarissa's uncanny identification with the unknown Septimus at a moment when her separation from others is stressed (283). What is common to all is the desire to create meaningful orders, to impose some kind of unity on random life.

*Mrs. Dalloway* brings such desire to the surface, acknowledging the limitations of our own unifying systems.[15] In doing so, it disturbs our orientation to the narrative, though not as flagrantly as *Jacob's Room* does. Just when we get comfortable in the minds of characters, we are made to acknowledge the "artificiality" of the narrative. The effect is analogous to that produced by the deceptive narrator of *Jacob's Room* who takes us to empty rooms and returns our attention to characters who have departed. In *Mrs. Dalloway* the narrative seems to mislead us as well. It allows us to accept, along with Peter, the death of Mrs. Parry, only to have her show up at the party, ailing but living. It turns Sally's pawned heirloom from a brooch into a ring that may not have been pawned after all, for she has it still.[16] Certainly these scenes re-create the sense of failed memory, allowing us to share the characters' confusion. Yet they also reveal the extent to which the past and the world are re-created "every moment afresh." That details can be changed without any disruption in the story suggests the narrative is not a transcription of a world apart. Thus, we cannot take the narrative itself for granted, for to do so is to accept the text as *about* a unified world or consciousness that exists independently of our means of constructing such unity. Like the meaning of character in *Jacob's Room*, the devices perceived as creating unity in *Mrs. Dalloway* function in more than one way. Their thematic implications depend, then, on the kinds of relations we single out. Unity is only one such relation.

By revealing and disturbing conventional relations to the characters and narrators, Woolf's fiction shows us that novels perpetuate certain concepts of self and world. As long as we recognize these concepts as part of a particular mode of discourse, and not just representative of a world apart or a consciousness within, then such shared literary strategies serve to promote communication and sustain community. It is when we separate these concepts from their shaping contexts and motives that they can be deceptive, limiting, even dangerous. As the narrator remarks in *Orlando*, such illusions are valuable and necessary; the mistake is forgetting they are illusions. If there is a danger in fiction, it lies not in the dissolution of character or in the decentering of the subject; rather, it lies in the possibility that its readers will unquestioningly accept its forms as indicative of the way things are in the world (as Isa and Giles do in *Between the Acts* when they define their marriage by the clichés of fiction) and that they will read all narratives in the same way, thereby corroborating and perpetuating a limited range of responses.

When we fail to attend to the different functions of narrative elements, our interpretations tend to focus on less relevant issues, such as determining whether a novel is normative or deviant, conventional or experimental

(I might add, modern or postmodern). This is the case with *Orlando*. Many Woolf critics consider *Orlando* to be an aberration. Usually, its differentness from Woolf's "mainstream" fiction (e.g., *Mrs. Dalloway, To the Lighthouse,* and *The Waves*) is attributed to its qualities of fantasy, parody, and mock biography (though *Jacob's Room* and *Flush* also can be read as mock biographies). But as with *Night and Day* and *The Years,* the unusualness of *Orlando,* looked at from another perspective, can be attributed to its reliance on "conventional" novelistic techniques, for in many ways Woolf's most fantastic novel is her most conventional. The narrator, Orlando's biographer, characterizes Orlando by means of her history, her house, her physical appearance, her social life, and her personality traits—clumsiness, love of solitude, and sensuality—much as Arnold Bennett might. The narrator gets us from one scene to another, one century to another, even one sex to another by providing transitions and explanations, where explanations are possible. Unlike Jacob, Orlando could never be described as an absence, for she is as vivid and vivacious as any Fielding or Defoe character. And the narrator is consistent and unambiguous (except, as with everyone in this novel, in gender). Even the plot is conventional in covering Orlando's travels, careers, social life, and marriage. Although Orlando's long life and wavering sexuality seem to defy biography, the novel trudges on in the biographic style. Since this fantastic novel can be described in conventional ways, it would seem that our usual distinctions between normative and deviant are of little use. What is major and what is minor, what is mainstream and what is marginal, what is conventional and what is original, change, like Orlando's sex, with time and circumstance.[17]

What this novel reveals, then, is the difficulty of making such distinctions about identity and language and narrative form, because there is nothing stable to measure them against. It is not that *Orlando's* playful surface has no point to it, as Daiches implies: "the reader should peruse [*Orlando*] with the surface of his mind, not pondering too deeply as he reads" (*Virginia Woolf* 103). Rather, its point *is* its playful surface. *Orlando* is a text about constructing lives, histories, and fictions. As such, it shows us the beneficial consequences, for self and society, of accepting these things as variable constructions, not stable forms.

The obtrusive narrator in *Orlando* brings the textual language and style to the fore. By emphasizing his use of symbols and brackets (14, 256), digressions and omissions (269, 253), by intruding to discuss his own art (65), by mocking his own method (266), and by characterizing his own readers (73), the narrator shows us not the inadequacy of language, as Naremore says, but its primacy, not the impossibility of constructing a life but its compelling necessity. Language and identity are closely related in this novel. Orlando is identified with language throughout: she writes at her poem for centuries, she is read like a book (25), she reviews her life in terms of her reading and writing, and she concludes that she is "only in the process of fabrication" (175). Just as Orlando's identity swings from the extreme of conventionality (Orlando as a boy slicing at the swinging Moor's head) to the extreme of eccentricity (Orlando as a woman discovering that she has three sons by another woman), so the language shifts from the transparent conventionality of clichés (to put it in a nutshell, by the skin of his teeth) to the opaque originality of Orlando and Shel's cypher language (Rattigan Glumphoboo). As the bombastic masque of the Three Sisters hyperbolizes Orlando's sex change, the exaggerated lyricisms, the hackneyed expressions, the strings of metaphors, and the self-conscious diction exaggerate the language of this text.[18] Yet at times the sexes shift places—"You're a woman, Shel!" she cried. "You're a man, Orlando!" he cried (252)—and so do the extremes of rhetoric. For what appears to be conventional and transparent in one context may become original and opaque in another.

For example, when the narrator must describe the passage of time, he suggests that such descriptions are common enough that little need be said:

> —but probably the reader can imagine the passage which should follow and how every tree and plant in the neighbourhood is described first green, then golden; how moons rise and suns set; how spring follows winter and autumn summer; how night succeeds day and day night; how there is first a storm and then fine weather; how things remain much as they are for two or three hundred years or so, except for a little dust and a few cobwebs which one old woman can sweep up in half an hour; a conclusion which, one cannot help feeling, might have been reached more quickly by the simple statement that "Time passed" (here the exact amount could be indicated in brackets) and nothing whatever happened. (97–98)

This is, of course, a mocking reference to Woolf's own "Time Passes" section of *To the Lighthouse*, which is considered the most original section of a most original novel. We see that identity is as variable as language, language as vulnerable as identity.[19] There is no norm for each. Both are based on making distinctions, yet these distinctions are not fixed by reference to anything stable outside them.

The text of *Orlando*, then, is as unstable as the sex of Orlando. The first words of the novel shake our certainty about anything in this text. We read, "He—for there could be no doubt of his sex," and immediately our doubt is aroused.[20] The stress on what is obvious makes it seem unnatural. The stress on an innocent pronoun makes it suspect. The shifting and blurring of sexual identities, of literary genres (novel, fantasy, and biography), and of literary and historical periods (from Elizabethan to Modern), along with the violation of ontological boundaries (in Woolf's use of historical figures, such as Pope and Dryden, as characters), threatens meaning brought about by fixed polarities and rigid classifications and by reference to stable categories in the world or innate differences between the sexes. Androgyny reflects this basic ambiguity, not only a sexual ambiguity, but a textual one as well. The androgyne, as Barthes says in *S/Z*, is a threat to meaning in breaking down the "wall of antithesis" that allows us to make meaningful distinctions (65). Yet not all meaning is threatened. To remain suspended between two beliefs is not to deny meaning; rather, it is to call attention to and to call into question one way of making meaning. Androgyny is not, as DiBattista argues, a freedom from "the tyranny of sex" (*Major Novels* 117) so much as a freedom from the tyranny of reference.

In *Orlando,* androgyny, transsexualism, and transvestism call into question not just conventional assumptions about sexuality but, more importantly, conventional assumptions about language itself. Waugh writes: "The question of the ontological status of fictional characters is ultimately inseparable from that of the question of the referentiality of fictional language" (*Metafiction* 93). In its rhetorical transports, Woolf's novel challenges the reference theory of meaning. In particular, it questions the notion that words get their meanings from things they refer to; the definition of words and categories by their essential traits; and the isolation of words and statements from their contexts of use in order to interpret them. The point of focusing on the marginal case (e.g., the transsexual) is to reveal the crucial decisions made in the application of a term or in the assumption of an identity. We can see this point most clearly in the famous clothes philosophy passage in chapter 4, the passage often cited as Woolf's theory of androgyny.

Now a woman and living in the eighteenth century, Orlando in this chapter becomes acutely aware of her sex as she faces a legal challenge to her property rights, as she parries the advances of the ship's captain and the archduke Harry, and as she contends with "the coil of skirts about her legs" (153). Initially unchanged by the sex change, or so we are told, Orlando now assumes a more feminine nature. Her biographer writes:

> The change of clothes had, some philosophers will say, much to do with it. Vain trifles as they seem, . . . they change our view of the world and the world's view of us. (187)

According to this philosophy, our identity is as changeable as our apparel. Clothes make the man, or the woman. The difference between men, and between men and women, would seem to be superficial. However, Orlando's biographer continues:

> That is the view of some philosophers and wise ones, but on the whole, we

incline to another. The difference between the sexes is, happily, one of great profundity. Clothes are but the symbol of something hid deep beneath. It was a change in Orlando herself that dictated her choice of a woman's dress and a woman's sex. (188)

That is, clothes do not *make* the woman but *mark* the woman beneath the clothes. But again the biographer continues. Two sentences later we find the famous androgyny passage:

> For here again, we come to a dilemma. Different though the sexes are, they intermix. In every human being a vacillation from one sex to the other takes place, and often it is only the clothes that keep the male or female likeness, while underneath the sex is the very opposite of what it is above. (189)

Placed in its context, this last statement not only contradicts the earlier assertion that Orlando's sex change has not affected his/her identity, as well as the other philosophy that says we put on our identity with our clothing, but it also contradicts itself. The biographer begins by saying that clothes are a symbol of something deep beneath, that is, one's nature or identity, and ends by remarking that often what is deep beneath is the opposite of the clothing above. In other words, the passage asserts both that clothes are natural and fitting and that they are arbitrary and deceiving. Such self-contradiction is not in the least surprising in this particular novel. What is surprising, however, is that, in appropriating this statement as Woolf's theory of androgyny, many feminist critics pass over the contradictions, accepting the statement at face value, taking the biographer at his word, which is to take his discourse for granted.[21]

The reason many feminist critics in particular have tended to appropriate Woolf's androgyny in this way can be found in their desire for a definition that corresponds to their concept of feminism. In other words, what most feminist critics want (in both senses of lack and desire) is a definition. They want to know who they are, to distinguish *us* from *them*, to identify the real feminist from the cross-dresser. But such a motive is very much at odds with Woolf's use of androgyny in *Orlando*. To resist defining androgyny consistently and to resist saying who Orlando really is, we must shift our mode of inquiry, from asking what Woolf's concept of androgyny means to asking what it means to present androgyny in these terms.

If we consider the above passage within its larger context, we see that Woolf is not arguing for one of two ontological theories—that is, that identity is fixed or identity is changeable, that sexual differences are natural or they are learned. Rather, *she is testing out the consequences of different concepts of language and identity*. To speak of rhetoric as either revealing or concealing, to speak of appearance as either natural or contrived, is to set up a false opposition; it is to assume that we can get beyond or beneath

the linguistic paradigm, in which rhetorical and sexual differences function, to some natural state, some natural discourse. Proving the contrary
is precisely the point of the vacillating rhetoric and epicene protagonist
of Woolf's novel. We can no more speak of *two* aspects of identity than
we can speak of *two* functions of language. At any one moment, for any
one motive, both are fixed; but each changes with changing purposes and
changing circumstances.[22]

In *Orlando,* then, clothing, identity, and rhetoric are not an ornamentation of something prior but an orientation to something else. What
matters is not what they mask or mark but what they enable the protagonist or the writer to accomplish. That is, what matters is not the nature of
the sign, the transsexual, but its position and function within a particular discursive situation. And so we must attend to the production of the
androgynous Orlando, not to her properties. If we return to the clothes
philosophy passage, we see that, in trying to distinguish the ways in which
Orlando has changed with the sex change and how Orlando embodies
traits of both sexes, the biographer ends up making stereotypical remarks,
for he can make such sexual distinctions only by relying on conventional
assumptions about sexual difference. The biographer's only recourse, then,
is to look at the particular case: "but here we leave the general question
[of sexual difference] and note only the odd effect it had in the particular
case of Orlando herself" (189). We, too, must attend to the particular case
rather than the general category.

To read this novel we need a conceptual model for narrative discourse
that enables us to discuss the novel not in terms of its relation to the theme
beneath or the world beyond but in terms of the multiple and shifting
relations among signifying systems, such as rhetoric, fashion, gender, and
genre. We need a dynamic model, not a dualistic one. If we adopt such a
conceptual model, we must attend not only to the various relations among
changing historical periods and rhetorical styles but also to the changing
sexual metaphors. By employing three metaphors for sexual identity in
*Orlando*—androgyny, transvestism, and transsexualism—Woolf shows us
that there are different ways of talking about identity, different kinds of
appropriateness, different functions of language. When we fail to specify
the kinds of distinctions we are relying on (as Sandra Gilbert does, in
"Costumes of the Mind," by equating these metaphors), our conclusions
become suspect. Woolf knew all too well that any language she could use
was already embroiled in certain conventional assumptions about gender
and identity. By changing metaphors for sexual identity, and by divest-
ing Orlando of her property and her patronymic, Woolf does not liberate
identity but exposes the categories by which identity is determined and
legalized.[23] What is at issue here is a language that sets up opposing alter-

natives (Gilbert's) and one that plays out various relations (Woolf's). Such an epicene novel is possible when different functions of language are tested out rather than one function being taken for granted.

Like Orlando's poem, fiction, identity, and history are palimpsests, bearing their plural pasts within them.[24] Because we cannot locate innate sexual traits or essential literary values or eternal metaphysical truths in the face of changing attitudes, conventions, and paradigms (whether scientific, literary, or psychological), we must continually posit and undermine, affirm and doubt, yield and resist (O 155). Oscillating exploration is the method of *Orlando*.

Androgyny, then, is a refusal to choose. The androgynous vision is paratactical, not dichotomous. It affirms a "fertile oscillation" between positions.[25] The androgyne defeats the stereotype, "the word repeated without any magic, any enthusiasm, as though it were natural, as though by some miracle this recurring word were adequate on each occasion for different reasons" (Barthes, *Pleasure of the Text* 42). Androgyny defeats the platitude, and the norm. But it does more than expose conventional forms; it also exposes the process of producing these forms.

The problem with the stereotype, the platitude, and the norm is not that they are false or trite in themselves but that they are false or trite in being detached from the contexts that give rise to them. Within the parodic context of *Orlando*, the original and lyrical "Time Passes" becomes a tedious and grandiloquent way of saying simply that "time passed." Within the fantastic context of *Orlando*, the critical commonplace of the fact/vision dichotomy becomes banal. And what enables Mr. Pope's scathing remark on women's characters (a remark so famous that the biographer can omit it) to become a commonplace about women is its being loosed from its generating context, which was this: Orlando inadvertently offended Mr. Pope by dropping a sugar cube "with a great plop" into his tea (214). What appears to be a witty remark in one context may be a petty retort in another. Unmoored from their contexts, literary standards, social values, and sexual traits appear to be incontestable; yet they are responses to particular historical and rhetorical situations. Taking Woolf's statement of androgyny from its context in *Orlando*, repeating it as an unambiguous truth about human nature, runs the risk of turning it into a platitude. What gives the statement its force are the contextual, textual, and sexual relationships in which it plays its part. After all, "brilliant wit can be tedious beyond description" (196).

With the many literary quotations, genres, and periods that compose this text, with the exaggerated string of metaphors and images produced by the narrator and by Orlando, this novel might seem to be seeking the appropriate aesthetic form, much as Orlando constantly searches for the right metaphor. However, Orlando discovers, in desperately seeking the irreducible linguistic episteme, that one cannot "simply say what one means and leave it":

> So then he tried saying the grass is green and the sky is blue and so to propitiate the austere spirit of poetry whom still, though at a great distance, he could not help reverencing. "The sky is blue," he said, "the grass is green." Looking up, he saw that, on the contrary, the sky is like the veils which a thousand Madonnas have let fall from their hair; and the grass fleets and darkens like a flight of girls fleeing the embraces of hairy satyrs from enchanted woods. "Upon my word," he said . . . , "I don't see that one's more true than another. Both are utterly false." (101–2)

Poetry and nature, language and self, are learned together.[26] This is the point of the vacillating narrative and the epicene protagonist of *Orlando*. It is not a new form, new words, new "being" that are needed but a new understanding of how forms and words and beings behave. Orlando's diuturnity is not a testament to some common human nature; rather, it is a revelation of a common past and of a common activity, the life-sustaining impulse to create fictions.

If the "new novel" (whether Georgian or postmodern) fails, it is not because it is inadequate to its task of describing the world or self, for as the biographer reminds us, we go on communicating despite (or because of) the imprecision of our language. If it fails, it can only be because no one responds. No sooner has Orlando finished her poem than it clamors to be read, for what is the text—"the thing itself," as Orlando calls it—but "a voice answering a voice" (325). Private poetry, of a Rhoda or Isa, soon palls; we need the dramatic voice of a Bernard or Miss La Trobe. "A voice answering a voice" describes the self as well as the text, the self as text. Orlando, like Jacob, Clarissa, and Bernard, needs an audience. The androgynous self becomes a metaphor for the dramatic self. It is a dynamic process, a metaphor for change, for openness, for a self-conscious acting out of intentions. The androgynous self is not a type but a response. Identity is always disguised in *Orlando,* not because the true self is running around "incognito or incognita as the case might turn out to be" (168), but because identity is formed in relationships, whether the relationship of self to other, of character to narrator, or of narrator to reader.[27]

Already, then, in *Orlando* Woolf has enacted a dramatic conception of self, history, and literature, as she does in her last novel, *Between the Acts*. The pageant of *Between the Acts* is a temporal, transient, communal act. It partakes of the past as well as the present moment; indeed, it perpetually renews the past in the present by breaking down artificial historical divisions and by immersing us in time, in the contingent, not looking to some absolute beyond time. The parodic strategy of La Trobe's play and of Woolf's *Orlando* proclaims "dramatic re-enactment" as the basis of their art. For Woolf, as for Flaubert, the mimetic function of art is closely related to mime, an exaggerated, parodic imitation and re-creation.[28] Because *Orlando* and La Trobe's village play reflect other literary acts, they affirm art as dramatizing the pageant of life, not as representing some stable reality distinct from the narrative and dramatic structures that enclose it. The relation of text to world, or character to individual, is only one relation among many. *Orlando* and *Between the Acts* dramatize the self and literature as acquiring significance within a history, within a plural past. Such works are not to be reread and reinterpreted only; they are to be re(en)visioned and re(en)acted. This revisionary act attests to the continuance, and accounts for the continuity, of the self, society, and literature.

Virginia Woolf's fiction does not react against a narrative tradition so much as it re-acts within narrative traditions. Woolf accepts neither the uniqueness of the individual nor the individual's submergence in some universal consciousness. Her character is neither individual (Proust) nor typical (Bennett), neither archetypal (Joyce) nor anonymous (Sarraute), because her character does not *represent* anything; rather, her character is *functional*. Like the arbitrariness of literary forms, the tenuousness of character in Woolf's fiction is due to the individual's relatedness and situatedness. Character and self, narrative form and literary language, are situated within various discourses and function within the contexts and constructs that enclose them. The character is as inseparable from its narrative and rhetorical contexts as the self is inseparable from its historical and social contexts.[29] A narrative does not just represent a world; it represents as well a mode of producing and a way of valuing that world.

By focusing on the problem of reading that Woolf's novels pose, I have attempted to show that Woolf was not offering a new type of character or narrator but was changing the ways we read characters and narrators. Her androgynous and her collective characters, and her anonymous and her multiple narrators, do not substitute for anything. Just as her conception of self makes disguise, imitation, and performance indispensable rather than irresponsible, so does her conception of the novel make highlighting the narrative surface essential rather than frivolous. The kind of reading I challenge assumes the world of Woolf's fiction is representational; my postmodern reading assumes it is rhetorical. Learning to read such novels as Woolf's in a new way is not to discover something "unsaid" or "hidden" in other readings or other narratives. Rather, it is like moving from the crowded city to the suburban spaces: one is surprised to find how many people are already there.

## NOTES

1. Bennett goes on to say that *Jacob's Room* is "characteristic of the new novelists" (*Critical Heritage* 113), by which he means, of course, the "high" modernists, not the "early" postmodernists. But what a delightful slippage in terms!

2. In her discussion of women's fiction, Nancy K. Miller comments that emphasizing what passes for neutral or standard in fiction is "a way of marking what has always already been said, of making a common text one's own" (343).

3. Hynes argues that Woolf was wrong to concede character as central in her debate with Bennett, suggesting that, had she not given in on this point, she may have won. For a detailed discussion of "Mr. Bennett and Mrs. Brown" that connects change in literary conventions to change in the representation of women, see chapter 1 of Bowlby's *Virginia Woolf: Feminist Destinations*.

4. For example, in *The Age of Suspicion*, Sarraute says that characters in the new novel are no longer empirical beings but "props." That is, they perform certain functions in the narrative rather than represent certain types, and they are constituted by the relationships into which they enter, not by the personality traits they possess (75–76, 85). In *For a New Novel*, Robbe-Grillet writes that the character with a proper name, a family, a heredity, and a profession belongs to the novel, which marks "the apogee of the individual" (27–28). The new novel, by contrast, "has renounced the omnipotence of the person" (29), as seen in Kafka's K., about whom Robbe-Grillet says: "he is content with an initial, he possesses nothing, has no family, no face; he is probably not even a land surveyor at all" (28).

5. The idea of some universal mind in which we all participate, a belief often attributed to Woolf, is undercut in *Jacob's Room* by Woolf's presentation of the British Museum as one enormous mind. The names of those most representative of this cultural mind (all male, as Julia Hedge notes) are emblazoned around the dome. Believing in the musuem's authority, Jacob seeks within its confines to prove his thesis on indecency, and Miss Marchmont seeks to justify her theory "that colour is sound, or perhaps it has something to do with music" (JR 108), though neither succeeds. The narrator contrasts that vast mind "sheeted with stone" with the bustle in the streets outside. In the attention paid both to those who live outside this dome and to the "unpublished works of women," or women's letters (JR 93), the narrative undercuts this static, closed notion of culture. *Jacob's Room*, as does *Orlando*, presents social and literary history as a bustling city, not a stone museum or one enormous mind.

6. Minow-Pinkney also notes that *Jacob's Room* is crammed full of objects: "too many objects present themselves . . . as signs to be read" (35). "The world becomes text," she continues; "it overloads, even overwhelms the observer with more and more signifiers" (36).

7. Jacob Flanders apparently dies in World War I. The suggestiveness of his name, as well as the narrative attention given to his empty shoes, his unoccupied room, and the forgotten crab in his bucket, tempts critics to allegorize this novel, as Fleishman does when he turns the crab in the bucket into "a symbol of man's fate" and Jacob's empty shoes into the waste of youth in World War I (46, 54). Yet such objects are not transparent signs but elements in a relation. And Jacob, like

Kafka's K., never seems to die because he never seems to exist fully, independently of his context. Jacob is not in the world but in the text. Robbe-Grillet discusses this tendency to allegorize seemingly insignificant and unconnected objects and events in Kafka's works (*For a New Novel*, 163–65).

8. Woolf herself finds hope where others see only despair. In "Mr. Bennett and Mrs. Brown," she describes the change in narrative conventions in terms of grammar and syntax: "Grammar is violated, syntax disintegrated" (CDB 115). In response to such change in characterization and narrative perspective Woolf writes: "In view of these facts . . . I am not going to deny that Mr. Bennett has some reason when he complains that our Georgian writers are unable to make us believe that our characters are real. . . . But *instead of being gloomy,* I am sanguine. For this state of things is, I think, inevitable whenever . . . the convention [of character] ceases to be a means of communication between writer and reader. . . . At the present moment we are suffering *not from decay,* but from having no code of manners which writers and readers accept . . ." (CDB 115; emphasis added). Without such a code of manners or an alternative way of talking about character, we must fall back on terms like *dissolve, decay,* and *decenter,* all of which suggest a narrow focus on the mimetic relation between character and individual rather than a broader focus on the narrative relations between writer and reader.

9. Bowlby comments as well on the analogy between reading a book and knowing a person (chap. 6). She argues that Jacob is an object of others' readings rather than an individual "in his own right" (101).

10. Other examples can be found on pages 146 and 153. I am often surprised that so few readers, besides Woolf herself, comment on how amusing *Jacob's Room* is. Taken in by the thematic reiteration of melancholy, sadness, and gloom, readers neglect the humor on the narrative level. (A notable exception is Little, in her essay "*Jacob's Room* as Comedy"). Woolf remarks in her diary entry of May 20, 1920, that *Jacob's Room* "is the most amusing writing I've done, I think; in the doing I mean" (Diary 2:40). The amusement "in the doing" makes for the amusement in the reading.

11. Jakobson defines the phatic function as follows: "There are messages primarily serving to establish, to prolong, or to discontinue communication, to check whether the channel works, . . . to attract the attention of the interlocutor or to confirm his continued attention" ("Linguistics" 92). This use of language is not intrinsic to postmodern fiction alone, but it is given preference in many postmodern works; it also accounts for the intrusions of the narrator and the ways in which the narrator calls attention to the use of language. This checking up on the channel of communication shows that such fiction does not take for granted either its status as discourse or its audience, a point Lyotard makes in reference to postmodern writing (75).

12. Exceptions to this common reading are found in several recent works. Minow-Pinkney and Bowlby both claim that the narrative devices of *Mrs. Dalloway* deny a unified subject. And Minow-Pinkney and Waugh (in *Feminine Fictions*) both discuss this novel in terms of female subjectivity and women's writing in particular, thereby shifting the terms of debate.

13. As Zwerdling points out, if the party is meant to unify, as Clarissa feels,

then Woolf has gone to great lengths to draw attention to those left out, such as Septimus, Rezia, Miss Kilman, and the street singer (127).

14. Bowlby comments that Elizabeth's position at the party, standing next to her father, puts her in the very position she had rejected earlier when she is idealized by being compared to natural objects (87).

15. Waugh says unity is "a desired ideal that all Woolf's novels confront and struggle to resist" (*Feminine Fiction* 115). Johnson acknowledges, "This hope for some ultimate unity and peace seems to structure the very sense of an ending as such"; then she critiques the implications of this desire for unity as they manifest themselves in Erich Auerbach's famous reading of *To the Lighthouse* (*World of Difference* 164–66).

16. Such strategies are common in postmodern fiction. For example, in García Márquez's *One Hundred Years of Solitude,* the narrator allows us to suppose that Colonel Aureliano Buendia dies before the firing squad, only to tell us a hundred pages later that he dies of old age. And in Robbe-Grillet's novels, objects singled out for attention often shift subtly as the novel progresses, like the billboard in *Le Voyeur* or the centipede in *Jealousy.*

17. Most critics rely on the contradiction between the conventional form and the unconventional subject matter in their analyses. They say *Orlando* shows the futility of the biographic fact and the necessity for the artistic imagination in depicting a personality (Naremore); that it explores the dichotomy of fact and fiction (Moore, *Short Season*); that it turns life into literature and literature into life (Fleishman). (As a fantasy, *Orlando,* of course, already self-consciously blurs the distinction between appearance and reality.) Whether they focus primarily on history or identity or gender, critics discuss *Orlando* in terms of a changing surface and a stable core. The conventional self changes but the essential self remains the same (DiBattista, *Major Novels*); the external circumstances change but the common life is eternal (Naremore). More recently, Knopp has challenged such readings by discussing how this fantasy "annihilates" such categories as normal/abnormal, natural/unnatural, healthy/maimed (30).

18. Such extremes of style and language compose *Between the Acts* as well, from the communal nursery rhymes to Isa's private lyrics, from the transparent conventional plots of La Trobe's play to the opaque emptiness of the stage, from Lucy's clichés to the Village Idiot's babbling—all calling attention to the spectrum of rhetorical possibilities.

19. Lanham points to a common "mistake" we make as readers: "We refuse to think 'life' as variable as literature" (43).

20. Bowlby also remarks on this doubt (50).

21. Recent exceptions to this common appropriation of androgyny are given by Knopp, Minow-Pinkney, and Bowlby. Knopp argues that critical attention to androgyny has neglected "more relevant discussions" of gender traits and sapphism (30). Minow-Pinkney attends to the contradictions in this passage and concludes that Woolf anticipated the poststructuralist view that gender, like language, is a system without positive terms (130). And Bowlby argues that the seemingly opposed hypotheses "turn out to be mutually implicated in such a way as to render undecidable, if not to obliterate, the distinction between them" (55).

22. In *Reading Woman,* Jacobus makes a similar argument in her first chapter, where she discusses *Orlando* in terms of language and clothing. In "Rereading Femininity," Felman discusses sexual identity as "conditioned by the functioning of language" (29).

23. DiBattista points out that "sex becomes a legal fiction, like paternity and property rights" (quoted in Minow-Pinkney 128).

24. The palimpsest has become a popular image. Hassan uses it for history ("The Question of Postmodernism," in *Liberations*), as did H.D. before him in *Helen in Egypt.* Gilbert and Gubar apply it to women's fiction in *The Madwoman in the Attic.* The metaphor suggests that what we often take as closed systems or linear progressions should be seen as a network of texts. This palimpsest metaphor, used for postmodern as well as feminist writing, should caution us against identifying certain structures as characteristic of one or the other mode of discourse and instead lead us to specify the kinds of distinctions we are making within this network of texts.

25. Lanham used the term *fertile oscillation* in a lecture on postmodern art, "The Literary Canon and the Post-modern Critique," delivered at the Penn State Conference on Rhetoric and Composition, July 1985. As an example, he used the sketch from Wittgenstein's *Philosophical Investigations,* vol. 2, which can be seen as a duck and as a rabbit (sec. 11). Postmodern art, Lanham argued, seeks to move from a monostable to a bistable view of the world, making "the mind as honest as the eye" in its ability to oscillate between two views. Bateson calls this a "binocular vision," one that provides a different kind of understanding, not just additional information. This kind of understanding, he says, enables us to distinguish among contexts, not to discriminate between two things (78–87, 133–34).

26. Kuhn writes that "nature and words are learned together" (191). Woolf expresses this view in her "or" constructions: "to call forth, or light up" (*Orlando*), "to found out, or make up" (*A Room of One's Own*). Creation and discovery are reciprocal processes. The term *episteme* comes from Foucault's early works, where he uses it to refer to the distinct governing principle of a historical period, not a totalizing force but a "set of relations."

27. In *Feminine Fictions,* Waugh discusses at length Woolf's relational concept of identity.

28. In discussing the concept of self underlying the pragmatism of William James and the linguistic philosophy of Wittgenstein, Lanham writes: "Our felt sense of selfhood, in such a view, comes from enacting a series of roles, building up a self from layers of dramatic reenactment" (129). This, in Lanham's view, is the basis of postmodern art. In "Flaubert and the Status of the Subject," Brombert discusses mimesis as mime in Flaubert's writing. This sense of miming is most clearly presented in *Between the Acts,* with its wordless drama and its cast of mummers.

29. Heath points out Sarraute's awareness of identity as historically and socially situated, not as absolute and fixed. For this reason, he says, Sarraute does not fix a character's identity, does not even name a character, because she sees individuality as merely a contrived distinction (48–49). Commonly in postmodern fiction, characters are revealed in terms of their literary and historical contexts. For example, the protagonists of Barthelme's *Snow White* must be read not only in relation to the

fairy tale but in relation to the time period as well, as brought out in the quotations from Mao Tse-tung and from television commercials interspersed throughout the text. Similarly, Fowles's characters in *The French Lieutenant's Woman* must be read in relation to their Victorian predecessors, as brought out in the epigraphs to each chapter.

# 3

## Narrative Structures and Strategies:
### From "the babble to the rhapsody"

But if there are no stories, what end can there be, or what beginning?

—Virginia Woolf,
*The Waves*

What is past is not dead; it is not even past.

—Christa Wolf,
*A Model Childhood*

Having considered the ways in which Virginia Woolf attracts attention to narrative strategies, I now want to consider the ways in which she organizes them into a plot structure. Elucidating different narrative functions is a first step. The next, as Fredric Jameson points out in his critique of structuralism, is to explain their relation to the completed narrative. "What is necessary," Jameson asks, "in order for a story to strike us as *complete?*" (*Prison-House of Language* 62). Considering this question from a functional point of view, not a thematic one, is the main focus of this chapter.

As with much postmodern fiction, the assumption that Woolf's novels are complete is often in question. Many Woolf critics concur with Joan Bennett's assertion that after writing *Night and Day* Woolf ceased to write stories. Just as she "abandoned the convention of character-drawing" with *Jacob's Room,* Bennett claims, Woolf "abandoned the convention of the story" (42). By "story" Bennett means a logically connected series of events progressing toward a conclusion. It is this logical connection and this sense of a conclusion that Bennett and others claim Woolf's narratives lack. Woolf's endings are often described as inconclusive (Bennett), suspended (Naremore), or false (Lodge).

Yet to say that Woolf's novels do not conclude is to risk saying that they are not really narratives, for ending is what marks a narrative sequence, a plot structure. "A narrative without a plot," writes Seymour Chatman, "is a logical impossibility" (47). All narratives do not mean or conclude in the same way, but they all mean or conclude in some way. Woolf employs a variety of concluding strategies, from the expected (the death or betrothal of the female protagonists in *The Voyage Out* and *Night and Day*) to the unexpected (the sudden death of the male protagonist in *Jacob's Room*); from the emphatic ("I have had my vision") to the understated ("For there she was"); from the placid statement ("The sun had risen and the sky above the houses wore an air of extraordinary beauty, simplicity, and peace") to the wild cry ("'It's the goose!' Orlando cried. 'The wild goose . . .'"). To categorize such endings as either "closed" or "open," either "conventional" or "arbitrary," is to set up a false distinction; for the point at which any narrative breaks off is, in some sense, arbitrary. It is, we might say, already a false conclusion. There are as many strategies for suspending an ending as there are for rounding one off, so we need not oppose suspended endings to closed ones. When we say that a novel's ending is definite or suspended, complete or incomplete, we have not yet said anything about how it *functions* in the overall narrative structure.

Woolf herself has complicated such simplistic distinctions. In "Mr. Bennett and Mrs. Brown" she distinguishes endings that are definite yet incomplete from endings that are suspended yet complete. In the first case, the reader must write a check or join a society to complete the novel (e.g., a Wells novel); in the second, the reader desires only to reread (e.g., *Tristram Shandy*). The difference, Woolf says, is whether the writer is interested in the text itself (formal concerns) or in what is outside the text (social concerns). Although Woolf herself sets up a false choice here (between form and content, aesthetics and politics), her comment makes us realize that her concern is for the point of the narrative: that is, for the motive of the writing and for the effect on the reader. One must consider the context of the ending, including the questions we are invited to ask and the comparisons we draw. We have only to compare Woolf's later novels with novels by Djuna Barnes and Nathalie Sarraute to see how much Woolf relied on Bennett's understanding of "story."

The question, then, is not how to classify Woolf's endings but what is at issue in any classification. To begin to answer this question, I want to consider some problems generated by classifying Woolf's novels in terms of their plot structures. The two novels that have caused critics the most trouble in this respect are *Night and Day* (1919) and *The Years* (1937), novels Woolf called "representational" and her critics often call "conventional." Each is discussed in terms of the classical novel—the social comedy and the family chronicle, respectively—and each arouses suspicion in those critics who try to classify the novels accordingly. Detecting a Woolf in Austen or Galsworthy clothing, critics discuss these novels in terms of appearances. David Daiches says of *Night and Day* that "the social comedy that *seems* to determine the *superficial* form of the book is not its *essence*" (*Virginia Woolf* 18; emphasis added). Jean Guiguet claims the novel's weakness is not its failure to correspond to a type of the classical novel, but its allowing the reader to *suppose* that it does (209). James Hafley claims that *Night and Day* is "a social comedy *pretending* to be a novel of ideas" (*Glass Roof* 34; emphasis added). This pretense makes the novel seem to some to be derivative, to others spurious.[1] Similarly, critics who debate whether *The Years* is a throwback to a more traditional form or an extension of Woolf's innovative novels focus on what the novel *seems* to be: *The Years* "seems . . . a reversion to traditional realism" (Fleishman 172); "seems a novel of fact, a family chronicle" (Richter 171); "appears to be traditional" (Daiches, *Virginia Woolf* 111). The difference is that while most critics feel *Night and Day* is an unintentional confusion of kinds, they suspect the pretense of *The Years* is deliberate. James Naremore, Bernard Blackstone, Phyllis Rose, and Victoria Middleton all discuss Woolf's refusal to shape a narrative and her deliberate destruction of a pattern, as if some natural narrative shape imposed itself on the writer, requiring a great effort to be resisted.[2]

Trying to account for these novels in terms of a conventional narrative form, critics must either dismiss these suspiciously conventional novels as deviations from Woolf's innovative ones or dismiss the deceptive conventional surface for the innovative form beneath.[3] However, the fact that critics as different as Daiches and Naremore can employ the "same" standards (unity of structure) and rely on the "same" distinctions (traditional vs. modern) while reaching opposing conclusions—Daiches affirms that there is "nothing startling" in the technique of *The Years* (*Virginia Woolf* 112); Naremore insists its technique is "strikingly unorthodox" ("Nature and History" 246)—suggests that our criteria are variable and our distinctions unstable.

Recognizing such variability, Woolf clarified her concept of structure in her diary recounting of a discussion with T. S. Eliot in which she "taxed him" for the discontinuities in his poems (Diary 2:67–68). According to Woolf, Eliot explained these as the suppression of unnecessary explanations, for intelligent readers (those in the tradition, we might say) will make the connections themselves. This kind of discontinuity differs from Woolf's in that it depends on some fundamental system of belief or some shared educational and literary tradition that enables the reader to provide the right connections. Woolf's use of discontinuities, in contrast, explores and discloses the ways in which the reader makes those connections. In the story "An Unwritten Novel," for example, she draws attention to her omissions as well as to the kind of thing omitted: "But this we'll skip; ornaments, curtains, trefoil china plate" (HH 11). Even the title calls attention to such devices: "unwritten novel" does not refer to some phantom novel but to the process of unwriting it, taking it apart to show how it could be put together. That is, Woolf forces the reader to scrutinize the particular system that allows certain connections to be made.

As we have seen in the preceding chapter, one effect of Woolf's narratives is that they make us self-conscious about our critical terminology and common assumptions. Consequently, the critics cited above are right to suspect their classifications of Woolf's novels. However, most critics allay their suspicions by resorting to the appearance versus essence hierarchy to resolve contradictions in narrative structure. Too often critics believe they have explained contradictory narrative elements by means of their classification of the novel; therefore, they neglect to explain the relations between their classification of the novel's form and their assumptions about the functions it performs.[4] By redefining what is merely the surface appearance and what is really the essence beneath, they stop short of more precise descriptions of Woolf's narrative structures. They read them in the same way. Thus, while we credit Woolf with changing the novel tradition, we do not give enough credit to her own changing novels.[5]

Classifying novels is not the problem. The problem arises when we forget that our classifications enable us to make certain kinds of distinctions and when we assume that we are describing, in Woolf's words, "the thing itself before it has been made anything" (TTL 287). One function of the postmodern strategies we have been concerned with is to remind us that the novel is something we help to make. Postmodern novels invoke conventions of the classical novel to expose their relations to certain kinds of themes and certain concepts of reality.[6] As a result, they throw into confusion readings based on a theory of representation, which displace the text toward something else—for example, the structure of society or some norm for narrative—thereby setting up a correspondence between the structure of the novel and some pregiven standard of measurement. Accounting for narrative change in terms of dualistic distinctions, such as the surface/depth or the one-to-one correspondence model, is not wrong, but it is not always very useful. A postmodern reading enables us to make other kinds of distinctions: more explicitly, it shifts our focus from what the novel says and how it says it to what the novel does and how it comes to say anything. When postmodern fiction suspends the ending, then, it does not tell us something about the world or the novel as it is or should be. Rather, it tells us something about the effects of certain narrative structures and strategies on the novel and the world. If *The Years* relies on an open ending rather than the rounding off we find in *Night and Day*, it is not because Woolf refused to shape her narrative or rejected outmoded narrative conventions. Rather, it is because *The Years* presents a different kind of structuring with different kinds of effects. When we apply Jameson's question ("What is necessary in order for a story to strike us as *complete?*") to Woolf's novels, we are not asking, What does Woolf's suspended ending mean? but, What does it mean to suspend the ending?

In the pages that follow I explore the effects of different structural possibilities in Woolf's most "representational" works. In doing so I show how Woolf was questioning and challenging the reading habits and critical assumptions that depend on a theory of representation, and how much these habits and assumptions guide our readings of her novels, even when we praise her for having rejected them, even, in fact, when we claim to have rejected them ourselves. By offering another explanation for why Woolf abandoned *The Pargiters,* the early version of *The Years,* I suggest an alternative approach to the structures of *Night and Day* and *The Years,* one that enables us to make more relevant kinds of distinctions than those between the conventional and the innovative novel or the appearance and the essence. My reading of *The Pargiters* points to the changes in Woolf's thinking that make any discussion of these seemingly conventional novels suspect when we rely on *the same kinds of distinctions in each* or when we trace *a change from one kind of text to another,* as if only the properties of novels changed, not the concepts of narrative and world bound up with them.

Commentaries on *The Pargiters* most clearly reveal this critical reliance on the surface/depth dichotomy, whether critics are discussing narrative structure or personal psychology. Giving preference to representation leads many critics to take the discourse for granted, to read through the structure and strategies of *The Pargiters* to the repressed subject matter beneath.[7] While I do not deny that Woolf often relied on this surface/depth or appearance/essence dichotomy herself, I do deny that she always, characteristically, accepted such distinctions and that these distinctions always hold for our own critical discussions of her works.[8] Such dichotomies are useful starting points, as long as we resist the urge to valorize one term over the other and as long as we eventually move beyond setting up oppositions to explaining the exchanges between terms. In fact, as *The Pargiters* shows, Woolf doubted and questioned her own reliance on dichotomies, throwing such oppositions into confusion.

*The Pargiters* is the novel-essay portion of *The Years,* as editor Mitchell Leaska subtitles it. According to Woolf's diary, it originated in a speech given to a group of professional women (later revised and published as "Professions for Women") and was linked in her mind to *A Room of One's Own:* "I have this moment, while having my bath, conceived an entire new book—a sequel to *A Room of One's Own*—about the sexual life of women"

(AWD 161–62). Woolf's avowed motive in this work is to reveal sexual repressions, those restrictions on the sexual life of women and men that lead them "to turn away and hide the true nature of the experience" (TP 51). The essays attempt to analyze what the narrative chapters dramatize by pointing out the powers "that lay beneath the surface" of daily life (32). That is, the novel-essay form was originally conceived as a structure that depends on and reveals a dichotomy between what is surface, superficial, and conventional and what is deep, significant, and natural. Two years after recording the inception of this work, Woolf wrote in her diary that she was "compacting" *The Pargiters* by "leaving out the interchapters," that is, the essays (AWD 189). These revisions became *The Years*.

Leaska provides the standard interpretation for why Woolf abandoned the novel-essay. Drawing on Woolf's "New Biography," he borrows her own terms *granite* and *rainbow* to argue that she could not combine truth of fact and truth of vision, essay and novel, or the solid empirical surface and the intangible psychic depth: "For Virginia Woolf, the truth of fact and the truth of imagination simply would not come together in that queer 'marriage of granite and rainbow.' Essentially, this means that the whole idea of the 'Novel-Essay,' this 'novel of fact,' was abandoned by February 2 1933; and from that date on, the novel form [of *The Years*] would govern the design" (TP xvii). In his discussion of *The Pargiters*, Leaska treats the fictional scenes as objective correlates of the "governing ideas" and repressed feelings analyzed in the essays. He assumes that the language of the essay portions, the "explicitness of prose" (TP xviii), is unequivocal and transparent, allowing us to see how these controlling ideas have been transformed, ornamented, or disguised in the fictional parts. In doing so Leaska relies on distinctions between fact and fiction, essay and novel, "didactic discourse" and dramatic discourse that are not only untenable from the perspective of postmodern fiction but that Woolf found did not hold, distinctions that in fact are already blurred in the First Essay.[9] He assumes, as do most critics of this work, that explicit language is honest; indirect prose, duplicitous. (This is one assumption Woolf exposes in *The Pargiters* when she says that Edward's bias for explicitness and exactness in poetry is a learned response, not necessarily the correct one.) Leaska concludes that what is so unique about *The Pargiters* is that it gives us both the "fictional specimen" and the explanation of it (TP xx). And, he argues, by tracing the evolution of the controlling ideas we can see why Woolf had to discard this form that did not fit her subject matter.

We must ask, however, if the novel-essay form of *The Pargiters*, in which Woolf presents fictional scenes and then comments on them, in which she combines "poetic dramatization" with the "explicitness of prose" is really unique to *The Pargiters*. It seems that many of her essays do just this; that is, they trace or analyze her own presentation of a fictional scene or her own reading of a passage of fiction. In this sense, then, *The Pargiters* may not represent a unique, and eventually unsuccessful, form but a commonly used approach.

Comparing *The Pargiters* with *A Room of One's Own*, we can see that it is not a *form* Woolf abandons but a *motive*. The two works share several structuring devices: fictional scenes are framed by explicating essays in which the narrator comments on what has taken place in these scenes to an imaginary audience. In *A Room of One's Own*, Woolf's motivating questions (What are the conditions necessary for artistic creation? What are the effects of tradition, or an absence of it, on the woman writer?) are related to the informing question of *The Pargiters*. Only whereas in *The Pargiters* Woolf looks at the effect of traditions (educational, social, familial) on female nature, in *A Room of One's Own* she looks at their effect on the female writer. In *A Room of One's Own* the focus on writing throughout allows the fictional scenes to "work in and out of" the essays or analytic parts; in *The Pargiters* the focus on "being" (social self and true self) leads to the formal division between drama and analysis. As the narrator of *A Room of One's Own* keeps shifting its identity along with its method of investigation, we sense that the truth being sought and the traditions being questioned are multiple and shifting as well. What is factual and what is fictional, what is of "granite-like solidity" and what is of "rainbow-like intangibility," is an operational distinction in *A Room of One's Own*, not a given distinction, as in *The Pargiters*. The point of tracing her own methods and explicating her own fictions in *A Room of One's Own* is to invite us to look *at* the various approaches and how they posit a truth, to look *at* conventions and traditions. The point in *The Pargiters*, on the other hand, is to expose restricting conventions and traditions that thwart female development, so that we must look *through* these to something stable beneath. The fictional scenes in *The Pargiters* are meant not to disclose our ways of knowing but to expose repressions on our being. In other words, whereas in *A Room of One's Own* Woolf focuses on different concepts of the truth and different rhetorical accesses to it, her concern in *The Pargiters* is with seeking the suppressed truth, the genuine feeling, that is covered over by conventions. It is this motive for writing, rather than the form of writing, that Woolf abandoned with the novel-essay.

When we look at the differences between the fictional chapters and the essay chapters, as well as the difference between the motivating strategy of *A Room of One's Own* and that of *The Pargiters*, the problems generated by the essays become apparent. In the essay sections Woolf tries to distinguish the powers "that lay beneath the surface of the Pargiter family" (TP 32), the conventions that "hide the true nature" of experience (51), the natural and the highly artificial (52), the genuine emotion expressed in a genuine way and the imitative feeling based on conventions (69–70, 83). In the Second Essay, for example, the narrator discusses those instinctive (because learned) responses that make us conceal sexual feelings and experiences, as Rose conceals the pillar-box incident. The narrator goes on to discuss those novelistic conventions that have evolved from such repression, conventions that restrict what the novelist can say: "All the novelist can do, therefore, in order to illustrate this [repressed] aspect of sexual life, is to state some of the facts; but not all; and then to imagine the impression on the nerves, on the brain, on the whole being, of a shock which the child instinctively conceals, as Rose did" (51). If we read this as saying that the novelist brings to consciousness what is unconscious because it is repressed, then "all the novelist can do" must be meant ironically, for this would be quite a lot: the novelist as psychoanalyst. But if the novelist could express, and thus eliminate, those crippling repressions and lay bare the true experience or the natural self, then the goal of the novel would seem to be the elimination of its own necessity, much as the psychoanalyst cures the patient and eliminates the need for further analysis.[10] However, we can read "all the novelist can do" literally and see the novelist's task as selecting and arranging from a variety of conventions and facts in order to investigate how these particular ones affect individual responses. In this case the novelist's goal is not to express the experience that is not conscious ("to *express the inexpressible*") but to dramatize how we become conscious of certain experiences (in a sense, "to *unexpress the expressible*"; Barthes, *Critical Essays* xvii). The novelist, then, neither liberates truth nor discovers it; rather, she or he produces a truth-effect. That is, the novelist's concern is not with what truth is but with how truth is posited.

What Leaska observes as Woolf's dilemma in *The Pargiters*—in writing about repressions and taboos she would disprove their existence—reveals the very problem of thinking in terms of repressions. Leaska's second explanation for why Woolf abandoned *The Pargiters,* one that grows out of the first granite/rainbow explanation, is that the "explicitness of prose" could not convey the "restrictive taboos" that are Woolf's subject, for in expressing taboos explicitly, Woolf would disprove their repressive effects. Because of her subject matter, then, she was forced into being a "pargeter" (TP xix). According to this reading, the novel of vision is not opposed to the novel of fact as a different kind of truth (as Leaska's first explanation suggests); instead, this reading opposes facts or truth to lies or disguises. Rather than change his own conception of Woolf's text in response to his two incompatible explanations, though, Leaska shows how Woolf became a "pargeter" in *The Years,* one who conceals and covers over, in order to reveal repressions indirectly.[11] But repressions do not necessarily inhibit our "natural" expressions. Michel Foucault's question in *The History of Sexuality* pertains here: If sexuality is repressed, why have we been writing about it for so long? Ironically, the work in which Woolf desired to reveal how sexual instincts are repressed turns out to be one of the most explicit treatments of sexuality in her writings. This is because repressions are part of a particular discourse, one that relies on the very surface/depth hierarchy that Woolf eventually abandoned but that critical interpretations like Leaska's continue to use. The strategies Woolf employs to frustrate the desire to prevail (e.g., indirection, equivocation, and fragmentation) may produce repressions as an effect. Thus, what most critics identify as repressions that necessitated Woolf's indirect, discontinuous, and duplicitous narrative strategies in *The Years* could well be *the thematic structures generated by the kinds of discursive strategies with which Woolf was experimenting*.[12] What began as a study of sexual repression and social taboos in *The Pargiters* turns into a testing out of what Woolf calls the "layers" of discourse in *The Years*.

I want neither to impose my reading on Woolf's novel-essay as a more "accurate" one nor to dismiss Leaska's reading entirely; rather, my desire is to expose the very doubts and contradictions that Woolf faced, the doubts and contradictions generated by the fact/vision, surface/depth dichotomies, and to note as well the critical consequences of relying on these dichotomies. Although Woolf writes in "Professions for Women" and *The Pargiters* as if one could dispose of restraining conventions and release the true self, she also doubts this view and comes more and more to acknowledge the primacy of conventions, as the essays begin to sound more and more like the novel chapters. Throughout the six essays she runs into difficulties in analyzing the fictional chapters in terms of generalized polarities (male nature/female nature, social repressions/natural instincts, conventional responses/genuine feelings) and turns instead to particular dramatizations: "But so complex and important an emotion can scarcely be analysed effectively. Perhaps a quotation from the novel may help to bring the scene into a better perspective" (TP 38); "and perhaps the best way to illustrate feelings which he himself could scarcely analyse would be to quote a scene" (83–84).

We can see in several places Woolf's awareness of the instability of her polarities and of the problem with her motivating strategy. In the typescript of "Professions for Women," she writes of killing the Angel in the House, the stereotype of women's familial and social roles that had once restricted what she could write about:

> And now when the Angel is dead, what remains? You may think that what remains is something quite simple and common enough—a young woman. . . . Having rid herself of falsehood, so we might put it, she has now

only to be herself. . . . But what is "herself"? I mean, what is a woman? I assure you, I don't know; I do not believe that you know. . . . All I can tell you is that I discovered when I came to write that a woman—it sounds so simple, but I should be ashamed to tell you how long it took me to realise this for myself—is not a man. (TP xxxiii)

This is the view Woolf expressed years before in a *Times Literary Supplement* review, "Women Novelists."[13] She does not deny differences between male and female writing or experience, only that we can define these differences or specify some correspondence between writing and experience. "Much depends," she writes, "upon training and circumstances" (TP 158). In the Fifth Essay, as the narrator's voice becomes more ironic and playful, more like the narrator of *A Room of One's Own* or the biographer of *Orlando,* she shows that one mode of discourse may conceal what another clearly reveals: though the door between the dining room and the drawing room may be closed, though male attitudes toward female intellectual powers may not "reach Kitty directly in the vivid and racy language which [men] used over the port and cigars" (TP 124), still, the message gets through in other symbolic forms.

With this awareness, presented not only through statements in the last two essays but through the shifting tone and structure of the essays as well, Woolf could not persist in the clear-cut divisions between essays and scenes that were meant to reveal the deep ideas beneath the surface forms. Nor could she persist in the dichotomy of genuine feelings and false conventions that inspired the essay-novel divisions. If changing contexts and changing conventions are so vital, then we cannot speak of what is natural and repressed; and we cannot define the right relations between the sexes, between self and society, or between writing and experience. At stake in this text, then, is not freeing the true nature from conventional forms but exposing the seemingly natural as conventional and disclosing our tendency to accept certain conventions as natural and normative. The upshot of all this is not that we cannot posit more useful conventions or that we must deny any relation between writing and experience; rather, we discover with Woolf that we must learn to distinguish among different kinds of conventions and different kinds of relations.

My point is this: it is not that Woolf cannot mix genres, for she does it all the time (e.g., in *A Room of One's Own* and *Orlando*); it is not that she cannot combine two kinds of truth, for truth is an effect of method. The discrepancy exposed in the course of *The Pargiters* is not between novel and essay, fact and vision, or granite and rainbow, as these apply to different properties of things; nor is it between truth and rhetoric. The discrepancy is between two modes of thinking, the substantial and the relational. As Woolf discovered that the surface/depth distinction does not always hold, she questioned the concept of the world as substance and the narrative as illustration on which such distinctions rest. What makes the difference is whether we accept reality as stable and substantial, as Kitty does (TP 151), or as a "play of forms" (Culler, *Pursuit of Signs* 13). A sentence in "The New Biography" that may be more useful than the granite/rainbow distinction so often quoted by critics and applied to Woolf's novels is the one that indicates the concept of reality shared by these new biographers: "They have no fixed scheme of the universe, no standard of courage or morality to which they insist that [the subject] shall conform" (GR 153). It is the lack of a fixed conception of the world and the adoption of a relational mode of thinking that affects these writers'—and Woolf's—thinking about narrative and throws into confusion the structure of *The Pargiters*. And when the concept of the narrative changes, so does the meaning of the terms we apply to it.[14]

Here we see the problem of reading posed by *The Years* for critics who read these different narrative structures in the same way. Woolf began *The Pargiters* with an empirical approach, distinguishing features—the conventional and the natural, the permanent and the transient, the contingent and the necessary, the profound and the superficial—in a static world. In *The Years* her approach is conceptual, distinguishing forms of relations—repetition, imitation, transference—in a dynamic world. In such a discourse, variable functions replace determinate qualities. We can see Woolf experimenting with a different set of strategies and a different conception of reality in her diary entries on these two works. When she first conceived of *The Pargiters* in January 1931, she was finishing *The Waves* and, as she puts it in her diary, prodding the uses of prose "from the chuckle, the babble to the rhapsody" (AWD 161). This prodding of language use motivated her writing in *The Years*. As Woolf revised *The Pargiters* into *The Years,* she became increasingly concerned with "layers" rather than polarities (AWD 209, 215, 248), with contrast and change rather than stasis and continuance (AWD 206, 243, 248), with drama and its "particular relation with the surface" rather than surface and depth (AWD 209, 214, 236). By the "surface value" of drama Woolf implies what is publicly enacted, not what is immediately given. In *The Years,* dramatic performance is not a metaphor for life but a strategy for staging various relations among self, language, and world and for exploring the ways we get from one set of conventions to another. Investigating communication itself, that is, the behavior of language in the world, *The Years* gives us everything from "the babble to the rhapsody."

My understanding of why Woolf abandoned *The Pargiters* has consequences, of course, for my reading of *The Years*. But more than that, it enables us to see *the conceptual differences generated by structural differences*. It shows us that we cannot make the same critical moves in different texts and that we cannot count on any one element meaning the same thing from one text to another. Leaska's explanations assume we have a more thorough knowledge of *The Years* because *The Pargiters* reveals to us what has been omitted, suppressed, and disguised in the revised version. Such a reading rests on a Cartesian concept of knowledge: it assumes that knowledge is cumulative and that facts are "out there," like coins scattered on the dusty road of life, which we gather as we progress, becoming richer with every step. Leaska's desire is like North's in *The Years:* to do away with the presumed "gap" between "the word and the reality," to defeat difference, and to control sense (308–9). An example is his treatment of objects in the novel. Leaska traces the recurrence of the chair with gilt claws, which belongs to Maggie and Sara Pargiter's family, and provides an elaborate thematic interpretation of this seemingly innocent object ("Woolf, the Pargeter").[15] While his readings may be plausible (indeed, he even suggests his connections are "obvious"), they ignore the countermovement of the narrative, the way it works against such consistent representations by testing out various strategies.[16] Leaska treats repetition as thematic emphasis and as an accretion of meaning. But repetition is also a rhetorical strategy and structuring device that calls into question the very origins and ends of meaning Leaska seeks.

The structure and strategies of *The Years,* in contrast, present a different kind of understanding. Woolf's use of discontinuities, repetitions, and parodies in this novel conveys a Kuhnian concept of knowledge: it assumes knowledge is configurative and that what we identify as facts affects the character of what we know. While Leaska's reading would have the text appear to say one thing while really saying something else, the narrative shows instead how saying one thing can mean different things at different times. When the child Sara mimics her father's words, they no longer have the same meaning or produce the same effect (TY 98). This novel, then, calls forth the concept of narrative structure advocated by Barbara Herrnstein Smith: "Not only is an entity always experienced under more or less different conditions, but the various experiences do not yield a simple cumulative (corrected, improved, deeper, more thorough, or complete) knowledge of the entity because they are not additive. Rather, each experience of an entity frames it in a different role and constitutes it as a different configuration, with different 'properties' foregrounded and repressed" ("Contingencies of Value" 12). The issue is not whether or not these objects represent something in the world but how the structuring of these objects presents a certain understanding of the world. A critique of representation, as postmodern novels are said to provide, does not mean the end of representation. Leaska's assumptions about what is obvious and what is hidden take for granted what is at stake in this narrative: What can we say is obvious? How do we know when something is obvious (a transparent surface) and when it is opaque (masking concealed depths)? That is, Leaska must go one step further and explain why his moves are called for in this particular narrative.[17]

To understand this conceptual difference produced by different narrative structures, we can contrast the use of images in *The Years* and *Night and Day,* especially those objects associated with the past. In the earlier novel, the relics of the past are contained in a separate room, a kind of shrine to the past as it is figured in Katharine's poet-grandfather. Characters move into and out of that room, but the relics within remain stationary. The past serves as a background in *Night and Day.* So many scenes occur in the room with the relics, such as Katharine and Ralph's first conversation and Katharine and William's break-up. The past is a standard or model against which to measure the present. It is a tradition providing stability and continuity in the midst of social change. It also provides belief, even if that belief is "faith in an illusion" (ND 232). The past is a conception of life we can either accept or question; in either case, it is absolute, autonomous.

In *The Years,* however, we get a different concept of the past. Here the past infiltrates the present, just as the present reconstitutes the past. Different objects associated with the past—such as the chair with gilt claws, the walrus pen holder, and the mother's portrait—recur in various contexts throughout the novel. At times they seem to disappear for good (Eleanor loses the walrus pen holder), only to turn up again (it is found on Crosby's mantlepiece). The past is a perspective on the present. It is not coherent, static, and self-contained but contradictory, dynamic, changing as the present changes. It is a complex of competing and conflated value systems. The past in *The Years* is not a model for the present but a function of the present. A unified history of objects, actions, and manners in *Night and Day* gives way to a heterogeneous history of perspectives and relations in *The Years.* Successive images are purposive, then, but they do not necessarily represent the same thing from one chapter to the next. Missing in the structure of *The Years,* with its repetitions and its lack of connections, is the sense of a univocal and teleological development that Stephen Heath says is missing in Sarraute's narratives (*Nouveau Roman* 54), the kind of development that many readers miss in postmodern novels. There is continuity without progress, coherence without unity, ending without certainty.

It is in this sense that we must read the frequently cited 1914 section of *The Years.* This section repeats "it was impossible to talk" (178, 179, 180); it presents many people talking to themselves (182, 183, 185) or mimicking the speech of others (177, 184, 185); and it provides a brief version of Bernard's "world without a self" (185–86). For these reasons, it seems to confirm, as Margaret Comstock ("Loudspeaker") and others note, the failure of communication. And yet, in this section, stories finally get told (189, 194, 200), party guests cooperate in staging a scene (194) and in constructing a story (200), and the self is always on stage (176, 177, 194). From thwarted conversations to completed stories to collaborative productions to meditative silence, this section displays a variety of discursive strategies. It reveals the diversity of language use: the ability of language to unite people and to prevent union, and its tendency toward both originality and banality. When Victoria Middleton says *The Years* is an "exemplum" of the effects of writing under repression, she misses this point. The novel does not teach us "the *adverse* effects of constraints upon selfhood and creativity" (Middleton 171; emphasis added). On the contrary, it demonstrates the *ineluctable* ones.

Belief in a repressed natural self, and in a stable past and a present in opposition to it (the concepts that structure *Night and Day*), encourages many critics to read *The Years* as a rejection of the authority of the past for the authenticity of the present. For example, Comstock reads the repeated references to the "ordinary voice" in the 1914 section as the natural, authentic, or personal voice, as opposed to the "loudspeaker voice," the authoritarian or conventional voice. This ordinary voice, Comstock says, must be found in order for the individual to be free of repressions, to establish a natural relationship with others, and to exist in harmony with society. The broken speeches, the repetitions, and the clichés show the need for individuals to free themselves from "prohibitions against speech" if the human race is to grow to maturity ("Loudspeaker" 255, 258). Yet "ordinary" can mean typical (characteristic) and mundane (trite), common and commonplace. Woolf's word choice is not innocent; her meaning is not obvious. The numerous clichés, repetitions, banalities, and recitations in this novel make it difficult to distinguish what is natural from what is conventional, who is innocent from who is implicated. Indeed, the novel shows us that what we assume to be personal may well be an expression of what is interpersonal or communal. Even Sara's poetic outbursts often turn out to be a pastiche of quotations.[18] Woolf reached this insight in *The Pargiters*. When Edward writes his poem to Kitty, it is not a question of whether he expresses a genuine emotion through conventional forms or whether his emotion, based on his reading of Greek poetry, is merely imitative and thus not genuine. His emotion *is* imitative in that what we take to be a genuine response is posited by or an effect of a particular convention, that is, a particular mode of discourse and a particular literary and linguistic heritage. There is no "ordinary," in the sense of natural or normative, relation between self and other, for such a relation can exist only through discursive and symbolic systems such as language, social conventions, and cultural traditions. We know how to enact a relationship only by imitating or repeating certain formulas. We can extrapolate from these formulas, but we cannot eliminate them entirely.

It is not that the mimicking in this 1914 section is inauthentic, expressing a lack of real feeling or a loss of one's essential self; rather, such imitation is essential, constituting feelings and self. The question, then, is not how to find our ordinary (natural) voice but how to situate ourselves within an ordinary (common) language. The echoes, the parodies, the repetitions, and the mimicry present a language that belongs to everyone yet is no one's possession. We are all implicated in this verbal network. Woolf's use of street musicians, street sounds, and street speakers (like La Trobe's use of common folks and common items in her pageant, like John Cage's use of common sounds, and like Andy Warhol's use of common objects) produces a public spectacle.[19] Mutual participation, not authoritarian prohibition.

Eleanor's questions in the following passage suggest this sense of a common pageant, which implicates all in the performance: "Does everything then come over again a little differently? she thought. If so, is there a pattern; a theme, recurring, like music; half remembered, half foreseen? . . . a gigantic pattern, momentarily perceptible? The thought gave her extreme pleasure: that there was a pattern. But who makes it? Who thinks it? Her mind slipped. She could not finish her thought" (TY 282). Many critics cite this passage as support for Woolf's unifying vision, her faith in a pattern behind the cotton wool of daily life. Yet in the context of this novel, it is not the unified pattern that is stressed but the numerous questions. This passage brings to mind the audience's response to La Trobe's play: Whom to thank? Whom to make responsible? The impossibility of finding the one responsible, or of tracing the pattern to its origin, implicates all in this social production. The repetition and parody draw attention to the lack of an origin(al) that so many critics continue to posit and seek. The recitations and banalities counter claims to either an authentic or an authoritarian voice—that is, to any voice (or any culture) completely in possession of itself. The narrative strategies of *The Years* do not represent the effects of authoritarian controls; rather, they call into question the possibility of any completely authoritative expression as well as any absolutely free expression. In a world where everything echoes and reverberates, no one has the first, or last, word.

With this perspective on Woolf's changing conceptions of narrative and history in *The Years* and *Night and Day,* we can now look at the endings of these two novels in terms of their different concepts of plot structure. *The Years*, like *Night and Day*, does narrate a succession of events, but the succession displays a different narrative patterning from that of *Night and Day*. Or rather, it reveals the difference between the structure (grammatical form) of narrative and the effect (persuasive force) of narrative.

The world of *Night and Day*, as its title suggests, is substantial and orderly, the "and" marking the boundary between two realms, bringing them together while keeping them separate. As many critics have pointed out, the novel moves from the civilized drawing room to the disruption of this stable world and back, at the end, to a vision of order. This concept of reality, based on distinct divisions, engenders the narrative conflicts between right and wrong relations, truth and falsehood, freedom and restriction, illusion and reality, night and day. The language of *Night and Day* reinforces these dichotomous distinctions: the day world is the "antechamber" to the world of night (319); Mr. Hilbery presides at the "interregnum" between the old order and the new (433); Katharine and her mother serve as "ambassadors," shuttling between the past and the present, mediating between the old generation and the new (188, 442); and, in the last paragraph of the novel, Katharine stands on the "threshold" (460). Such words divide this world into separate realms, with literature functioning as a bridge between past and present or between private and public worlds. In this substantial world the self is an opaque sphere (256, 456–57); "it's being and not doing that matters" (44, 104). Contemplating the conflict between solitude and society, the worlds of night and day, Katharine asks, "Was it not possible to step from one to the other . . . without essential change?" (306). At the end Katharine feels the riddle has been answered. In her hand she holds life, a globe "round, whole, and entire" (455).

If reality is seen as given and substantial, then this question of one's essential being is important. If reality is seen as dynamic and relational, then acting in the world takes precedence over being, and it is acting that Woolf stresses in *The Years*. The recurring references to parody (5, 98), pantomime (177), chorus (184), masks (194, 224, 311), caricatures (242, 297), comedy and farce (264, 269), curtains and scenes (124, 194), actor and critic (313) bring out not just a dramatic motif but a narrative strategy that turns this world into a pageant like La Trobe's in which everyone participates. Life as spectacle, play, ruse. Speech is "echoed, or parodied" throughout as characters repeat each other's words, as if learning a language. Conversations occur "over and over again." Thoughts and memories echo throughout the novel, shared by different characters at different times. The repetition and parody, so insistent in *The Years*, makes role playing essential; and the pervasiveness of this performative strategy in

the speech, the point of view, and the patterning of the novel makes it
not a theme (e.g., the loss of meaningful communication) but a change
in the concept of art's function. In the closing section of the novel, we
get multiple points of view, a speech delivered in many voices, and a song
sung in discordant tones. Yet the uncertain ending of *The Years* does not
necessarily represent an uncertain future in the face of World War II or
the dawn of a new, nonauthoritarian social order (two common thematic
readings); rather, it is a *structural necessity* in a narrative that conceives of
history and story as a dynamic complex of relations.[20]

In other words, the endings of *The Years* and *Night and Day* are in
keeping with the rhetoric of the narratives. The relations between natural
self and conventional self, between private realm and public, and between
past and present are dichotomized and absolutized by the language and
structure of *Night and Day,* so that these pairs are treated as enduring distinctions and take on transcendent value. The relations in *The Years* are
contextualized by the novel's language and structure (imitation is compre-
hensible only in context), so that these distinctions are functional and their
value contingent. Thus, the patterns of images cannot "mean" in the same
way, and the narratives cannot end in the same way. This understanding
has consequences for our reading, for if the dichotomies that structure
*Night and Day* do not function in the same way in *The Years,* then we cannot conclude, as Rachel Blau DuPlessis does, that the public and private
realms in *Night and Day* are integrated in *The Years.* Such a reading implies
that *The Years* resolves the problem in *Night and Day* of how to reconcile
the public and the private life. On the contrary, *The Years* removes the
problem by relying on a relational way of thinking rather than a substantialized one. When Howard Harper says *The Years* longs for certainty and
order, when James Naremore says it seeks a harmonious relation between
self and society, and when Avrom Fleishman tries to solve the riddle posed
by the song, they rely on the substantialized mode of thinking evident in
*Night and Day* and *The Pargiters.* Such orders, such harmony, and such
solutions are possible only in a positivistic world.

As opposed to the change from one vision of order to another in *Night
and Day,* in *The Years* change manifests itself as new sentences (313) and
new combinations (226). It is a collaborative effort, not a private achieve-
ment.[21] For this reason the novel's ending cannot be contained, cannot
be summed up, and, more important, cannot be appropriated by any one
person, group, or reading. What is at issue in these narrative structures is a
world that can be contained, controlled, and perfected versus a world that
is constantly being rehearsed.

To read *The Years* as a representation of the way things are in the world
(Leaska, "Woolf, the Pargeter"; Middleton) or as the way things should

be (Comstock, "Loudspeaker"; Squier, *Virginia Woolf and London*) is to answer the questions Woolf raises in this novel and in her diary entries of this time: Whose point of view is right? (TY 199) Whose view of the world will we accept? (185) If we alter the structure of society, what then? (AWD 247) Establishing a new order or the right relations necessitates exclusion, the very patriarchal or authoritarian gesture Woolf resists in *The Years*. It requires defining the self apart from the social and linguistic orders in which it plays its part, the very thing she discovers in *The Pargiters* cannot be done. Woolf says she "distrusts reality," uncertain whether it is substantial or shifting (AWD 138). She believes "there is no certainty" and "no absolute point of view" (TG 12–13). And she desires a system that does not shut out (AWD 183). Therefore, she calls into question what is perceived as lying "outside" the realm of discourse and grounding language and literature. Woolf does not tell us what a novel is or should be; instead, she shows us how it functions in the world. To appreciate these novels, then, we do not need the right classification of them or the right conception of narrative. Rather, we need an approach to narrative that enables us to specify the kinds of distinctions possible in different kinds of discourse, an approach that neither rejects nor privileges representation but sees it as one relation among many.

The strain felt in many readings of Woolf's novels is due less to the duplicitous form of her narratives than to her critics' effort to make everything fit a form. They try to locate the same narrative structure everywhere in Woolf's canon; and by doing so, they elide an important point that emerges through Woolf's changing structures: namely, *different narrative structures evoke different kinds of reality*. Thus, the change from Woolf's concept of reality expressed in *Night and Day* to the concept produced in *The Years* can be seen as the kind of change that is conducive to a feminist textual politics, not as the goal of Woolf's feminist quest from the beginning. *The Years* no more ends Woolf's quest for "literature itself" than it answers her question, What then? (AWD 247).[22]

What I have attempted to demonstrate in this chapter is that identifying characteristic features in order to classify texts is only a first step. The next is to consider their functions within their narrative contexts and the implications of these for our understanding of language, narrative, and reality. In other words, we cannot rely on a particular narrative element representing the same structure of beliefs from one narrative context to another. For this reason, as I state in the Introduction, it is misleading, and even potentially dangerous, to sort out features that are outmoded, conventional, or authoritarian from those that are appropriate, authentic, or liberating. That point is worth repeating here. One can imagine a narrative in which multiple protagonists or a suspended ending served authoritative or authoritarian ends. Indeed, debates over whether postmodern novels are neoconservative or radical stem from this very possibility. Although the aesthetic principles of *The Years* may oppose authoritarian positions, they do so not as individual elements—for example, multiple protagonists, suspended ending—as Comstock and DuPlessis argue, but by their elaboration into a narrative structure. A relational, not a representational, approach to narrative allows us to investigate society without first deciding on the right order, the best structure, or the correct reading.

I do not want to reduce Woolf's narratives to one kind of structure but to bring out into strong relief the kinds of structuring she has used. Neither do I want to praise the ending of *The Years* over the ending of *Night and Day* but to relate endings to narrative contexts. It is not a question of choosing between two things but of finding the strategy that enables us (and that enabled Woolf) to move from one to another: one narrative structure to another, one mode of thinking to another, one use of language to another. The suspended quality of Woolf's narrative structures is due to the contingent character of her narrative strategies, which depend on the particular contexts and conventions being questioned and explored. As such, these narratives show us not the truth that lies beneath the surface of conventions but the ways conventions can both restrict our behavior in society and enable us to continue functioning in it. Like Sterne's endings, and many postmodern ones, Woolf's suspended endings encourage rereading with new emphases and new values.

We sense in works like *Orlando, The Waves, The Years,* and *Between the Acts*—as in works like *Watt, In the Labyrinth, The Golden Fruits,* and *If on a Winter's Night a Traveler*—the exhaustion of any one narrative structuring. This exhaustion is felt in the repetitions of lines, images, and actions; in the mirror reflections; in the renewed beginnings; and in the bricolage endings. But this exhaustion is not a theme in Woolf's narratives, as Ihab Hassan says it is in Beckett's (*Liberations* 190); it is a strategy, *a way to keep narrative forms from becoming abiding formulas.* By making narrative structures disposable, not by disposing of certain "outdated" structures, Woolf has kept her narratives from exhausting reality and has resisted an authoritarian system. She has not changed the ending of narrative structure but the narrative structuring of endings.[23] What Woolf has stressed is not narrative systems and social schemes but exchange and enactment, changing and acting, many voices and multiple roles.

## NOTES

1. Marcus picks up on this quality of *Night and Day,* but whereas others see this pretense as a weakness, she turns it from a flaw in design into a successful strategy,

focusing on the "tone of serious playfulness" and the "comic theme of lying" ("Enchanted Organs" 98, 101). Comparing *Night and Day* with *Orlando* and *Flush,* Marcus turns this "confusion of kinds" into a deliberate ploy to challenge the history, ideology, and literature of our culture, "the way in which literature shapes our expectations of life" (98).

2. While *The Years* is usually compared with *Night and Day* as being more "traditional" than Woolf's other novels, it has also been compared with *The Waves,* from its publication (de Selincourt's 1937 review that Woolf favored) to more recent analyses (e.g., Fleishman; Richter).

3. The fact that many feminist critics, such as Minow-Pinkney and Bowlby, give scant attention to *Night and Day* in their discussions of Woolf's subversive form suggests that they find it "suspiciously conventional." Katherine Mansfield dismissed it as "a lie in the soul" (Diary 2:45). On the other hand, Marcus finds something subversive beneath the deceptive conventional surface ("Enchanted Organ").

4. Smith argues this point throughout her article "Contingencies of Value," particularly in her discussion of "the mutually defining relations among classification, function, and value" (13).

5. Blackstone's response to *The Years* exemplifies at once critics' acknowledgment of change and their reluctance to change. The point of *The Years,* he says, is How to think differently? Yet in dismissing this novel as the obverse of Woolf's great works, Blackstone resists this invitation to change.

6. An obvious example is Fowles's use of different endings in *The French Lieutenant's Woman* and his narrator's discussion of the different effects of these endings. In *For a New Novel,* Robbe-Grillet writes that a linear plot moving toward a definite conclusion (i.e., the kind of plot associated with the classical novel) imposes "the image of a stable, coherent, continuous, unequivocal, entirely decipherable universe" (32). To relinquish such a narrative pattern is not simply to reject conventions that no longer fit but to question the concept of reality on which these conventions depend. In *Snow White,* for example, Barthelme's statement, "Try to be a man about whom nothing is known" (18), invokes James's advice to the writer, "Try to be one of the people on whom nothing is lost" ("Art of Fiction" 11), thereby serving to undermine James's belief in the realism of the character and the authority of the author (cf. Graff 52–53).

7. Commentaries on *Night and Day, The Pargiters,* and *The Years* rely on distinctions between the "superficial form" and the "real stuff" (Daiches, *Virginia Woolf*), the "surface drama" and the "essence" (Love), the "insignificant surface" events and the significant repressions beneath (Richter). The most blatant example of this bias against the surface (whether of narrative or of society) is Blackstone's dismissal of *The Years:* "everything is on the surface, is meaningless" (202).

8. In her diary entries during the early stages of *The Years* (e.g., 1932), and in her typescript of "Professions for Women," which engendered *The Pargiters* (see TP xxvii-xliv), Woolf often sounds like her critics when positing such distinctions.

9. The fact/vision dichotomy is complicated from the very beginning of *The Pargiters,* wherein the first full paragraph shows us that there are different kinds of facts (e.g., historical and personal) and, we would suppose, different kinds of vision.

10. My description of the psychoanalyst is based, of course, on the American psychoanalytic practice that Jacques Lacan opposed.

11. For a similar critique of Leaska's reading strategy, which relies on the assumption of a repressed desire or truth to be revealed, see Caramagno's "Manic-Depressive Psychosis and Critical Approaches to Virginia Woolf's Life and Work" (20).

12. Narrative strategies such as repetition, fragmentation, and indirection in the novel portions of *The Pargiters* and in *The Years* are interpreted by critics in one of two ways: either as intentional strategies that enabled Woolf to reveal sexual repressions indirectly, or as unconscious strategies that enabled her to avoid painful, hostile, and/or sexual feelings. In reading the changes from the novel-essay to the novel in terms of how Woolf masked her true feelings and her real intentions, critics like Leaska, Radin, and Squier (*Virginia Woolf and London*)assume the different narrative structures of these works are about the same subject. They assume *The Pargiters* is the truer version because it is the earlier one. Thus, Radin interprets Woolf's toning down of her outbursts against the patriarchy, her trend toward balancing opposing views, and her undercutting of her own positions in *The Years* as a moral failing rather than as a rhetorical strategy. By looking to *The Pargiters* for what *The Years* could have been (and, by implication, what it was intended to be), she reads the novel as failed statement or flawed representation, not as a specific set of strategies producing certain thematic implications.

13. In "Women Novelists," Woolf discusses two kinds of sexual tyranny: one is "the tyranny of what was expected from their [female] sex"; the other is "the tyranny of sex itself" (CW 25). That is, she does not discuss female repression and male freedom but different kinds of repression and "what appears, perhaps erroneously, to be the comparative freedom of the male sex from that [second] tyranny" (25). Her point is similar to Flax's, in "Postmodernism and Gender Relations in Feminist Theory": "In a wide variety of cultures and discourses," Flax writes, "men tend to be seen as free from or as not determined by gender relations" (629). Flax argues that such a view is erroneous, leading us to treat the male as the norm, the female as the "other."

14. In *Philosophical Investigations,* Wittgenstein says that a new language game embodies a new form of life, not a new arrangement of the same form. In *On Certainty,* he writes: "When language-games change, then there is a change in concepts, and with the concepts the meanings of words change" (#65). This change from a substantial way of thinking to a relational way is one that Jameson associates with the change from positivism to structuralism (*Prison-House of Language*) and that Thiher identifies with postmodern fiction that puts to the test, as he says, the language theory of Saussure, Wittgenstein, and Derrida. In doing so, such fiction calls into question the notion of the essence of narrative and its representation of a given world.

15. Leaska connects the seven references to the chair with Colonel Pargiter, adultery, and ceremonies. It represents, therefore, "the masculine, patriarchal world of Victorian England" and "the guilty claws of a crippling paternalistic world in which human values are subordinated to solemn and sterile abstractions" ("Woolf, the Pargeter" 185). For a discussion of the significance of "things" in terms of

"the representation of historical change" in *The Years*, see Bowlby, *Virginia Woolf: Feminist Destinations*, chap. 7, in which she deals with some of the same issues I raise here.

16. Heath on Robbe-Grillet, Freedman ("Kafka's Obscurity") on Kafka, and Jameson ("Flaubert's Libidinal Historicism") on Flaubert all discuss the problem of representational readings of these authors' texts. Such readings reduce the plurality of the text to a single, unified relation, and thereby ignore the text as a testing of possible forms. Therefore, structure is discussed as a reflection of narrative theme rather than as what generates thematic concerns.

17. Ellis writes: "And any claim that in a given unique situation a particular move is the right one must begin a general discussion of the factors that distinguish this situation from one in which the move would be the wrong one" (6).

18. For example, at Sara and North's dinner, we believe at first that Sara is creating poetry in response to North's account of his African experiences, only to find that she is "quoting from his letters" (TY 244).

19. Waugh comments on the effect of such parody and popular arts: "The use of parody and the assimilation of popular and non-literary languages in metafiction thus helps to break both aesthetic and extra-aesthetic norms. Because both languages operate through very well-established conventions, however, the reader is able to proceed through the familiar to the new. The text is freed from the 'anxiety of influence' (Bloom 1973) by the paradoxical recognition that literature has never been free, cannot be 'original,' but has always been 'created' or produced" (*Metafiction* 67). This is Woolf's point: not to reject outmoded conventions but to get from well-established conventions to new ones. In *The Years*, as in *Orlando* and *Between the Acts*, she seems to seek not an authentic voice but a more "comprehensive language" (Barthes, *Critical Essays*). This is what Kristeva sees as the point of postmodern fiction ("Postmodernism?"). Granted, certain classes and races of people are conspicuously absent in Woolf's public spectacle, and in saying that this language belongs to "everyone," I don't mean to suggest that everyone shares the same power over language. As I go on to suggest, Woolf's vision of society is hardly a unifying one. My point is not to make Woolf into a spokesperson for an egalitarian social vision or to fault her for her class bias, two common responses to Woolf's writings. Rather, my point is to note the implications of certain narrative strategies in her writings and the kinds of conclusions they allow for—even if those implications are not the ones we would like Woolf to approve.

20. Critics make much of the uncertain ending of *The Years*, with the disturbing children's song, the melodramatic dawn, and Eleanor's question, "And now?" But this novel not only ends on a note of uncertainty, it also begins on such a note: "It was an uncertain spring. The weather, perpetually changing . . ." (5). This beginning undercuts critical accounts of the novel's progression from a stable past to an uncertain future, or from the control of the past to the freedom of the future.

21. The title of *The Years*—like those of Kafka's *Castle*, Robbe-Grillet's *In the Labyrinth*, and Calvino's *Castle of Crossed Destinies*—gives us not the subject but the situation of the novel. The difficulty of reaching a conclusion in the sense of a summing up is due as much to the structure of the discourse as to the structure of society. Any conclusion must be drawn in awareness of our situation in the years

(the historical context) and in *The Years* (the narrative context). Such a text encourages us to look at the multiple relations between a textual organization and a social organization, of which representation is only one.

22. Here we can see the implications of the kind of argument I make in the Introduction. To define feminist criticism, we need not agree first on the right conception of language or the right theory (e.g., the American empiricist vs. the French poststructuralist); rather, we need to change our tasks as critics so that to practice feminist criticism we do not first have to agree on any one concept of language, text, self, or society. This belief distinguishes my own work on Woolf from some other post-1985 works, such as those by Waugh and Hirsch, that do seek agreement on a certain concept of writing or self. But more importantly, the kind of reading that results from accepting this belief in a variety of positions enables us to test out the practical consequences of Woolf's changing strategies rather than simply to praise them as a more "genuine" form of writing.

23. Writing on the structural features of Beckett's trilogy, Wolfgang Iser makes a similar point about the effect of these texts that "consume their own beginnings": "The fiction which Beckett is constantly questioning shows that, in fact, we are alive because we cannot settle anything final, and this absence of finality is what drives us continually to go on being active" (268–69).

# 4

## Woolf's Nonfictional Prose:
### *Exploring Prose Discourse as Aesthetic Phenomenon and Social Product*

And what a partial view: altering the structure of society; yes, but
when it's altered?
— Virginia Woolf,
Diary, 1935

The observable social bond is composed of language "moves."

— Jean-François Lyotard,
*The Postmodern Condition*

Throughout the preceding three chapters, I have elaborated a different way
of responding to Woolf's changing narrative strategies based on what I
refer to as postmodern assumptions and expectations concerning the function of prose discourse. In particular, I have shown that the assumptions
bound up with the reference theory of meaning and a mimetic theory of
representation are the sticking points in our analyses of Woolf's novels,
for her novels test out different notions of how language and narratives
function. One charge my approach is open to is that it neglects other
kinds of relations—for example, social, political, economic, sexual—in its
attention to language theory and textual strategies. What worries many
feminist critics in particular is that the kind of functional and task-oriented
approach I elaborate here cannot change the way things are in the world.

Of course, this was the charge leveled against Woolf's writings, especially in the 1930s when writers such as Auden and Spender were producing overtly political and polemical works that made Woolf's writing, by
comparison, seem detached, indifferent, even a bit quaint. Woolf defends
herself quite well in a late essay, "The Leaning Tower," in which she turns
the table on these poets and precariously tilts their tower. She says the
poets of the thirties are detached in that the very privileged position from

which they condemn the social order is built on the sins of that society: private property and class oppression. To abuse that society while profiting from it, Woolf argues, is to engage in "scapegoat beating" and "excuse finding" (M 141). Failing to recognize their own complicity, these poets, in her view, reify society, separate themselves from it, and attack. Woolf's is a different response and a different relation to that society, not only because she has not had the same privileges as those men, but also because her view of society differed from theirs: "A writer has to keep his eye upon a model that moves, that changes, upon an object that is not one object but innumerable objects" (M 128).

Feminist critics over the past decade have defended Woolf's writings against charges of social irresponsibility or political indifference, yet their defenses often downplay the significance of the different kinds of relations that Woolf discloses in "The Leaning Tower" and that we have been exploring in Woolf's fiction. In this chapter I want to test out the social and political consequences of the relational way of thinking about self, narrative, and reality that I have been at pains to bring out in Woolf's writings. To this end, I focus on Woolf's nonfictional essays of the thirties—in particular *Three Guineas* (1938), *The London Scene* (1932), and "Street Haunting" (1930)—that raise the question of the social and political value of her writing and that explore the relations between aesthetic forms and social-economic forces. By testing my reading against other—namely, feminist—critics, I argue that the problems generated by their readings come from accepting a reified view of society and a positivistic view of language. As Ludwig Wittgenstein might put it, the trouble is that we still think about things (*Blue and Brown Books* 38).[1]

In her book-length essay *Three Guineas*, Woolf attempts to answer the question put to her in a letter from a society soliciting funds for the prevention of war: How are we (specifically, educated women) to prevent war? In the process of answering that letter, and before making her contribution, Woolf responds to two other requests for money, one to rebuild a women's college, the other to help women obtain employment. Thus, *Three Guineas* specifically links war to sex and class oppression, singling out "the daughters of educated men" (Woolf's avowed audience) as "the weakest of all the classes in the state" (16). It is easy to see why the essay is often read as a companion piece to *The Years* (published a year earlier). Support for this connection comes from Woolf's diary entries (e.g., AWD 284) as well as from the symmetry of the argument that in abandoning the novel-essay *The Pargiters*, Woolf split it into the novel *The Years* and the essay *Three Guineas*. The important question, though, is not whether or not these works are related but what is the nature of the relation between them. Here my reading of *The Years* can prove useful in demonstrating that the significant connection between these works is less their indictment of a particular social system, as is so often assumed, than their similar ways of responding to such a system and their ways of making us self-conscious about such responses. Whereas many critics read *Three Guineas* looking for the fundamental ground of patriarchal tyranny, Woolf investigates the complex of conditions in which tyranny can function: the psychological, the historical, the economic, and the linguistic.

One could argue that the best-known essay on Woolf's *Three Guineas,* and one of the most extensive discussions of it, is Jane Marcus's "'No More Horses': Virginia Woolf on Art and Propaganda." It is certainly the first article that attempts to explain the complex position Woolf has expounded in terms of "the relations between class, sex, and art" (282). As the title implies, Marcus's goal is to reconcile Woolf's objection to using "art to propagate political opinions" (TG 190) with Woolf's own "coupling of art and propaganda" in *Three Guineas* ("'No More Horses'" 266). Although Marcus attends to the complexities of and the contradictions in Woolf's essay, neither dismissing its idiosyncrasies, as Quentin Bell does in his biography of Woolf (204–5), nor accepting its pacifist argument at face value, her essay is itself contradictory.[2] The reason for this is twofold. First, Marcus seeks to clear up the contradictions in Woolf's essay in order to articulate Woolf's committed "socialist, pacifist, and feminist" stance (267). Second, she accepts unquestioningly Woolf's opposition of art and propaganda, the "donkey work" of pamphleteers and the "thoroughbred" work of artists, just as she accepts the opposition of a language of fact and a language of fiction. Acknowledging Woolf's admonishment that art should not preach (AWD 182), and equating preaching with rhetoric, Marcus resolves the contradiction Woolf faced by pointing out the "inescapable logic" of Woolf's argument (279). Such logic, Marcus tells us, defeats the need for rhetoric and can allow the artist to propagate without preaching: "[Woolf] was truly an 'outsider,' for this is a complex position she expounds, although her lack of rhetoric makes her sound uncommitted" ("'No More Horses'" 269).[3]

When Marcus denies any rhetoric in *Three Guineas,* as she does several times, she seems to take Woolf literally, for throughout her essay Woolf insists that what she says is not mere rhetoric but is supported by facts. Yet Woolf also cautions us that neither facts nor opinions are ever "pure," that they are always "adulterated" by various motives (TG 111), so that Marcus's distinction between rhetoric and argument may not hold. And Marcus herself notes that *Three Guineas* is highly ironic and that early reviewers were led astray by taking Woolf at her word. Marcus wants to deny rhetoric because she wants to save Woolf from her own criticism of art that is committed to a cause, and also because she wants to argue that Woolf only sounds uncommitted while in actuality she was passionately committed to her stance against tyranny, patriarchy, and oppression. But it is Woolf's rhetoric, I argue, that has allowed her not just to sound uncommitted but *to remain uncommitted to any one position,* thereby enabling her to investigate the complexities of tyranny and to change the very structure of responses that not only perpetuates domination but also informs Marcus's approach. Woolf's rhetoric resists the search for a noncontradictory and committed position that Marcus undertakes.

As a "random and tentative" essay that gives its author "the right to wander" that she desired (AWD 279, 253), *Three Guineas* is itself a rhetorical device. Thomas De Quincey defines the rhetorical essay as an attempt not to carry out a sustained attack but to consider all aspects of the subject in question in its myriad and complex relations. The rhetorical essay confronts doubts, inconsistencies, and objections; it conveys less the clarity and precision of logic than the "flux and reflux of thought" (xxiv).[4] Indeed, the aim of rhetoric is to stimulate thought: "Where conviction begins," De Quincey says, "the field of Rhetoric ends" (82, 92). As a rhetorical exercise, *Three Guineas* attends to the tensions and instabilities in the social-political environment; and, in attempting to work through these, Woolf experiments with different responses to them. The conflict raised in *Three Guineas* is not between logic and rhetoric or art and propaganda, as Marcus sees it; rather, the conflict is between different attitudes toward rhetoric and differing views of what politically responsible behavior is.

To neglect Woolf's rhetoric is to miss Woolf's point: we must change our commitment to certain kinds of responses before we can change the tyrannical social order now threatening men through fascism as it has long threatened women through patriarchy. The desires to possess, to publicize, and to prevail—that is, those desires that indicate pride in and certainty of one's position—can produce tyranny as an effect. Of the many rhetorical devices Woolf uses to resist those desires, the most salient and pervasive is repetition, in all its aspects: anaphora, anadiplosis, and repetend; reprise, recapitulation, and recurrence. The highly repetitive structure of *Three Guineas* functions in various ways. It conveys the sense of the "flux and reflux of thought." It suggests the old song "round and round the mulberry tree" that becomes in Woolf's essay a metaphor for our devotion to property as the hub of our social, economic, and political system (TG 68, 76, 86). It is a highly ironic device that signals the lack of accomplishment and direction that women are accused of by various authorities cited throughout the essay. And it exhausts the argument of the essay, resisting attempts to reduce it to a progression of logical propositions and undermining any final position, for to impose a position on others would be fascist.

And so in the end Woolf gives her guinea away gratis, without attaching any conditions (164) and thus refusing to exchange it for something else, be it promises, power, or publicity.[5] Likewise, she gives her essay away gratis by admitting that any suggestions she has offered are vague, idealistic, impractical, and complicated by social conditions. She asks no compliance from us. Even the concept of an Outsiders Society precludes requisite beliefs that would mark one as an insider to the Outsiders Society. (The absence of the possessive case is, in this instance, telling.) Woolf says over and over that as an outsider she has no desire to speak (5), indeed, "no right to speak" (37), and yet, like a Beckett character, she goes on speaking. Such garrulousness calls into question both the restrictions imposed on and the indifference and detachment professed by the outsider.[6]

Woolf reveals in *Three Guineas* that there is no real choice for outsiders within the social-economic system *as it now functions,* for the system continually circles back on itself, reinforcing and endlessly reproducing its own forms of production.[7] The choice Marcus sanctions, the Outsiders Society (an oxymoron), is not an alternative order but an instance of the instabilities in the present order. Oppositions set up choices; oxymorons confute them. It is not a program or a position but a problematizing disruption.[8] Similarly, the choice between private and public realms is not a real alternative, as Woolf realizes: "Behind us lies the patriarchal system; the private house, with its nullity, its immorality, its hypocrisy, its servility. Before us lies the public world, the professional system, with its possessiveness, its jealousy, its pugnacity, its greed. The one shuts us up like slaves in a harem; the other forces us to circle round the mulberry tree, the sacred tree, of property. It is a choice of evils. Each is bad" (TG 86). (The last two sentences reveal another kind of repetition, a type of pleonasm.) Although Woolf gives a guinea to the society for women's professional employment, and another to the society to rebuild the women's college, she faces the uncomfortable fact that these professional and educational institutions must function in response to the very system they would refute:

> And since that reality meant that she must rebuild her college on the same lines as the others, it followed that the college for the daughters of educated men must also make Research produce practical results which will induce bequests and donations from rich men; it must encourage competition; it must accept degrees and coloured hoods; it must accumulate great wealth; it must exclude other people from a share of its wealth; and, therefore, in 500 years or so, that college, too, must ask the same question that you, Sir, are asking now: "How in your opinion are we to prevent war?" (41)

How do we break out of this endless cycle? The answer lies in the very effect of Woolf's rhetorical strategies: to change the way we respond to and the way we conceive of the relations between things, such as insider and outsider, private and public realms, powerful patriarch and impoverished daughter, art and politics. Woolf refuses to play the game of assertion and denial, or accusation and defense, in *Three Guineas*. Instead, her essay chatters, repeats, digresses, and disperses its argument over three letters, numerous notes, and endless evidence. It thereby diffuses the opposition more effectively than by any "sustained attack" (Marcus). By evading the challenger's position, Woolf prevents the opponent from responding in the same terms. She changes the rules and the roles of this game by advocating a change in our responses to patriarchy, capitalism, and tyranny, so that the dominant power (whether father, dictator, or property owner) can no longer control by its established means of control. What response does Woolf recommend? Instead of confrontation and attack, evasion and decampment. Instead of anger, laughter: "Pelt the [mulberry] tree with laughter" (93); "Laughter as an antidote to dominance is perhaps indicated" (200). Woolf wants us to laugh, but Marcus is not amused: "*Three Guineas* is not in the least amusing" (277). Afraid that Woolf's essay will be dismissed as silly, frivolous, or irresponsible, Marcus resists the very strategies Woolf employs to disarm such criticism. But laughter is not opposed to righteous anger, as Marcus may fear; rather, it is a way of dealing with anger that does not fix us in the initially defining situation.[9] Laughter is a metaphor for a kind of response that changes the power game so that the dominant group must in turn change its own responses. To change rhetoric, not to avoid it, is to redefine politics. For Woolf, as for the Sophists, rhetoric is the politics of language use. *Three Guineas* is socially responsible, but its responsibility is not where Marcus would locate it: that is, it is not in its *lack* of rhetoric but in its very *use* of rhetoric as a training in language and politics.[10]

There is yet another way in which Woolf's rhetoric provokes laughter (literally as well as metaphorically) and functions to change our responses, one that leads us to the other essays considered in this chapter as well as to the next chapter on *Flush*. Woolf continually reasserts throughout *Three Guineas* that she must be brief, hasty, and rapid, for her interlocutor is pressed for time. Yet she drags out her arguments, reiterates the same points, begins over and over again. She trifles with time, which is such a precious commodity in this busy commercial society and which is of the utmost importance in this society on the brink of war. From the opening words of the essay, Woolf is anything but to the point: "Three years is a long time to leave a letter unanswered, and your letter has been lying without an answer even longer than that" (5). In an age of commercial production, De Quincey says, rhetoric would be attacked as "trifling with time" (100). In a capitalistic environment, what De Quincey calls this "boundless theatre of pleasures" where people are easily distracted, it would be difficult to find an audience for the rhetorician's performance, one that requires the audience's participation (97) and, we might add, the audience's patience. Here De Quincey has in mind one of the two types of rhetoric he distinguishes: not the argument with a "definite purpose of utility" but the "art of ostentatious ornament" (81–82). The first is considered significant; the second, a waste of time.[11]

This distinction is similar to one Woolf sorts out in her diary and tests out in her writing. And the relation between rhetoric and production is one Woolf explores in her *London Scene* essays. Only Woolf does not see commercialism as defeating rhetoric but as giving rise to a revival of it by necessitating "artificial display." In "The Docks of London" and "Oxford Street Tide" (the first two *London Scene* essays), Woolf turns this "boundless theatre of pleasures" and "the tide of public whim" (De Quincey's phrases) into a new stage for rhetorical display. In doing so she distinguishes types of prose discourse by their motives and contexts rather than by their ends (knowledge or power), as De Quincey does. Moreover, she demonstrates that playfulness and laughter are frivolous only within the context of a purposive theory of motive and a referential theory of meaning.

As Susan Squier clearly shows in *Virginia Woolf and London: The Sexual Politics of the City*, Woolf's *London Scene* essays do more than describe London life. For Squier, they reveal the ways in which Woolf used the city as setting, image, and symbol "to explore . . . her experience as a woman in patriarchal society" and "to attain an authentic voice as a woman writer" (3).[12] Squier reads Woolf's *London Scene* essays, which were written for *Good Housekeeping* in 1931 and 1932, as a vehicle for social commentary and for exploring the relation between women and the working class.[13] Although Squier's socialist-feminist focus discloses the political significance of these descriptive pieces for Woolf's female audience, it does not allow her to move from the first essay, "The Docks of London," to the second, "Oxford Street Tide," without seeming to shift her own critical position as well as her assessment of Woolf's position. These two essays are clearly linked; however, the social commentary Squier pursues does not provide the connection but, indeed, obscures it. Squier's reading, which seeks out the appropriate social position and the right relation between aesthetics and politics, leaves me with two questions: What other relations between Woolf's aesthetic use of the city and her "sexual politics of the city" might we posit? What kinds of connections does Woolf make between the controlled activity of the docks and the wild confusion of Oxford Street? In giving us two perspectives on the commercial system of modern

London, the "severely utilitarian" temper of the docks and the "garishness and gaudiness" of Oxford Street, Woolf explores prose discourse as an aesthetic phenomenon and a social product. In so doing she tests out the complex relationship between writing styles and material circumstances. A postmodern perspective better enables us to articulate this relationship.

From this perspective, these two essays can be seen as enacting the life-long debate Woolf carried on in her diaries between two motives for writing and two corresponding styles: writing from deep feeling and a sense of purpose, what she called "the gift when it is serious, going to business," and writing from a sensual delight in the combinations of words, or "the mere gift, unapplied gift" (AWD 134). The first motive requires a controlled, conscious, and transparent prose style; the second creates a "glittery" (Woolf's term), self-conscious, and ostentatious prose style, what Woolf called her "florid gush" (AWD 24). It is this tendency in her own writing that Woolf tries to come to terms with in her diary debates, for in an age that values writing that is clear, sincere, coherent, formal, and urbane, verbal play is seen as "superficial" (AWD 68), "pretentious" (AWD 25), or superfluous—as Woolf well knows. "*An Unwritten Novel* will certainly be abused: I can't foretell what line they'll take this time. Partly, it's the 'writing well' that sets people off—and always has done, I suppose. 'Pretentious' they say; and then a woman writing well, and writing in *The Times*—" (AWD 25).

In the thirties, this debate became particularly acute as Woolf came to terms with the popular success of *Flush* and assessed the value of a dramatic style versus a demonstrative one while writing *The Years*. Although throughout her diaries she maintains the distinction between playful writing for its own sake and purposeful writing for the sake of an ending, she presents a series of alternations between these views rather than a sustained argument for any one. She valorizes neither motive because she does not reduce the different motives to opposing ones. There is purpose in verbal play, and controlled prose can come to be as mannered and pretentious as the "florid gush." It is Woolf's critics, like Squier, who polarize different motives, perspectives, or styles into opposing ones, creating for Woolf a choice she did not need to make. Woolf saw her self-conscious style, her "writing against the current" (AWD 40, 297), as a necessary response to the prevailing standard for prose, but she did not promote any *one* alternative style. By playing out a spectrum of possibilities for prose writing, Woolf avoided the need to polarize differences and to choose between two alternatives.[14] In "The Docks of London" and "Oxford Street Tide," Woolf surveys two urban areas representing two aspects of economic production and two motives for composition in order to explore how a certain rhetorical form affects our worldview, how a certain economic order affects our rhetorical response to the world.

"The Docks of London" develops as a series of contrasts: between the romance of the ships coming from India, Russia, and South America and the squalor of the dockside, the "dwarf city of workmen's houses" (LS 8); between the green fields and "pleasure making" of the past and the desolation and labor of the present (9); between the trash dumps at the docks and the stately buildings at the hub of the city (10). Such contrasts, however, are not simple oppositions. Church spires mingle with factory chimneys; the functional movement of the working crane and the practical rows of barrels and crates provide an aesthetically pleasing rhythm and order. This dockside scene is presented in terms of changing "perspectives" and changing "proportions." Without the "proper perspective of sea and sky behind them," the ships, "tethered" to the docks, lose their romance; in the dim lighting of the warehouses, the efficacious wine vaults appear to be a vast cathedral (8, 13).

As Squier remarks, all this is presented from the point of view of the observing aesthete, one who is concerned with perspectives and proportions, with symmetry, order, and rhythm. This point of view suggests that the concern of the essay is broader than the kind of social critique Squier privileges. Squier responds to this aesthetic point of view only in terms of how it weakens the social criticism, not in terms of how it links aesthetic concerns with social ones. "The Docks of London" presents the city as an aesthetic composition, one that is constructed "in the common interest," which is that of the "buyers" (LS 11). Because of its orientation toward consumers, this composition is structured according to a utilitarian purpose: "Oddities, beauties, rarities may occur, but if so, they are instantly tested for their mercantile value" (11). Though there is beauty in this composition, it is "thrown in as an extra" (13). What matters is "the aptness of everything to its purpose" (12). Pleasure, it seems, is excluded from an economy of production: "for all is business; there are no pleasure boats" here (7); "Now pleasure has gone and labour has come" (9).[15] Style, by implication, is superfluous in a purposeful composition: "Use produces beauty as a bye-product [*sic*]" (13). The docks represent, then, not just a means of production and a social order but an attitude toward the production of meaning as well. That attitude represents the moral standard of writing that Woolf discusses in her diaries and that De Quincey means by the rhetorical essay with "a definite purpose of utility": the standard that values a work in terms of how clearly and efficiently it meets its ends. The comparison of the wine warehouse with a cathedral (by means of which the narrator brings out an element of beauty and atmosphere in this scene) suggests that this practical system is a new religion, something accepted as a first principle rather than questioned as a product itself: "We might be priests worshipping in the temple of some silent religion" (LS 13). Yet as the penultimate paragraph reveals, this whole system, which seems to

govern our lives, is dependent on and structured by our needs and desires: "Our body is their master" (14). If we were to changed our needs,
our values, our attitudes, or our perspectives, "the whole machinery of
production and distribution would rock and reel and seek about to adapt
itself afresh" (14). As the shifting contrasts show, it is not a simple matter
of the economic system controlling our tastes or of our tastes dictating
the system; rather, it is a complex relationship, a continual shifting of the
relations between human desires and systems of production.

Squier grounds her reading of "The Docks of London" on two passages not found in the final version. She argues that Woolf, in her revision
of the first passage, toned down the facts by detaching herself from the
workers, eventually eliminating the social criticism (*Woolf and London* 54).
In revising the second passage, Woolf deleted a metaphor that divided
the city into masters (upper class and male) and housemaids (working
class and female), that is, along gender and class lines (55–57). Why did
Woolf omit or drastically revise these passages of social criticism that so
clearly revealed the sexual politics of the city? Squier provides two explanations. One, in her oscillation between "conflicting identifications"
(Squier's terms), Woolf shifted from identification with the workers as
outsiders (an identification based on her gender) to identification with
the privileged class as insiders (an identification based on her heritage)
because of the "uncomfortable empathy" and sense of powerlessness produced by the former (55). Though Squier can understand such feelings,
she laments that shift from outsider to insider because it has weakened the
social criticism. The second, more hostile explanation is that in the final
version Woolf capitulated to the "consumer mentality" of her middle-class
audience. The ending of "The Docks of London," Squier concludes, is
one of resignation and complacency (57). This Squier cannot understand.

Squier's understanding is limited by her narrow concept of social criticism. She must lament the changes that obscure, if not lose, the connection between gender and class as weakening the essay considerably. Unless
Woolf identifies with outsiders, how is she to place herself as a woman
writer in a patriarchal society without succumbing to patriarchal values?
This is, of course, the very question raised in *Three Guineas*. Woolf suggests an answer to this question, through what she does, not through what
she says. Squier's focus prevents her from seeing this answer, prevents her
from asking what these changes have done to the point of the essay. What
is the final version trying to effect? Squier looks at what the essay *could
have been*—and, by implication, what it was *intended to be*—not at what
it *does*. She looks at the essay as a failed statement, a flawed representation, not as a speculative process and a performative strategy.[16] She rightly
perceives that in this essay the narrator's position shifts from outsider to

insider; however, this shift can be seen not as a failure of nerve but as a change in perspective, from observing aesthete (detached) to aesthetic participant (involved). (This is a change Squier notes with approval in the essay "Oxford Street Tide.") Woolf's emphasis on her narrator's relation to this dock scene is hardly a pretext. Where Squier senses self-congratulation at the end, Woolf may well be conveying complicity, a recognition of the writer's implication in this social system. And consideration of one's audience is not a weakness, as Squier implies, but a necessary component of the writing process, perhaps the preeminent rhetorical strategy. Writing to and for a particular group is not dishonest, it is unavoidable.

Woolf's identification with her audience and her insider role provide several important insights into her understanding of the writer's activity. First, they show her recognition of the complexity of the relation between literary production and economic production. Second, they show her awareness that the writer cannot choose to step outside the social-economic system to judge it, for one is as much a product of it as apart from it.[17] Finally, they show her change in focus in these essays, from social critique along gender and class lines (as the drafts suggest) to consideration of various cultural systems—economic, social, literary—and the relations among them. Rather than polarize the writer's roles—outsider versus insider, feminist versus aesthete—and be forced to choose between them, as Squier does, Woolf explores the relations between them. She studies the connections between politics and aesthetics, not only in these essays, but in other writings of the thirties as well.[18] Rather than seeing prose writing as simply reflecting and critiquing the social-economic reality in its content and theme, as Squier seems to, Woolf reveals the ways writing expresses, exploits, and exposes a society's systems of production. From a postmodern perspective, these essays can be read in terms of "the politics of language as a material and social structure," the position Toril Moi identifies as the strength of poststructuralist theory like Julia Kristeva's, as well as a position holding "considerable promise for future feminist readings of Woolf" (*Sexual/Textual Politics* 15). In other words, *Woolf explores the kinds of social contexts that make certain kinds of prose writing operable and certain kinds of critical responses tenable.* She does not set up a simple correspondence.[19]

Woolf's change in perspective from detached observer (outsider) to complicitous participant (insider) in "The Docks of London" anticipates the change in perspective between "The Docks of London" and "Oxford Street Tide": from aesthetic observer to "appreciative observer" (Squier's distinction); from the single perspective in "The Docks" to the double perspectives of the detached moralist and the sympathetic narrator in "Oxford Street." The two essays must be read together to grasp Woolf's point. The utilitarian temper of the docks—"every commodity in the world has been examined and graded according to its use and value" (LS 12)—supports the "blatant and raucous" buying and selling on Oxford Street by providing the products to be sold here. The first paragraph of "Oxford Street Tide" discloses the relation between the two parts of London:

> Down in the docks one sees things in their crudity, their bulk, their enormity. Here in Oxford Street they have been refined and transformed. The huge barrels of damp tobacco have been rolled into innumerable neat cigarettes laid in silver paper. The corpulent bales of wool have been spun into thin vests and soft stockings. The grease of sheep's thick wool has become scented cream for delicate skins. And those who buy and those who sell have suffered the same city change. Tripping, mincing, in black coats, in satin dresses, the human form has adapted itself no less than the animal product. Instead of hauling and heaving, it deftly opens drawers, rolls out silk on counters, measures and snips with yard sticks and scissors. (16)

The "city change," with its play on "sea change," expresses the transformation of one value system into another. The above passage, for instance, highlights the change from substance to style in contrasting the bulk of the docks—*huge* barrels, *corpulent* bales, *thick* wool—with the airy, sensual quality of Oxford Street—*silver* paper, *thin* vests, *scented* cream. At the end of "The Docks of London," the narrator remarks that the "only thing . . . that can change the routine of the docks is a change in ourselves" (14). In "Oxford Street Tide," we see this change not in the "essential self" or in the social-economic system but in attitude, motive, and rhetoric. Woolf brings out the differences between these two urban spaces through contrasts and juxtapositions, not through explicit commentary. In the docks all activity is ordered by the buyers' interest; in Oxford Street all is arranged from the sellers' interest. In the docks one is concerned with measurable substances; in Oxford Street one is concerned with style. In the docks everything is anchored; in Oxford Street everything flows. The buildings on the docks are dismal, forlorn, coarse, and low-ceiled; the buildings on Oxford Street are bright, glittery, high, and airy. And humans adapt to the change. Only the moralist (whose voice is absent in the univocal world of the docks, where all functions according to a moral standard of efficiency and practicality) "points the finger of scorn" at the vulgar commerce in this multivocal Oxford Street (16). The moralist prefers to withdraw to perform his "more sublime rites" in Bond Street (16). However, whether in Bond Street or Oxford Street or the docks, one is implicated in this system of production. And Woolf understands that the style of Oxford Street depends on the products of the docks.

The activity of Oxford Street, then, is different from, but not opposed to, the activity of the docks. "Oxford Street Tide" develops as well by a series of comparisons and contrasts. The effect of this street on the observer is expressed in two contrasting images: the "glutinous slab" and the "perpetual ribbon" (17). At times the activity of Oxford Street "coagulates"; then "it streams again" (18). What appears to be solid and cohesive is constantly shifting and dissolving. Oxford Street is a puzzle (with a definite shape) that "never fits itself together" (always shapeless; 18). Likewise, the sellers of present-day Oxford Street are compared with the aristocrats of old. Both press gifts on the populace, as if gratuitously yet always in exchange for something else. What has changed over the years is not the exchange system but the objects exchanged, the objects of our desires. Where the old aristocrats dispensed gold and bread in exchange for votes, the modern aristocrats provide sensation in exchange for shillings: "Only their largesse takes a different form. It takes the form of excitement, of display, of entertainment, of windows lit up by night, of banners flaunting by day" (18). In other words, Oxford Street is "a breeding ground . . . of sensation" (17), not a world of substance and purpose, as a final contrast makes clear: the solidity and permanency of the structures of old (the world the moralist values) are contrasted with the flimsiness and transitoriness of modern structures. Where the aristocrats of old wanted to build lasting structures (whether grand estates, literary masterpieces, or eternal values), the aristocrats of today build structures for the moment only.

The moralist finds the "flimsy abodes" in this world of "yellow cardboard and sugar icing" ostentatious, irresponsible, and reprehensible (19). The appreciative observer, however, accepts this world as governed by a different motive, expressing different values:

> The charm of modern London is that it is not built to last; it is built to pass. Its glassiness, its transparency, its surging waves of coloured plaster give a different pleasure and achieve a different end from that which was desired and attempted by the old builders and their patrons, the nobility of England. Their pride required the illusion of permanence. Ours, on the contrary, seems to delight in proving that we can make stone and brick as transitory as our own desires. We do not build for our descendants . . . but for ourselves and our own needs. We knock down and rebuild as we expect to be knocked down and rebuilt. It is an impulse that makes for creation and fertility.[20] (19–20)

Disposable structures—economic, social, and literary—can accommodate changing values and changing circumstances. Things that are not built to last are not meant to be accumulated (like the products at the docks) but re-created; they are not meant to be possessed finally but only momentarily. This, then, is a difference between the docks and Oxford Street. The structures of the docks are built according to a utilitarian purpose, making considerations of style superfluous: the fungus in the wine vaults, "whether lovely or loathsome matters not," is welcome "because it proves that the air possesses the right degree of dampness for the health of the precious fluid" (13). The structures of Oxford Street, by contrast, are built for style, which is essential here: "Everything glitters and twinkles" (17). (One of Woolf's modifiers for her playful writing is "glittery.") Instead of accumulating useful products, Oxford Street values using things up, selling things quickly, changing things frequently. But Oxford Street is not simply the ornamentation of the drab world of the docks; it is a different orientation to that world. When comparing these two urban spaces, one must account for their different orientations and the different responses they evoke.

The difference between the docks and Oxford Street is not primarily between a hierarchical and an egalitarian social order, not between a repressive environment and a liberating one, but between a centralized society and a multivalent one. What keeps the dock system going is the "authority of the city," its solidness and diuturnity: "This [the center of London] is the knot, the clue, the hub of all those scattered miles of skeleton desolation and ant-like activity" (LS 10). "Knot," "clue," "hub," all suggest a structure built around some stable core, some core of meaning. This world of permanent structures ensures the continuance of the economic system. But what if, Woolf wonders, the city is not authoritative but charming? What if it is not built to last but built to pass? The morality of Oxford Street is of a different orientation. As Barbara Herrnstein Smith writes, "To understand the ethics of verbal transactions we must appreciate its economics" (*Margins of Discourse* 105).[21] Oxford Street presents the social-economic functioning associated with postmodernism and referred to as the consumer society, or "the society of the spectacle" (Jameson, Foreword vii). Oxford Street flaunts its diverse values, accepts its own impermanence, and exaggerates its own functioning—and thereby reveals the values, the function, and the transitoriness of the docks as well. The motive compelling the social investigations in these essays is the differing rhetorical approaches themselves; therefore, the social representation is an effect of the writing, not the thematic core or the objective ground. The status of the referent (the social order) changes with the change in the rhetorical form itself—with a change, we might say, in the method of investigation and the means of investment. "The Docks of London" and "Oxford Street Tides" problematize the assumed distinction between these two rhetorical approaches, the purposive and the playful, and between these two functionings of the social-economic order. What changes is not just Woolf's vision of society but her use of language.

The city, then, stands for more than the social-economic system of patriarchy and capitalism; it suggests the aesthetic orders and attitudes that are necessarily tied up with this social-economic system. But it is not just that the rhetorical approach affects our understanding of this system; rather, the form of that system affects language use as well. And the economic system of this capitalistic society is one that produces *excess*. In the docks the excess takes the form of substances. "The Docks of London" presents a world surfeited with products, weighted down with commodities: "malodorous mounds," "fresh heaps," "barges heaped," "long mounds," the "dumps get higher and higher, and thicker and thicker," "the buildings thicken and heap themselves higher," "the sky seems laden with heavier, purpler clouds," "barrel is laid by barrel, case by case, cask by cask, one behind the other, one on top of the other, one beside the other in an endless array" (9–11 passim). The images of piles, heaps, mounds, and rows present a mass of products stacked up, ready to be exchanged for something else, while the comparative adjectives suggest that such products are continually accumulating, that the excess is excessive. It seems that this consumer-oriented, ends-oriented composition leads to ever more products (goods, programs, conclusions) to be marketed. Yet from a utilitarian perspective, which is the temper of the docks, excess is undesirable. Efficiency is valued in this kind of system: words that form exact meanings (14), actions that are quick and effective (14), ends accomplished without waste (11), everything being provided for (12). Nothing must be superfluous. Activity is controlled—everything is "set down accurately," "set in its right place" (11)—implying not only a practical efficiency but a moral judgment as well.[22] So when the narrator of "The Docks of London" (the one Squier says *capitulates* to these values) describes not just the mounds of products to be made into billiard balls and umbrellas and exchanged (i.e., what is appropriate to this economic scheme) but focuses outrageously and immorally on the waste products and the trash dumps (i.e., what is immoderate and immoral because it cannot be appropriated into the system of production), she exposes what the docks prefer to hide or ignore. The docks, then, prepare us for Oxford Street in two ways. All those useful products stockpiled at the docks need the marketplaces provided by those "palaces" of Oxford Street. But if there is a glut on the market, if this commercial system produces too many goods, too much superfluous waste, then a different attitude from that of the moral, utilitarian one is necessary if the whole system is not to sink under its own unidirectional, end-oriented purpose.

This different attitude, one presented in much postmodern writing, is seen in Oxford Street. Here, too, we are in a world of excess: "there are too many bargains, too many sales, too many goods" (16). All those products produced ingeniously (skillfully) by trade must be disposed of ingeniously (cunningly) by markets. In the docks, trade may be "ingenious and indefatigable beyond the bounds of imagination" (12); in Oxford Street, imagination is ingenious and indefatigable beyond the bounds of trade. And so the excess of Oxford Street is in the form of style, a by-product of the utilitarian activity of the docks. Since there is so much to use up, lavish display becomes as important as the products displayed. Oxford Street flaunts its process of exchange. The images of glowing windows, plush carpets, and bright colors present everything as on display, enjoyable in its display. The concern here is with things being used, not just with things that are useful. It is not that Oxford Street has no products, only that they carry no weight. Excess is flaunted; superfluity is brandished. (*Superfluity* here is meant in all three of *Webster's* definitions: excess and oversupply; something superfluous; and luxurious living habits and desires.) Its styles are ephemeral and its structures disposable, not because Oxford Street is irresponsible, but because it is responsive to circumstances, particularly to a consumer society. The utilitarian attitude of the docks depends on the universalization of standards and the possession of products; the rhetorical attitude of Oxford Street depends on the transitoriness of standards and the momentary enjoyment of things. Their interests are not the same. The common interest of the docks is that of the social benefit; *interest* is meant in an economic sense. The common interest of Oxford Street is that of "an excess above what is due" (*Webster's*), *interest* in the sense of entertainment, "the decoration and entertainment of human life" (LS 19). Thus, the bustle and glitter of Oxford Street cannot be celebrated as an alternative to the world of the docks, for in part it upholds that world: the palaces of Oxford Street "are overwhelmingly conscious that unless they can devise an architecture that shows off the dressing case, the Paris frock, the cheap stockings, and the jar of bath salts to perfection, their palaces, their mansions and motor-cars and the little villas out at Croydon and Surbiton where their shop assistants live, not so badly after all, with a gramophone and wireless, and money to spend at the movies—all this will be swept to ruin" (20). "All this" refers to capitalistic society in its multiform aspects, including the dwarf city of workmen's houses as well as the middle-class villas. Thus, this flaunting of excess and of style, this ostentatious, self-conscious, and playful display not only mocks the docks by exposing its immoral, unseemly excess but depends on and shores up that system as well. Oxford Street keeps the system of production alive, assures its continuation, but also ensures its change.[23]

The change from one section of London to another is a change in our conception of and response to discourse and reality: from a positivistic world of referential reality to a stylistic world of rhetorical reality; from a substantial view of meaning production to a functional one; from a concern with bricks and cement to a concern with architectural form (a change signaled in Woolf's revisions of "The Docks of London" that Squier regrets so much). Such a shift is brought about by a change in language use, a change alluded to not only in terms of the different attitudes toward purpose and style but also in a passage on language use near the end of "The Docks of London": "Even the English language has adapted itself to the needs of commerce. Words have formed round objects and taken their exact outline" (13–14). The narrator goes on to discuss some slang terms that "have formed naturally" over years of use in dockside labor. More generally, this passage reveals an attitude toward language that Woolf explores in other essays, such as "Craftsmanship" (1937), as well as in her diary entries debating playful versus purposive writing. This positivistic attitude toward language values words for what they can be exchanged for, that is, what they substitute for in the world. Its reality is referential, a source of subjects and themes. Its use of language respects a transparent prose style in which the expression represents precisely the writer's purpose. The language of the docks produces results in the sense of a useful statement, which is "a statement that can mean only one thing" ("Craftsmanship," DM 201). At the end of the paragraph on language, the narrator comments: "Dexterity can go no further" (LS 14). If the world is seen to be stable, if human values and desires are seen to be eternal, then such a transparent prose is suitable.

But if one suspects, as Woolf does, that reality may be shifting (AWD 138), and if one accepts an impermanent, passing world (LS 19–20), then a self-conscious prose is necessary to stress the way reality changes in response, in part, to changes in language use. This is the attitude expressed in the "play side" of Woolf's writing; language is valuable in itself, style is significant, "the sentence in itself beautiful" (AWD 183). Emphasis on rhetorical flourish over referential use is what Oxford Street displays. Its reality is rhetorical, a matter of verbal (as well as visual) constructs. As opposed to the limits of dexterity, here "discovery is stimulated and invention on the alert" (LS 20). Though both kinds of expression are purposive in that each has its point, the language of the docks is concerned with substantial results, the language of Oxford Street with creative strategies. A change in our attitude toward language use is what Woolf advocates in *Three Guineas*. There she argues both for using up words that have lost their usefulness because society has changed (a word such as *feminist*) and for explaining "exactly, even pedantically" what one means by a word in a particular "context" (a word such as *free*), because words can mean more than one thing (116–17).

Although I agree with Squier that Woolf celebrates Oxford Street, I do not agree that Woolf presents Oxford Street as a liberation from the social-economic order of the docks; rather, in "Oxford Street Tide," she assumes a different attitude toward that order and makes a different use of it. The celebration is a response to the system, a response that calls attention to its devices and desires, a response that, like much postmodern art, neither accepts nor dismisses the supporting structures of society but exaggerates their functioning so they can be noticed, and changed. This change in attitude is signaled by Woolf's change in narrative perspective.

Woolf responded to London life much as Lucy responds to Giles, "expressing her amazement, her amusement, at men who spent their lives buying and selling" (BA 47). In "Oxford Street Tide," as in *Between the Acts,* Woolf presents a "positive use of mass culture," as do many postmodern writers (Arac xxiii), but not necessarily the "new egalitarian political vision" that Squier finds in that essay (*Woolf and London* 59). We must ask whether or not Oxford Street is more egalitarian than the docks: after all, the "great Lords of Oxford Street" are better off in their mansions than their shop assistants are in their "little villas out at Croydon," and these assistants are better off than the bank clerk's wife who has "only fifteen pounds a year to dress on," and she is better off than the thief who is "a lady of easy virtue into the bargain" (LS 20–21). Oxford Street, it seems, is not an egalitarian society so much as a multivocal spectacle. And Woolf does not present Oxford Street as a new political-economic order that can supplant that of the docks; rather, she explores and questions the presumed opposition between them. More specifically, her critique of property is much more far-reaching than either Marcus or Squier perceives. Woolf objects not only to private property as the hub of the capitalistic system but also the conception of the social world as property, property to be accumulated, possessed, stored, protected, raided (Marcus, *New Feminist Essays*), or cleaned (Squier).[24]

By seeing these essays primarily as social criticism, Squier puts Woolf in a self-contradictory position. To condemn the activity of the docks while celebrating Oxford Street would be to ignore their common ties and thus mask their complicitous relationship. Had she done so, Woolf would resemble a poet of the thirties. Indeed, from her reading of "The Docks of London" as a capitulation to middle-class values, we would expect Squier to be less than enthusiastic over Woolf's appreciation of Oxford Street's middle-class marketplaces. If, that is, Squier's readings were consistent. It seems Squier would have preferred that Woolf criticize the commercial system when touring the slums of the docks but praise it when strolling the middle-class Oxford Street. So who is changing allegiances? Who is capitulating to middle-class values? Squier wants Woolf to assume the role of the finger-wagging moralist in "The Docks of London" by withdrawing from the activity of the docks in order to scorn it, yet to mock the moralist's role in "Oxford Street Tide" by knocking those who stand apart and judge. But Woolf refuses to assume this "outsider" position finally, morally.[25] So Squier herself plays the role of the moralist in "The Docks of London" by scorning it, dismissing it, even masking it to assert "Oxford Street Tide" as a more appropriate representation, to turn the supposedly new egalitarian vision of that essay into a "normalizing moralism" (Gallop, *Daughter's Seduction* 11). My point is not to insist on a consistency in Squier's writing that I resist imposing on Woolf's but to show how Squier's desire for a consistent view in Woolf's essays has led to contradictions in her own and caused her to miss the very implications of Woolf's *changing* views. Squier's reading treats reality as univocal and referential even while acknowledging Woolf's preference for treating reality as multivocal and rhetorical. In other words, Squier's reading belies her claims, and her critical method conflicts with her aims.

My point is this: If these essays were merely reflections of a particular social order or vision, then we could compare their representations and judge between them. But if, as I argue, they represent not different social orders alone but differing responses and approaches to the social world, then they cannot be judged *on the same terms,* as if their goals were the same.

Considering these essays in terms of different aesthetic considerations and different responses to social-economic circumstances not only allows us to avoid being caught in a contradiction but also enables us to understand the social implications of the differing motives and methods Woolf has explored. Certainly Woolf prefers the bustling, hustling Oxford Street to the efficient, practical docks, but not because Oxford Street opposes the docks. Woolf approves of Oxford Street for adapting to changing circumstances, for baring its devices, and for listening to a thousand "incongruous voices." She applies these qualities to the docks by having her aesthetic observer notice what is usually hidden or dismissed in this world: the trash dumps of waste products, the "rarities and oddities" that are cast aside, the aesthetic delight in a utilitarian production. The narrator's imagination is stimulated by the refuse and the excess. In this way, Woolf does not offer us a choice between opposing value systems, economic systems, or prose styles; rather, she shows us how to read writing and reality in different ways. She therefore avoids assuming the didactic and moralizing voice she so wanted to avoid. Her playful prose, as presented in terms of Oxford Street, is not a repudiation of purpose so much as it is a stance against certainty, against a moralizing egotism, against the desire to prevail that she recognized as the patriarchal position as well as the position one could be forced to assume in any attack on the patriarchy. By playing out a spectrum of possibilities in her prose, Woolf emphasizes the importance of change: "I rather think the upshot [of this "fluent and fluid" style] will be books that relieve other books: a variety of styles and subjects: for after all, that is my temperament, I think, to be very little persuaded of the truth of anything—" (AWD 134). An artificial, self-conscious style, a text that calls attention to its devices, has this advantage: it flaunts its own impermanency and thus the impermanency of the social structure with which it is bound up.[26] What is self-consciously contrived cannot harden into a permanent order or a prescribed form. Ironically, Squier's feminist reading is consistent with the attitude toward language use that governs the world of the docks, the world Squier would reject, the attitude Woolf questioned, and the reading Woolf has challenged.

In "Street Haunting" we can see clearly how Squier's approach implicates her in a position she would have Woolf repudiate and how it fosters the kind of reading Woolf resists. In this essay Woolf presents the activity of the street (Oxford Street again) from the writer's point of view. As in "Oxford Street Tide," we are in a world of spectacle, of dramatic scenes, choric voices, and fantastic displays. Woolf describes the city in terms of its dazzling, entertaining aspects: "the glossy brilliance," "the carnal splendour," "the bright paraphernalia of the streets" (DM 23, 24). Even the lives of the less fortunate, the "maimed company," are presented theatrically, in terms of the "fantastic," not the "tragic," in terms of spectacle, not polemic (26). Again, Woolf stresses the perspective and motive of the writer: "Passing, glimpsing, everything seems accidentally but miraculously sprinkled with beauty, as if the tide of trade which deposits its burden so punctually and prosaically upon the shores of Oxford Street had this night cast up nothing but treasure. With no thought of buying, the eye is sportive and generous; it creates; it adorns; it enhances" (27). The narrator is not adopting the perspective of the prosaic, punctual, and practical world of "The Docks of London" but of the diverting and dynamic world of "Oxford Street Tide." The narrator is one who participates and passes on, not one who stands outside and condemns from her secure, rightful position.

Yet Squier, in her reading of "Street Haunting," would have Woolf step outside and judge, relinquish her identification with insiders. Squier asserts that this observing eye is "*unable* to move beyond such surface appreciation" (*Woolf and London* 46; emphasis added). On the contrary, the observer is *unwilling* to move beyond surface appreciation; or rather, the narrator recognizes the significance of the stylistic display and therefore refuses to see it as masking a deeper truth or as subordinate to some higher (moral) standard. Squier complains: "The stroll through London leaves [the narrator of "Street Haunting"] neither morally, spiritually, nor politically changed, but *merely* entertained" (47; emphasis added). And again: "the experience of other lives is *merely* diverting, not enlightening" (48;

emphasis added). *Merely* trivializes what Woolf valorizes in this particular essay and in "Oxford Street Tide": entertainment, pleasure, and delight in display.[27] Thus, Squier exposes her own utilitarian purpose, what Woolf in "Street Haunting" calls "the accustomed tyrant": "One must, one always must, do something or other; it is not allowed one simply to enjoy oneself" (DM 32). In these lines, Woolf pleads with her reader, in this case Squier, to let her off the hook of moral purpose, one conceived as univocal and unidirectional, abjuring the complex and the difficult (SCR 119). She wants the "unapplied gift," not the gift when it is "going to business." Squier's persistence in this moral reading that Woolf's narrator resists attests to the fact that we have indeed become accustomed to the tyrant purpose, for we take for granted a purposive theory of motive. In order to condemn, one must speak in one voice and from a firm, fixed position (outsider, authoritarian, tyrant). But the joy of street haunting is escaping the confines of the self, a unified self compelled by circumstances (DM 28–29), to give free rein to the "varied and wondering" self, to enact various roles, and to live other lives: "And what greater delight and wonder can there be than to leave the straight lines of personality" (35).[28] A role-playing self does not require an appropriate social order to support it. It changes with changing relationships. Ironically, then, Squier is the moralist, the tyrant, the slave to purpose. And it is her polarization of identifications that creates this self-contradictory position. By enacting different roles, Woolf keeps her position flexible, in motion, and open to change.

The problem with Squier's reading is twofold: it seeks in Woolf's essays a repudiation of the social-economic system that in part shapes them and of the authoritarian, utilitarian values associated with this system; and wherever it fails to turn up such a repudiation, it judges those essays in terms of the very purposive, authoritarian, fixed position that Woolf rejects and that feminist readings would also want to decry. Squier privileges representation, takes language for granted, and sees the social order as a problem on the level of subject and theme. In other words, she accepts the positivistic view of language that the docks represent while rejecting the social order and values that give rise to and arise out of such a view of language. Woolf, by contrast, emphasizes expression, flaunts rhetoric, and treats the social order in its relation to writing styles as a play of forms.[29] Her concern is not with representing reality to reveal its nasty side (a motive she herself attributed to many modernist writers, including Eliot and Joyce) but with disclosing and probing the forms by which the real is posited and expressed, that is, with dramatizing the possibilities of discourse. In other words, Woolf's feminism or socialism does not take the form of a naive identification of women and workers as "oppressed" groups; rather, it reveals the kind of understanding that encourages us to see these groups as "oppressed" in the same way and the various kinds of oppression we must learn to distinguish among.[30] Woolf does not promote outsiders over insiders; instead, she shows us that such terms are bound up with the very kind of thinking that perpetuates the social-economic system she explores. For this reason Woolf theatricalizes Oxford Street, with its horrid tragedies, its street magicians, its Hollywood sets, and its dramatic monologues, thereby avoiding the moralistic tone that would put her into a position to speak for others. This dramatic conception of reality, like the dramatic conception of the self in "Street Haunting," a conception Woolf expresses more and more in her later writings (*Orlando, The Years, Between the Acts*), encourages verbal play, rhetorical display, and flexible forms. The bustling, showy Oxford Street reminds us, as Woolf says, "that life is a struggle; that all building is perishable; that all display is vanity" (LS 22); indeed, this whole glittery display can be burst by a "vigorous prod with an umbrella point" (19). And so the narrator of "Oxford Street Tide" cannot end with a thematic statement: "it is vain to try to come to a conclusion in Oxford Street" (22). *In* Oxford Street, not *on* it. It is not just the kind of motives and values we find in Oxford Street that defeats any conclusion but the writer's own position in that world. It is not that all conclusions at all times are vain but that conclusions must be drawn with as much awareness as possible of the writer's own historical and rhetorical situation.

Where Squier would have Woolf simplify the relation between these two urban spaces, dismiss one and celebrate the other (dismiss one in order to celebrate the other), Woolf understood that the more comprehensive and complex a vision is, "the less it is able to sum up and make linear" (AWD 238–39). What enabled her to grasp the relations among various signifying systems was her very avoidance of a feminist form or an outsider position (one taken up as an end, that is) that would erroneously assume we can free ourselves from restraints and that would turn differences into polarized positions. "Writing against the current"—the kind of writing Woolf identified with her playful, fluid prose—depends on that current, takes place within it, not on the marginal shoreline. Such writing, such opposition, must be continually enacted, never prescribed and codified. The marginal position is not a place to which we are consigned or a defensive from which we conduct our raids. The marginal is the relation at stake in the language games we play.[31] As Woolf shows in *Three Guineas*, thinking of the world as property and dividing it into private and public realms offers no real choice for women. As her diary entries reveal, she was well aware that writing against the current can be restricting and tiresome when it becomes personal, egotistical, or insistent; that is, when it becomes a writer's possession or when it becomes identified as the possession of a particular group, a particular class or sex. Thus, Woolf could not advocate a new society or an appropriate literary form, but she could promote new ways of valuing society and literature. In a 1935 diary entry on a Labour party meeting, Woolf writes: "and what a partial view: altering the structure of society; yes, but when it's altered?" (AWD 247). Woolf distrusted fixed structures; she preferred to consider flexible relations. Society must be changed over and over, must never be allowed to settle into a position. Such a view has implications for our readings. Where Woolf's readers usually look for the thematic, purposive element in her social essays, we might do better to seek out, as Woolf often did, the rhetorical element in the social order.[32]

The moralistic, purposive attitude toward writing presented in "The Docks of London" is not wrong, but it is often taken to be the appropriate attitude rather than one attitude among many. To accept this attitude, as Marcus and Squier seem to do, we would have to accept two assumptions: the positivistic assumption of empirical stability and the reference-theory assumption of some correspondence between language and empirical reality. In the first place, we would have to agree on a common ground to fight over; and in the second place, we would have to agree on a use of language capable of achieving our common ends. Put another way, agreement on the proper use of language must depend first on agreement about the status of reality, and that is just what is in question.[33] Our changing language is a paradigm for our changing society, but it does not follow that a particular literary change will correspond to a particular social change. And here the relation of art to politics becomes fraught with difficulties, for the artist, no matter how passionately she believes in a political goal, cannot turn her art into a means toward that end, not because it would be morally wrong to do so, but because *there is no simple relation to be drawn*. To deny a simple or reductive relation between literary revolution and social revolution is not to deny *any* relation between the two. Certainly, we do not want to argue naively that particular kinds of textual innovations necessarily convey a particular political effect, as Toril Moi claims Kristeva does at times (*Sexual/Textual Politics* 170–71). But that is not to say that changes in the literary and linguistic code do not bring about, or at least make visible, changes in the social-economic order and the historical-cultural consciousness. While it is ludicrous, if not dangerous, to believe that literary revolution is the primary or most effective agent of social change, as Nancy Fraser argues (204), it is equally ludicrous, if not dangerous, to believe that "poetry makes nothing happen," as Auden later came to believe ("In Memory of W. B. Yeats"). Both modernist theories of art's autonomy (art for art's sake) and socialist or feminist theories of art's commitment (art for revolution's sake) depend on the concept of art and life as separate realms of experience; both depend on the form/content or inside/outside dichotomy. To reject such concepts is not to reject political commitment or to deny the politics of language use but to accept that every artwork enters into a variety of relations and that, as Moi says, "the same aesthetic device can be politically polyvalent, varying with the historical, political and literary context in which it occurs" (*Sexual/Textual Politics* 85). And it is this important insight that feminist criticism has given us. Feminist critics have shown that what at one time was thought to be apolitical art in comparison with other art of the time (e.g., Woolf's writings of the 1930s compared with Auden's and Spender's) can come to be very political indeed with a change in audience and, I argue, a change in motivation—a change we have come to call *postmodernism*.

Robbe-Grillet had in mind this lack of a simple relation between art and politics when he wrote that the artist "can create only *for nothing*" (37). Woolf would have agreed that the artist cannot exchange her work for something else. In this sense, the artist's work is concerned with the "pragmatics" of rhetoric. Pragmatics deals with the analysis of any language situation "as an unstable exchange between its speakers" (Jameson, Foreword xi). Thus, more important than its predictive value in relation to the reality represented is its pragmatic value in relation to the issues raised. "Postmodern knowledge," writes Lyotard, "is not simply a tool of the authorities [or the outsiders, I might add]; it refines our sensitivity to differences and reinforces our ability to tolerate the incommensurable" (xxv).[34]

Such tolerance is what Woolf's writing strives for, not tolerance of all views, but tolerance for what cannot be simply compared on the same terms. Woolf explores the kinds of distinctions we can make and the kinds of relations we can enter into in any particular social situation. As a result, she gives us no one answer to the question raised earlier: How can we change the social-economic system in which we are implicated? Indeed, she shows us that we cannot answer this question once and for all but that we must answer it again and again. We must continually question in what ways our actions shore up and in what ways they subvert the social system. We must constantly analyze our own behavior in relation to certain defining social relations. And we must be wary of any one program, whether political or literary. As Woolf says in *Three Guineas,* programs and labels do not fit the heterogeneity of human life; nor, Lyotard points out, the "heterogeneity of language games" (xxv):

> Josephine Butler's label—Justice, Equality, Liberty—is a fine one; but it is only a label, and in our age of innumerable labels, of multi-coloured labels, we have become suspicious of labels; they kill and constrict. Nor does the word "freedom" serve, for it was not freedom in the sense of licence that they wanted; they wanted, like Antigone, not to break the laws, but to find the law. Ignorant as we are of human motives and ill supplied with words,

let us admit that no one word expresses the force which in the nineteenth century opposed itself to the force of the fathers. (TG 157)

Woolf's project, political and literary, was neither to "break the laws," that is, to reject established social or literary conventions, nor to "find the law," that is, to codify new, more liberating conventions; for once such conventions are changed, the important question still remains: And now? (TY 331). Instead, her project was to trace the laws, to find the connections, and to remake them over and over again. In this sense she seems to have shared a postmodernist insight: "The social bond is linguistic, but it is not woven with a single thread" (Lyotard 40). In place of a representational theory, with its evaluative categories of adequacy and accuracy, a postmodern theory relies on the insights of Wittgenstein: the point of writing is not to produce new models but to generate change in behavior and thinking (Jameson, Foreword vii-ix).

In her essays of the 1930s, Woolf undertakes a study of possible prose strategies for different motives and circumstances. She asks not how writing reflects the world but how different styles work in the world: how material circumstances affect style, how style affects our view of material circumstances. Changing viewpoints and methods can be seen as a strength of Woolf's essays in the psychoanalytic sense that Jane Gallop defines strength, as flexibility, not as a firm position (*Daughter's Seduction* xi). The strength of Woolf's writing is its refusal to simplify and its awareness of its own relation to the signifying systems it exposes. It refuses to be anchored to the docks of London but flows with the tide of Oxford Street.

## NOTES

1. In particular, I consider the readings of two prominent feminist critics: Jane Marcus and Susan M. Squier. Marcus is, undoubtedly, the best known and most influential feminist critic on Woolf, as her collections of feminist essays that I discuss in the Introduction well testify. And Squier deals directly with the social and political function of Woolf's essays considered here in *Virginia Woolf and London*.

2. Marcus explains the "mule" and "horse" distinction in such a way as to show its inapplicability to Woolf's essay (267), then she goes on in the next paragraph to grapple with this distinction in *Three Guineas*. She calls *Three Guineas* satirical, then quotes Woolf to argue that such a complex position defeats satire. She compares Woolf's essay style with Sydney Smith's in its wit and humor, then asserts that Woolf's essay is not in the least amusing. And she calls Woolf's essay "passionate" at one point, "unemotional" at another (273, 278). There is a point to the contradictions in Woolf's essay, but contradictions do not function in the same way in Marcus's.

3. It is somewhat unclear whether Marcus is referring to the essay Woolf pub-

lished in the *Daily Worker* or to the argument on art and propaganda in *Three Guineas;* yet later, she refers again to Woolf's "avoidance of rhetoric" in *Three Guineas* ("No More Horses" 274).

4. De Quincey was one of Woolf's favorite authors, and many of his remarks about writing in these essays can be found in Woolf's essays on him, in particular, "De Quincey's Autobiography" (SCR) and "Impassioned Prose" (GR).

5. The concept of exchange is discussed in greater depth in conjunction with *The London Scene* essays in this chapter and in relation to *Flush* in the next chapter. In *Three Guineas,* Woolf points out the power of the wealthy giver to impose terms on the poor recipient and even gives way to the impulse herself throughout the essay, making the act of charity both gracious and pernicious (48).

6. This view of the outsider's position not only refutes the thirties poets' kind of detachment but also seems to confirm the postmodernist's sense of involvement. In *The Postmodern Condition,* Lyotard writes: "No one, not even the least privileged among us, is ever entirely powerless over the messages that traverse and position him at the post of sender, addressee, or referent" (15). Choosing a certain position or response to these power relations means "choosing how society can answer" (13). Sharing this view may be one reason Stimpson calls the author of *Three Guineas* "the postmodernist Virginia Woolf," not only because of her call for an Outsiders Society, but, more importantly, because of her wariness of essential unities, common identities, dominant discourses, and right positions that would impose some kind of consensus on the outsiders ("Nancy Reagan Wears a Hat").

7. Waugh also points to Woolf's recognition in *Three Guineas* that women in particular have little to choose at the present (*Feminine Fictions* 125).

8. Solomon-Godeau makes a similar point in "Living with Contradictions." When the market is into every form of production, she says (as in Woolf's capitalistic London), then "the notion of an 'outside' of the commodity system becomes increasingly untenable. . . . a critical practice must be predicated on its ability to sustain critique from within the heart of the system it seeks to put in question" (207). I elaborate on this point later in this chapter.

9. This is a point Linda Orr made in a lecture on Kafka's use of humor, delivered at the University of Virginia in the fall of 1986. Bakhtin, in *Rabelais and His World,* claims laughter as a subversive strategy as well. In chapter 2 of *The Pinter Problem,* Quigley discusses how we can impose a different kind of context on a potentially threatening situation to force our adversaries to respond differently. "It would seem," he writes, "that relationships are subject to verbal negotiation, even verbal imposition, in ways of which we may not be fully aware, while being constantly engaged in the process nevertheless" (49).

10. Lanham and Cassirer both discuss the Sophists' teaching of language as training us in ways of behaving, responding, and surviving in our social and political world. The Sophists emphasize out the pragmatic function of language, the way it compels certain responses and prompts certain actions, rather than the positivistic use of language to identify states and to name things in the world beyond. In a society where there is a lack of agreement on what the world should be like and where there is an inequity in the distribution of power, learning to use language

"to promote the responses one wishes to receive" is not irresponsible but crucial (Quigley, *Pinter Problem* 50–51).

11. This is very similar to an argument Robbe-Grillet makes in *For a New Novel* when he discusses our tendency to consider the style of a piece of writing as "innocent," as "no more than a means" to the raison d'être of the work, "the story it tells" (30). The story is judged not by how entertaining it is but by how convincing it is. Telling a story to divert, says Robbe-Grillet, is considered by many to be "a waste of time" (34). While this distinction between writing to divert and entertain and writing to convince and reassure seems arbitrary, it does point to the different conceptions of reality bound up with these different motives: writing to convince accepts the world as redeemable and "convertible into cash" (Robbe-Grillet 29); writing to divert accepts it as changeable and "subject to verbal negotiation" (Quigley, *Pinter Problem* 49). See chapter 5 for more on this concept of wasting time.

12. In the rest of this chapter and in the next, I articulate my approach in terms of Squier's reading because she is the only Woolf critic to give any sustained attention to these writings on London's social-economic system. By testing out my reading against Squier's, I argue against the untenable position her reading puts Woolf in, but I also want to acknowledge the significance for Woolf criticism of Squier's attention to these particular works and issues.

13. With the exception of "Portrait of a Londoner," these essays are collected in *The London Scene,* first published by Frank Hallman in 1974.

14. Squier recognizes this tendency in Woolf's writing in her reading of *Mrs. Dalloway:* "Yet careful study of the novel suggests that [Woolf] wanted to do more than merely juxtapose two opposed ways of living; rather, she wanted to transcend the very habit of thinking in dualities, and to criticize a society based upon such habitual polarization" (*Woolf and London* 93). Though it is doubtful that one can *transcend* a mode of thinking, one can reveal the limitations of thinking in terms of dualities, which is my goal here.

15. In *The Daughter's Seduction,* Gallop writes of Irigaray's reading of Freud's theory of sexuality: "questions of pleasure are excluded . . . in an economy of production" (67).

16. Pechter points out a weakness in the new historicists that I point out in the feminists considered here. They see power as reified "in a particular set of dominant institutions" rather than as potential in a variety of discursive strategies. One indication of this view, Pechter notes, is the way these critics "ignore the contrasting rhetorical situations of the texts they discuss" (297).

17. Squier acknowledges this situation in her comment on Woolf's language in "Street Haunting": "To condemn Woolf because she reproduces in her language the voice of the dominant culture is to condemn her for a tautology. She speaks in the language of the culture which has oppressed her because, as a contemporary woman writer, she has no other language" (*Woolf and London* 49). Squier seem to recognize the writer's necessary implication in cultural systems; however, she simplifies the complex relations Woolf explores by speaking in terms of oppositions, that is, dominant and muted languages. Squier implies, then, that such complicity

is an unfortunate situation, even an error we can now correct. Woolf, by contrast, seems to argue that it is not a matter of overthrowing the "dominant" language but of learning to use language in more than one way.

18. Naremore, Middleton, and Radin all bring out this connection in *The Years*.

19. In *For a New Novel*, Robbe-Grillet points out the difficulties with the kind of social criticism Squier pursues: "Of course, the idea of a possible conjunction between an artistic renewal and a politico-economic revolution is one of those which come most naturally to mind. This idea, initially seductive from the emotional viewpoint, also seems to find support in the most obvious logic. Yet the problems raised by such a union are serious and difficult, urgent but perhaps insoluble" (35).

20. This is not a simple historical contrast between past (traditional) values and present (modern) ones, for the values of the past persist in the modern moralist. Nor is it a simple contrast between permanent and impermanent value systems, for permanency is an "illusion" produced by certain values. And the first-person plural refers not to members of a certain class or gender only but to those sharing an age and an attitude. In other words, we are not talking about an absolute distinction but a variable and contextual one.

21. Smith continues: "That means we must appreciate that language *is* action, both speaking it and also listening to it, and that it always operates through the use and control of other people. Like all other economic markets, the linguistic market is never an altogether free one: it can be rigged, and it can be floated with counterfeit currency; the exchanges are not always conducted between those on an otherwise equal footing and, when attended by the machinery of political power, the control exerted and services exacted through language can be literally killing. We sometimes speak of language as a *game*—in the sense that, like games, it is a form of behavior governed by rules. But, in that sense, so is trade, so is politics, and so is war. If they are games, they are all games that are played for real" (*Margins* 105). This passage gets at the point of Woolf's investigation not only of these different sections of London but also of the different effects of different language games.

22. Austin writes: "Accuracy and morality alike are on the side of plain saying that *our word is our bond*" (10). The concept of excess is discussed further in the next chapter.

23. In my discussion here, I implicitly take issue with a common choice foisted on postmodernism. Either postmodernism is subversive of existing literary conventions and social-economic structures and is celebrated as such, or postmodernism is complicitous with existing social, economic, and commercial systems and is denigrated as such. Graff and Newman both represent the latter view quite clearly, Lyotard and Jardine (*Gynesis*) present the former, perhaps less clearly, and Jameson seems to hover somewhere in between, but leaning toward the latter. This kind of choice is similar to the one set up by feminist critics of Woolf who want to celebrate Woolf's works that seem to resist the social system while dismissing as weak or evasive those works that seem to comply with the system. My pragmatic position is to refuse this kind of choice and to demonstrate that what is perceived to be complicitous in one context can be resistant in another, and what is touted

as a liberating gesture may rely on the same kind of rhetoric and the same kind of activity as the position it claims to oppose. Compare Hutcheon's position in *A Poetics of Postmodernism*.

24. In her chapter on *Flush,* Squier compares Flush's "marginal position in human society" with Elizabeth Barrett Browning's in patriarchal society (125) and concludes that only from such a "marginal position in the social household can any serious housecleaning be done" (136). But the question is, does Woolf want to do some serious housecleaning? I do not mean to agree with Forster (*Virginia Woolf* 9), who remarks that Woolf eschewed politics because she felt men should clean up their own messes. Rather, I argue that Woolf resisted the notion of society as a household or a piece of property. Not only does such a notion lead to provincial attitudes (the economic problem is England's problem, or America's problem, or Germany's problem) but it also fosters the desires she criticizes in *Three Guineas* and the attitudes she criticizes in the thirties poets. Woolf writes, "as a woman, I have no country. As a woman I want no country. As a woman my country is the whole world" (TG 125). She expresses an attitude toward society that is associated with a postmodern culture: worldly rather than provincial, exoteric rather than elitist, performative rather than territorial.

25. In an essay on De Quincey, Woolf writes that the prose writer who "has a practical aim in view, a theory to argue, or a cause to plead" adopts "the moralist's view that the remote, the difficult, and the complex are to be abjured" (SCR 119). Such a motive for writing compels the writer to "express himself as clearly as possible in order to reach the greatest number in the plainest way" (119).

26. Jameson makes a similar comment on Barthes' style: "The very function of the style's artificiality is to announce itself as a metalanguage, to signal by its own impermanence the essential formlessness and ephemerality of the object itself" (*Prison-House* 154). The object itself, I suggest, is not simply the language of the text but the social order bound up with it.

27. Recall Woolf's "mere gift, unapplied gift" (AWD 134). Similarly, Squier reads Woolf's revision of one passage in "The Docks of London" as transforming her harsh description of slum conditions into a "visual discomfort" and an "architectural disorder," and she complains that "facts . . . have melted into atmosphere" (54). Squier seems to privilege facts (hard, measurable substances) over atmosphere (style and rhetoric).

28. Commenting on what she sees as the modernist, particularly Bergsonian, conception of identity expressed in "Street Haunting," Waugh says: "It carries, however, what seem to be *post*modernist reverberations in the insistence on the illusory wholeness of the subject, a dispersed subject rather than one defined in terms of organic coherence" (*Feminine Fictions* 95).

29. Discussing the various theories that compare art with play, Cassirer distinguishes between the two activities by stressing that "the child plays with *things,* the artist plays with *forms*" (164). Writing on Jameson's critical approach, Culler distinguishes the relationship between a literary work and its social-historical reality not as one of "reflected content" but rather as "a play of forms" (*Pursuit of Signs* 12–13).

30. Discussing the change in political questions (and, I would add, critical

questions) brought about by postmodernism, Ross asserts: "there are no necessary links, for example, between the interests of women and the interests of workers. These links have to be *articulated* . . . from contest to contest, and from moment to moment" (xiv). It is this postmodern insight that I see informing Woolf's *London Scene* essays.

31. Lyotard writes: "We know today that the limits the institution imposes on potential language 'moves' are never established once and for all (even if they have been formally defined). Rather, the limits are themselves the stakes and provisional results of language strategies, within the institution and without" (17).

32. Lanham observes that, in discussing the relation between literature and life, we often "search for the dogmatic ingredient in literature rather than the stylistic ingredient in life" (82). In his lecture on postmodern art at the Penn State Conference on Rhetoric and Composition, July 1985, he used the purpose/play contrast to distinguish modern seriousness from postmodern play.

33. In *The Pinter Problem,* Quigley writes: "Mutual certainty about language is also certainty about a shared reality" (62).

34. Flax would seem to concur: "Feminist theories, like other forms of postmodernism, should encourage us to tolerate ambivalence, ambiguity, and multiplicity as well as to expose the roots of our need for imposing order and structure" (643).

# 5

## *Flush* and the Literary Canon: *The Value of Popular Appeal*

> That silly book *Flush*—oh, what a waste of time!
>
> —Virginia Woolf,
> Diary, 1933

> Never stay up on the barren heights of cleverness but come down into
> the green valleys of silliness.
>
> —Ludwig Wittgenstein,
> *Culture and Value*

At the time Woolf was writing her *London Scene* essays, she was also working on *Flush*, her mock biography of Elizabeth Barrett Browning's cocker spaniel. Upon its publication in 1933, *Flush* was an immediate popular success, Woolf's best-selling novel in England and a Book-of-the-Month Club alternate selection in America (Kirkpatrick 57; Majumbar and McLaurin 5).[1] And that very popularity has contributed to the novel's critical neglect. In fact, *Flush* may well be the only text by Woolf that no critic has yet made a case for as canonical, whether in terms of Woolf's modernist canon or her feminist one. That lack of distinction is its mark of value for my reading. As the only novel by Woolf to have received very little critical attention, *Flush* raises useful questions about the value of popular appeal and about the relation of high art to popular art. Such a relation is, of course, a prominent issue in postmodern criticism. In this chapter I want to attend to the implications of my readings of Woolf for our concepts of the literary canon and literary value and thereby reconsider our common assumption about the dissolution of boundaries between elitist art and popular culture in postmodern and feminist writing.

My method throughout has been to focus on a particular problem in Woolf criticism, noting the difficulties in the common approaches to it and drawing on a postmodern aesthetics to reconceive the issue at hand. That pattern must be altered here, for the issue under consideration—how to deal with *Flush* and its popular success—is a non-issue in Woolf criticism. The common response is not to deal with it at all.[2] And so, I begin instead by focusing on an argument frequently made in postmodern, as well as feminist, criticism and use *Flush,* as a popular text, to reconceive the terms of that argument.

A common characterization of postmodern art is that it effaces the boundary between high culture and popular culture, intermingling elements of a modernist or elitist aesthetics with a popular or commercialized one. Such intermingling can be seen, for example, in the use of popular genres, such as the spy novel or the romance, by postmodern writers like Calvino and Fowles, or in the cultural bricolage of works by Barthelme and Acker, and Woolf's *Between the Acts* (see chap. 1). It is often argued (as I argue in the Preface) that, whereas modernist art defines itself *against* mass culture, commercial society, and popular appeal, postmodern art defines itself *in relation to* popular culture. For example, Patricia Waugh remarks that postmodernism and feminism "have embraced the popular, rejecting the elitist and purely formalist celebration of modernism" (*Feminine Fictions* 3). Here elitist or modernist art is linked to purely formal concerns, while popular or postmodern art is seen to integrate art with everyday life (6). By mixing high and popular culture, Waugh notes, these writers democratize art by recuperating the marginal and undermining canonized forms.

And yet, as both Michael Levenson and Joyce Wexler argue, modernist writers were not all, or always, writing against the populace or popularity; and as Laura Kipnis and Lawrence Grossberg assert, postmodernism has not always been on the side of the populace, nor has it necessarily been popular. Moreover, E. Ann Kaplan raises an important question for our task here when she asks in "Feminism/Oedipus/Postmodernism: The Case of MTV" whether or not this dissolution of the boundary between high art and popular culture is "the same" in a commercial context as in an academic one (34). It would seem that such oppositions and reconciliations between the high and the low are never simple, that there is more to be said about this relation. Thus, I ask what difference it might make to look at this relation from the perspective of *Flush,* Woolf's commercial success, rather than from the perspective of *Between the Acts,* an academic text, as I have done in chapter 1.

Such a perspective requires a different approach, one to be found (as we will see) in a popular aesthetics as well as in postmodern theory. Andreas Huyssen, for example, approaches this issue somewhat differently, and more usefully, when he argues that postmodernism bears a different relation to the categorical (not absolute) distinction between high art and popular art than does modernism. It is not, Huyssen asserts, that distinctions between good art and kitsch (or between high art and popular art) can no longer be made but that reducing all criticism to "the problem of quality" reflects the modernist "anxiety of contamination," the modernist tendency, that is, to enforce such distinctions as a way of defining and assuring its own autonomy, self-sufficiency, and vanguard position (vii-ix).[3] This change in relation, I suggest, can be seen in the shift from Nietzsche's thinking (often associated with modernism) to Wittgenstein's (often associated with postmodernism) as expressed in the following passage from Wittgenstein's *Culture and Value:* "Nietzsche writes somewhere that even the best poets and thinkers have written stuff that is mediocre and bad, but have *separated off* the good material. But it is not quite like that. It's true that a gardener, along with his roses, keeps manure and rubbish and straw in his garden, but what distinguishes them is not just their value, but mainly their *function* in the garden" (59e; emphasis added). Thus, if postmodern art challenges modernist values by drawing on popular culture, it may not blur distinctions so much as it reconceives our ways of drawing distinctions and reassesses, in Huyssen's words, our "canonized notions of quality" (ix). It is such a reassessment that I undertake in this chapter on *Flush*.

Considering the function *Flush* performs in Woolf's canon can effect a change in our way of valuing so that distinguishing absolutely between high art and popular art, canonical texts and marginal texts, or valuable fiction and worthless fiction is no longer worthwhile, no longer a valuable service rendered by critics and teachers of literature. If, in a canonical economy, value is produced by the process of "separating off" the wastes or impurities, then in considering the relation of *Flush* to the literary canon, it just might pay to read *Flush* not as a marginal text but as a waste product, the excess of a canonical economy.[4] The payoff of such a reading will take on a different economic value, the "yield" being measured not by the profits produced but by the by-products produced and "to yield something" meaning not to produce a solid return on an investment, that is, not to gain something, but to give up something, to relinquish a possession or a position. Reading *Flush* may lead to a noneconomical, what Barbara Herrnstein Smith terms a "noncanonical," theory of value ("Contingencies of Value" 7).

Since readers of *Flush* are nearly nonexistent, I must begin with a rough sketch of the novel.[5] The biography traces Flush's life from his puppyhood in the rural home of Mary Russell Mitford (chap. 1), to his seclusion in Elizabeth Barrett's bedroom at her father's Wimpole Street home (chap. 2), to his jealous confrontation and subsequent reconciliation with Robert Browning (chap. 3), to his kidnapping by Mr. Taylor's gang from lower-class Whitechapel (chap. 4), to his escape to Italy with the Brownings (chap. 5), to his death of old age in Florence (chap. 6). Not surprisingly, given my focus in this chapter, Woolf's book can be read as an allegory of canon formation and canonical value, for Flush's life tells us much about ways of valuing.

For example, Woolf devotes the first chapter largely to a discussion of pedigree, in both canine and human aristocracies. Good breeding comes about from the desire to preserve the purity of the "family" (whether canine, human, or literary), which means common ancestors and right alliances (F 7–8). And yet, the canine aristocracy seems much superior to the human; for if we are to distinguish between superior and inferior breeding, it is best to have definitive distinctions. What enables us to identify a good spaniel are visible traits—ears, noses, coats, topknots, or the absence thereof—while the signs of a human aristocrat are much less defined by virtue of being extrinsic, not intrinsic—the spelling of one's name, a coat of arms, or an income, all of which can be changed or bought or spent, unlike ears and noses and topknots. Thus, Flush can be considered a "pure-bred . . . marked by all the characteristic excellences of his kind" (10) because those traits are visible and unchanging, while the absence of clearly defined and visible standards allows a human aristocrat to lose his standing and authority and, worse yet, allows for impurities in breeding. What are the signs of such impurity? In Dr. Mitford's case, extravagance for one (8–9). Wasteful spending is the most fatal mark, for in Wimpole Street, which establishes the laws of good breeding, "such extravagance would not be allowed" (18).

Purity, efficiency, frugality, definitive standards, and right relations—these would seem to be the signs of good breeding. If *Flush* is an allegory of canonicity, then so far it would seem that Woolf is advocating some standard measurement of value for literary texts so that we might at once distinguish between superior and inferior works. However, the desire to draw such distinctions is what Woolf confounds in this novel. Even in the case of Flush, who has all the markings of good breeding, value proves to be contextual and variable. Flush is unaware of his status as an aristocrat of dogs until he moves to "the most august of London streets" (15). In Wimpole Street he learns that "dogs are not equal" (31) and comes to realize the privileges and penalties of his class: he drinks from a purple jar, but he is led on a chain. Even those intrinsic signs of the aristocrat, it would seem, depend on context and circumstance for their value. This becomes most apparent when Flush moves to Italy, where "there were no ranks" (112), and discovers that "the laws of the Kennel Club are not universal," that he must adopt a "new conception of canine society" (116–17). There Flush learns that freedom from rankings means freedom from tyranny (118) and that to be "nothing," to cut no figure in the world, is "the most satisfactory state" (135).

Flush's value, then, varies from context to context, in part because Flush is both a pure-bred (valuable in itself) and a commodity (valuable in what it can be exchanged for). That is, not just the lack of visible and universal standards undermines the aristocracy (or the canon), but so does the larger economy of value. Flush is not just a good cocker spaniel with the right markings, he is an economic good—something to be bought, exchanged, stolen, ransomed. In the country Flush's value is established when Dr. Pusey offers to purchase Flush, indicating that "there must have been something serious, solid, promising well for future excellence whatever might be the levity of the present in Flush even as a puppy" (13). Flush promises a good return in the future. Yet Miss Mitford refuses to sell him: "He was of the rare order of objects that cannot be associated with money" (14). This is an even greater testimony to his worth: Flush is priceless. As such, he becomes "a fitting token of the disinterestedness of friendship" (nothing is expected in return) and so Miss Mitford gives Flush to Miss Barrett as a gift (14). But once in the city, Flush is stolen, not because of his breeding, but because he is now the property of a lady. He is still of value, but the mark of value has changed: Flush's worth is determined by his market price, not by his markings. While the lesson of canonicity teaches us to distinguish literature that is worth our time from literature that wastes our time by identifying its distinctive, intrinsic, universal traits, *Flush* reveals that such value is variable. "All value," writes Smith, "is radically contingent, being neither an inherent property of objects nor an arbitrary projection of subjects but, rather, the product of the dynamics of an economic system" ("Contingencies of Value" 11). *Flush* shows us that aesthetic value (considered intrinsic) and economic value (determined by exchange worth) are "interactive and interdependent" (Smith 12). Flush is an aristocrat of dogs and a hot commodity; *Flush* is an aesthetic phenomenon and a social-economic product.

This interdependence of the two realms of value is foregrounded by Flush's kidnapping, which exposes the relationship between Wimpole Street and Whitechapel. The squalor, the violence, and the market transactions of Whitechapel exist "cheek by jowl" with "the most aristocratic parishes," throwing "doubts upon the solidity even of Wimpole Street itself": "Mixed up with that respectability was this filth" (F 78–80 passim). The relationship is not one of physical proximity and economic dependence only—"St. Giles's stole what St. Giles's could; Wimpole Street paid what Wimpole Street must" (81)—it is moral as well, as is made clear by Robert Browning's stand against the tyranny not just of thieves like Mr. Taylor but of patriarchs like Mr. Barrett.[6] Browning urges Elizabeth

Barrett not to perpetuate oppression by giving way to Taylor's demands for ransom: "So," reflects Elizabeth Barrett, "if she went to Whitechapel she was siding against Robert Browning and in favour of fathers, brothers and domineers in general" (93–94). Nonetheless, she goes to Whitechapel and pays the ransom, thereby giving way to and shoring up tyranny but also expressing a different value system. While Mr. Taylor, Mr. Browning, and Mr. Barrett are all concerned with what might be gained in this transaction—whether a sufficient monetary return (Taylor) or the correct moral position (Barrett and Browning)—Elizabeth Barrett is concerned with what might be discarded in the process—namely, Flush. Thus, we see that good values (liberty) and bad values (tyranny) cannot be so easily distinguished if Robert Browning, who liberates Elizabeth Barrett from her father's tyranny, sides with the father against Flush's liberty, and if Elizabeth Barrett, who is the last person to promote the tyranny of patriarchs, does just that to gain Flush's freedom. When it comes to values, context is everything.

In this sense *Flush* can be said to present what Stanley Aronowitz terms "the postmodern stance toward the canon": "good stuff is good stuff regardless of its pedigree" (26). As a mock biography, *Flush* undercuts the very value system that informs the biographer's craft, as well as the critic's, by revealing not only the variability and contingency of value (whether of the individual subject or the individual text) but also the implication of intrinsic (aesthetic) value in exchange (economic) value.[7] The interdependence of these two realms of value, which are so often considered to be opposing, is shown as well in Woolf's early motives for writing *Flush*. In fact, Woolf's changing use of *Flush* has as much to do with its subsequent evaluation as does its parody of canonical values. As Smith argues, a writer's process of composition not only throws light on the writer's own way of valuing literature but also prefigures readers' evaluations of that writing: "It will be instructive at this point to consider the very beginning of a work's valuational history, namely, its initial evaluation by the artist (here, the author); for it is not only a prefiguration of all the subsequent acts of evaluation of which the work will become the subject but also a model or paradigm of all evaluative activity in general" ("Contingencies of Value" 24). Therefore, in pursuit of the value of *Flush*, it will be instructive to turn to Woolf's initial evaluation of it as revealed in her diaries, letters, and other writings during the years she was working on this novel.[8]

Woolf began *Flush* in July 1931, as she was completing *The Waves*, and published it in early October 1933, when she was deeply absorbed in *The Pargiters*. (*Flush* was serialized in the *Atlantic Monthly* during July, August, and September 1933). During this time, it is important to note, she was also working on many other pieces, including her early versions of *Three Guineas*, her *Second Common Reader*, and, as mentioned, her *London Scene* essays. In a letter to Ottoline Morrell, dated February 23, 1933, Woolf has provided what many take to be the origin of *Flush*, in a sort of "family" joke: "Flush is only by way of a joke. I was so tired after the Waves, that I lay in the garden and read the Browning letters, and the figure of their dog made me laugh so I couldn't resist making him a life. I wanted to play a joke on Lytton—it was a parody of him" (Letters 5:161–62). Similar comments scattered throughout her letters and diaries sanction the typical view of *Flush*, that it was a "diversion"—or, as Woolf put it, a "freak."[9] After writing a tough modernist work like *The Waves* or *To the Lighthouse*, so the conventional wisdom goes, Woolf needed to unwind with something frivolous, like *Flush* or *Orlando*. But the desire to unwind and to play a joke on Lytton Strachey were not Woolf's only motives for writing *Flush*. In fact, her earliest references to the book make no mention of Strachey or relaxation but focus instead on two very different motivations. In a diary entry for August 16, 1931, the first mention of *Flush*, Woolf writes: "It is a good idea I think to write biographies; to make them use my powers of representation reality accuracy; & to use my novels simply to express the general, the poetic. Flush is serving this purpose" (Diary 4:40). For Woolf, then, *Flush* was not pointless but served a purpose, a purpose *The Years* served as well; both pieces provided relief, not from hard work, but from *one* kind of writing. But a month later, Woolf reveals yet another motivation in a letter to Vita Sackville-West in which she requests a picture of Vita's dog:

> That reminds me—have you a photograph of Henry? I ask for a special reason, connected with a little escapade by means of wh. I hope to stem the ruin we shall suffer from the failure of The Waves.
> This is the worst publishing season on record. No bookseller dares buy. (Letters 4:380)

In short, Woolf wrote *Flush* to sell.

In other words, nearly a year before Woolf raised the issue of *Flush* as a joke and a diversion, she took it seriously as a literary exercise and a profit-making enterprise. Certainly, these early motives do not supersede the later ones, but they do form an often neglected part of that work's valuational history, in particular, the intermingling of aesthetic and economic values. Yet critics have taken one set of evaluative remarks by Woolf—that *Flush* was silly, a joke, a waste of time—as the definitive assessment of the value of that work, thereby obfuscating the very relations at issue here.

To cite Smith again, evaluative acts, including the author's, represent "a set of individual economic decisions, an adjudication among competing claims for limited resources of time, space, energy, attention"—or, of course, "money" ("Contingencies of Value" 25). Not only did Woolf have many "competing claims" on her time while writing *Flush,* but her use of those various projects also changed over time. In fact, when we look at what happened in the intervening year between Woolf's initial evaluations that took *Flush* seriously and her later ones that dismissed it as a joke, we find that *The Waves* sold—six weeks after writing to Vita predicting its failure, Woolf wrote to her American publishers thanking them for a $950 check (Letters 4:399)—and that *The Pargiters* began to consume more and more of her time, allowing her to exercise her representational powers and sharpen her social critique. That is, the functions *Flush* initially served were being fulfilled elsewhere, which is not to say that *Flush* no longer served any purpose; rather, Woolf began to emphasize the joke and the freak of writing *Flush,* giving that work a different value for herself and setting up the possibility of a different value to be gained by reading it. And the death of Lytton Strachey in January 1932 may well have changed the point of the joke.

All these changes clearly demonstrate what Smith means by "paradigm of evaluative activity":

> The work we receive is not so much the achieved consummation of [the entire process of composition] as its enforced abandonment: "abandonment" not because the author's techniques are inadequate to his or her goals but because the goals themselves are inevitably multiple, mixed, mutually competing, and thus mutually constraining, and also because they are inevitably unstable, changing their nature and relative potency and priority during the very course of composition. ("Contingencies of Value" 24)

Such competing and changing goals are what our canonized notion of value cannot account for, focused as it is on the end product rather than the composition process, and concerned with distinguishing between the good and the mediocre rather than among various functions. But if we consider the many claims on Woolf's time while writing *Flush,* and her changing uses of that book, we see that what we get in *Flush* is less the "abandonment" of a project that did not pay off than the "excess" of a composition process that changed over the two years Woolf worked on the novel. Thus, I want neither to deny that *Flush* is silly nor to accept its silliness as a sufficient reason not to take it seriously as a work of literature.[10] Indeed, when we look at the entire twenty-five-month period of *Flush*'s production and initial reception, rather than isolating a few comments from Woolf's diaries, we discover not only a complex valuational history but a more conflicted aesthetics than critics of Woolf have yet considered. Such a conflicted aesthetics, I argue, cannot be accounted for in any useful way by simply attaching a label (e.g., feminist or postmodernist) to Woolf's works.

Once Woolf "abandoned" *Flush* with its publication in October 1933, it became a popular success, one she predicted yet dreaded: "Flush will be out on Thursday & I shall be very much depressed, I think, by the kind of praise. They'll say its 'charming' delicate, ladylike. And it will be popular. . . . And I shall very much dislike the popular success of Flush" (Diary 4:181). Such dislike of popular appeal is surprising, given Woolf's increasing attention to the reader in her fiction and in her criticism, a point I return to later in this chapter and in the next. Such a response to popularity is also atypical since Woolf's prepublication anxieties usually express her fear that no one will read her work or take her seriously. Moreover, Woolf's fear of popularity clearly shows that her early motivations have changed. If she wrote *Flush* to make money, as she earlier said, then its popularity would have been desirable. But if *Flush* were merely a joke, then surely its popularity could have been embarrassing to a serious writer, especially if she were seen as simply "a ladylike prattler" (Diary 4:181). That is, Woolf may have feared this *particular* image, for she worried that reviewers would find *Flush* "charming"—which they did: "A book of irresistible grace and charm," Rose Macaulay wrote in the *Spectator* (Oct. 6, 1933: 450); even "a little too charming," said the reviewer for the *Christian Science Monitor* (Nov. 18, 1933:8). And certainly the danger of the label *ladylike* is that reviewers would dismiss the work as trivial or minor—which they also did.[11]

One could make much of this connection between the ladylike and the trivial, the feminine and the ornamental, popularity and loss of virility, especially in a modernist literary tradition in which maintaining standards meant resisting popular appeal.[12] But my interests here lie elsewhere. I want to argue that it is not just this *particular* figure Woolf feared becoming but a figure in general, a figure bred by popularity, and it is her desire for change that can help to explain her anxieties about the publication of *Flush*.

The fact that Woolf was working on so many pieces during the years of *Flush*'s composition demonstrates that her goals as a writer were "multiple, mixed[, and] mutually competing." In addition to these various projects, however, we find in Woolf's diary at this time arguments for the very variety of motives and goals that her writings evidence. Over and over again, she stresses the value of *change:* "I believe in forever altering one's aspect to the sun" (Diary 4:125); "No critic ever gives full weight to the desire of the mind for change" (145); "I want to seethe myself in something new—to break the mould of habit entirely" (151); "One must grow

& change" (186; written in response to a negative review of *Flush*). *Flush*, it seems, is not so much the capricious text it is so often asserted to be as it is a consequence of valuing capriciousness.

Here we can see the consequences of my reading of Woolf's nonfiction writing of this time (chap. 4) for understanding her resistance to popularity in spite of her increasing concern with the relation of art to its audience. Woolf feared popularity, I suggest, because popularity breeds fame and fame fixes one in an image. In a diary entry in March 1932, in response to the publication of two new books on her work, Woolf cautions herself: "I must not settle into a figure" (Diary 4:85). And throughout *Three Guineas*, a book vying for her attention while she was writing *Flush*, Woolf disparages advertisement and publicity, which she associates with male desires for power, property, position, and prestige. "We must extinguish the coarse glare of advertisement and publicity," she writes, for the "limelight" freezes one in an image, much as headlights paralyze a rabbit (TG 131). That is, publicity inhibits change: "the power to change and the power to grow, can only be preserved by obscurity" (132). If *Flush* expresses Woolf's desire for change, her resistance to settling into a figure, and if publicity breeds fame and freezes one in an image, then Woolf might well have feared the popular success of *Flush*.

This "advertisement function," as Woolf argues in *Three Guineas*, partakes of a larger cultural economy bound up with property and profit, aspirations Woolf connected with patriarchy (TG 24, 76, 82, 86, 93). In a 1932 diary entry on *Three Guineas*, she reminds herself that "the male virtues are never for themselves, but to be paid for . . . what will pay" (Diary 4:95). By "what will pay," Woolf could not have meant just money, for she certainly was not against making money from her writing. Indeed, in response to Logan Pearsall Smith's attack on serious writers who publish in fashion magazines, she wrote to a friend: "What he wants is prestige: what I want, money" (Letters 3:154). And earning her own money was precisely what Woolf called the preeminent freedom for a woman, the only right worth fighting for (TG 117). Rather, by "what will pay," I would argue, she meant what will pay *off*, in the sense of leading to a firm position, that is, resulting in some product to be possessed or some position to be defended. The economic metaphor is a metaphor for an end-oriented value system, one that Woolf treats more fully in her *London Scene* essays and one that implicates an aesthetic system in a social-economic system. As we have seen in the preceding chapter, Woolf celebrates Oxford Street not just because of its egalitarian social order, mixing the high and the low, but, more importantly, because of its basis in different values and desires: the desire to build for the moment only, to produce disposable structures of value. This change of value can help to explain Woolf's desire to write for popular journals (such as *Vogue* and *Good Housekeeping*) despite her resistance to *Flush*'s popularity.

We can interpret Woolf's fear of being popular not as a fear of losing standards or status but as a fear of being solidified, a fear of the permanence that can come with popularity—or rather, a fear of the permanence associated with popularity in a certain economy, whether market or literary. This is, of course, what has happened to Woolf as she has become part of the literary canon: she has taken on a certain value by assuming a certain position, either the preeminent female modernist or the preeminent feminist writer. But in a different kind of economy, a noncanonical economy, one that values disposable structures and transitory desires, one that is open-ended, not end-oriented, popularity might well be associated with change, not fame, or with fashion, as something inevitable, not superfluous. In such an economy, as Andy Warhol once said of a postmodern world, everyone will be famous for a few minutes only, which means not just that everyone's time will come (presumably because of the growth of advertisement and the decline of standards) but that everyone's time must pass.

On the one hand, then, and from the perspective of some modernists, like Pearsall Smith and T. S. Eliot, popular success is undesirable because it is ephemeral, fashionable, spurious.[13] On the other hand, and from the perspective of Woolf and some postmodernists, like Pynchon, popular success may be undesirable because it makes one into a representative figure to be celebrated (the feminist modernist) or dismissed (the ladylike prattler). We see that popular appeal can be undesirable for other than canonical reasons (i.e., its transience, its complicity with the masses); in fact, it can be undesirable when it functions in a postmodern economy as canonical appeal functions in a modernist one, by promoting a certain representative writer, type of writing, or experience.[14]

Woolf's resistance to fame takes place in an economy (not just a capitalist market economy but a modernist literary economy) that makes such a stand untenable, and so it is not surprising to find that even as she disparages fame, permanence, and publicity, she values just those things. In July 1932, on the publication of her essay "A Letter to a Young Poet," Woolf writes: "my poet letter passes unnoticed," regretting its failure to attract attention (Diary 4:119).[15] Ironically, this essay, addressed to John Lehmann, advises the poet against publishing too early, against desiring fame, against becoming a figure. Woolf argues instead that since the poet is part of a larger literary tradition, a composite figure, not a unique personality, writing to satisfy the popular taste in literature is neither to court fame nor to pander to the populace; rather, it is to play a role: "There's no harm in it, *so long as you take it as a joke,* but once you believe in it, once you begin to take yourself seriously as a leader or as a follower . . . then you become a self-conscious, biting, scratching little animal whose work is not of the slightest value or importance to anyone" (DM 221–22; emphasis added). Later Woolf reminds herself, in response to a negative review of *Flush,* that "fashion in literature is an inevitable thing" (Diary 4:186); she might have added, "There's no harm in it, so long as you take it as a joke"—which she did. To take *Flush* as a joke might not be to dismiss it but to keep from taking oneself too seriously as a leader or figure, to keep from taking a firm position, to keep from attributing to one's writing a permanent value.

Woolf wanted her poet letter to be read to voice an alternative value system, the value of obscurity and change that she expresses in *Flush* as well as in *Three Guineas* and "Oxford Street Tide"; however, such a value system works against the desire to be read and remembered, which is necessary if one is to promote an alternative. The desire to write popular fiction without courting fame or pandering to the populace, and the impossibility of that task *within a certain economy of value,* is, if not the theme of *Flush,* then at least its occasion. The valuational history of *Flush* (which includes Woolf's many writings of that time) shows the extent to which *Flush* is the product of a complex and conflicted aesthetics, one that reveals those "divergent systems of value" so often elided, as Smith ("Contingencies of Value" 7) and Woolf (CR 49) argue, in discussions of canonical texts. Such a "complex and conflicted" aesthetics is what Janice Radway finds in the popular aesthetics of the Book-of-the-Month Club (537), the popular aesthetics that made *Flush* famous, the kind of fame that led to its critical neglect.

From the perspective of a popular aesthetics, one way to popularize art without pandering to the masses or the marketplace, one way to change the canonical economy without appealing only to a special constituency or market—in short, one way to discuss the relation of high art to popular art in a postmodern literary economy—is to shift from thinking in terms of a one-to-one relation between literature and its users to thinking in terms of a variety of such relations. According to Radway's study of popular fiction, the BOMC divides its "amorphous category of general fiction" into "serious" and "commercial," with serious books often being offered as alternate selections, as *Flush* was (526, 529). Ironically, Woolf's commercial success, a book she called "silly," would have been classified as "serious" fiction by the BOMC editors. As Radway emphasizes throughout her article, by offering serious fiction to its readers, the BOMC recognizes that different kinds of books serve different kinds of functions for different kinds of readers (520, 526). That is, while "commercial concerns" may predominate in the selection process, Radway says, the BOMC also seeks to appeal to a wide variety of readers, not just to the *mass* market, with its alternate selections. The BOMC functions, then, neither as an elitist organization selecting books on the basis of "a single set of criteria" and thereby perpetuating a certain set of values (apparently the view the BOMC holds of the academic institution) nor as "a homogenizing mass-market distribution operation pitched . . . to the lowest common denominator" (apparently the view the academy holds of the BOMC; 518, 523). In this sense the BOMC could be seen to endorse a solution Woolf offers in *Three Guineas* to women writers who want to appeal to the public without pandering to popular tastes: "Find out new ways of approaching 'the public'; single it into separate people instead of massing it into one monster, gross in body, feeble in mind" (113).[16]

By dividing the public and by dividing fiction, the BOMC recognizes that different books provide different "social contracts" between writers and readers. Therefore, the classification of a book like *Flush* as "serious" fiction (and this point would hold, in turn, for its classification as "silly" fiction) tells us not what *Flush* is (good or bad fiction) but how it should be read (Radway 527).[17] That is, the classification of a text is not a sign of its value and function but serves to create that value and function, a point Smith makes when she discusses the "mutually defining relations among classification, function, and value" ("Contingencies of Value" 13). The value of popular appeal, then, may lie not in the mixing of aesthetic elements, or in the renewal of high art through what Ford, in *The Good Soldier,* terms *intellectual slumming*. Rather, it may work the other way around: namely, the popular success of a book like *Flush* may allow for a different attention to it and a different use of it, one that enables popular or "silly" fiction to function differently in commercial society, providing a different kind of social critique from "serious" fiction, yet no less imperative for all its silliness.[18]

Discriminating among books in terms of various functions rather than limited criteria marks the difference, Radway says, between a popular and a high-culture aesthetics. (I make the point in chapter 6 that discriminating among books in terms of various functions also marks the difference between Woolf's criticism and most criticism of her day.) What function, then, did the BOMC perceive *Flush* would serve for the general reader, and does (or how does) that function differ from the function it serves for the academic reader? According to Radway's analysis of the BOMC readers' reports, serious fiction functions for the general reader as "a model for contemporary living and even practical advice about appropriate behavior in a changing world" (535). By contrast, as Radway and Smith both assert, the academic reader defines aesthetic value against such practical value. Academic readers privilege language over representation, the artful over the useful, or intrinsic value over practical application, while the general reader values literature for its representative experience, its usefulness, its prescriptions for living (Radway 534–35). When we look at the initial reception of *Flush,* the early reviews show that readers did find in that "silly book" what the BOMC editors say "serious" fiction provides the general reader: a sense of reality, a consistent personality, a new voice, entertainment, and quality writing.[19] And passages in *Flush* would seem to support the value of art for life's sake over art for art's sake, thereby promoting the book's popular appeal.[20] This kind of distinction also makes sense in terms of Woolf's academic canon. After all, those novels first canonized (i.e., cited, studied, anthologized, sanctioned by course syllabi and graduate reading lists) are those that seem highly self-conscious about language (*To the Lighthouse, The Waves, Mrs. Dalloway*), and those not given much critical attention until recently are novels that seem to be most "representational." In fact, this very charge was leveled against *Night and Day* and *The Years* and thereby kept them off those academic reading lists, for they did not adequately represent Woolf's modernism. Most importantly, Woolf's first diary entry on *Flush* (quoted earlier)—that it prompted her to use her powers of representation—suggests that she shared the values of a popular aesthetics.

And she did share them, but not because she valued practical purpose over language play, or representational writing over writing for its own sake, but precisely because she refused finally to distinguish between the two and instead engaged in several kinds of writing at once.[21] In fact, Woolf claims (ironically) that those who do try to make such a separation are the "middlebrows," the term often applied to the BOMC readers. In her 1932 essay "Middlebrow," Woolf argues that the "highbrow" (one concerned with the art of writing) and the "lowbrow" (one concerned with the art of living) are inextricably related. It is the middlebrow who tries to come between them by making a distinction between art for art's sake and art for life's sake (DM 177–79). In making such a claim, Woolf presents an argument against the middlebrows that sounds much like Radway's argument against the elite who dismiss the BOMC as a middlebrow forum. Radway asserts: "To label the Club middlebrow, therefore, is . . . to legitimate the social role of the intellectual who has not only the ability but the authority to make such distinctions and to dictate them to others" (518). Similarly, Woolf argues, to label a writer a highbrow and to dismiss her or him as such is to legitimate the social role of the middle-class intellectual who has not only the ability and the authority (as a teacher) but the audacity (as a snob) to make such distinctions and to dictate them to others, namely lowbrows (DM 180, 183). Specifically, Woolf deplores how the middlebrows market their materialistic values as moralistic ones, for in teaching literature to the lowbrows, the middlebrows seek "money, fame, power, or prestige" (DM 180)—that is, what pays (off).

My point here is not to quibble over highbrows and middlebrows but to argue, as Woolf seems to have argued, that there is no high and low, no superior and inferior, until there is a middle, a medial, a market—that is, until there is a need for trade, for exchange. Further, I want to show how misplaced such debates are once we concern ourselves with the various functions of literature rather than its formal criteria. Just as Woolf divided her literary interests among many kinds of writing, the BOMC divides its commercial interests among many kinds of reading. This refusal to codify any one approach to literature or to promote any one set of values is what Woolf's work shares with a popular aesthetics. Radway writes, "The BOMC has never formalized its definition of serious fiction, its characterization of what it offers within the category, or its criteria for selection" (527); thus, it has never codified a reading method either. This "ambivalence about the nature of serious fiction," Radway says, reveals the conflict between its goals of promoting diversity in literary tastes on the one hand and "search[ing] for enduring excellence" on the other (524, 528). But the BOMC's interest in fiction, like Woolf's, is not in its *nature* (its characteristics) but in its *function* (its uses). This is an important distinction, for the BOMC editors sound most like the academic readers they seem to oppose when they try to define serious fiction by its traits in order to distinguish it from trash. They fall back on the same kind of language as the academic readers use, disparaging "linguistic excess" or "lush" writing (such as romances display) and praising "economy, condensation, and precision" (Radway 528). That is, good fiction meets its ends efficiently; it does not waste time. As Radway suggests, such a distinction between good fiction and trash is a "function, perhaps, of these readers' training" in academic institutions (527). Most certainly it is also the function of a canonical economy. As Jane Gallop argues in "The Problem of Definition," purifying by getting rid of the excess, the trash, is "a structure that is very tempting whenever one is establishing a canon" and is "inextricably linked to the problem of definition" (121, 129).[22]

Thus, the kind of distinction between the academic and popular that informs much postmodern criticism, where postmodern art (in its connection to popular art) is seen to (re)integrate art and life (e.g., Waugh, *Feminine Fiction* 6; Kaplan 34) while modernist art (in its opposition to the popular and the practical) is regarded as "purely formalist" (Waugh), serves to maintain, not dissolve, the gap between the high and the popular. I agree with Lawrence Grossberg when he argues that much postmodern criticism ignores the popular despite its claims of a collapse of the difference between high art and popular art, so that critics end up reading popular texts the same way they read high-culture texts (177). But I am also arguing something else. Where popular art differs from modernist or elitist art may not be in its concern for representation and practical value rather than for form and technique. Indeed, I would argue that the concept of literature as representative experience, offering a model for appropriate behavior in a changing world, is the very concept on which our debates over the canon rest, not the concept identifying a particular *kind* of literature (i.e., popular). Those who defend the canon assume good literature represents enduring human nature and common experiences, while those who challenge the canon assume that texts worth reading represent the particular experiences of particular types of individuals in a particular social-historical milieu. Elizabeth Fox-Genovese writes that "attacks on the canon derive primarily from the perception that it does not adequately represent the experience and identities of most of those who are expected to study it" (132), while defenses of the canon often rest on the belief that those who study it must come to share a common experience and a shared sense of identity. That is, literature represents experience either because it transcends its time or because it represents its kind.

However much these views may conflict when it comes to arguments over the inclusion or exclusion of particular texts in the canon, they rest on the same general assumptions about literature: namely, literature conveys knowledge about the world beyond, conveys truths about human experience, represents characteristic lives. Thinking of popular (or marginal) literature alone in terms of representative experience, thereby leaving the problem of form to elitist (or canonical) art, may be the sticking place in our debates over the canon, preventing us from acknowledging "divergent systems of value" as well as different concepts of literature. Where postmodern writing differs from modernist writing, then, is in its functional conception of literature and in its heterogeneous conception of mass culture. Once we accept that books perform many different functions for different audiences, and that mass culture is not one body or mind, then it no longer makes sense to distinguish popular and elitist art on the basis of any *one* criteria. Postmodernism not only bears a different relation to the "categorical distinction" between high and popular culture, as Huyssen says (viii), but it challenges the kind of thinking that assumes some single relation between art and experience, or art and its users. In other words, we might say, more usefully, that postmodernism does not *collapse* the distinction between the popular and the high culture but rejects the concepts of literature and culture on which such a distinction rests. To reject the distinction between popular culture and high culture is to abandon certain beliefs, such as the belief that literature is about life; it is not, however, to make a new claim about the *real* nature of that relation.[23]

The attempt to draw some clear-cut distinction between the valuable and the worthless, the "serious" fiction and the "trash," is the gesture of canon formation, while the attention to various functions for various people in various circumstances works against this kind of evaluative activity. Thus, the BOMC may function like the academy whenever it tries to establish a "single set of criteria" (whether distinctive features or distinctive functions) to differentiate two types of fiction. But if a popular aesthetics refuses a clear-cut separation between art and life, if it is made up of contradictory values, as Radway suggests, then it would seem that the search for its characteristic features or its absolute difference from the academic aesthetics would work against its very economy. A popular aesthetics, then, is not other than or opposed to a high-culture aesthetics but part of the same economy, yet it may function to expose what that economic system prefers to hide or ignore, that is, the refuse of the canonical economy. *Any* canon has its refuse, waste products that both attest to and give the lie to its efficiency and its purity. As "waste," *Flush* serves an important function in the literary economy to the extent that it reveals what canonical readings ignore, "an evaluative system . . . constructed of contradictory elements" (Radway 537), and thereby promotes different kinds of reading. The promotion of different kinds of reading has been my goal throughout this book, and as we will see in the next chapter, it was Woolf's goal as a critic.

We are now in a position to reconsider the different uses of fiction by general and academic readers. I turn, therefore, from the general reader (BOMC members and *Flush*'s early reviewers) to Susan Squier, perhaps the only academic reader besides me to give *Flush* any sustained attention. I (re)turn to Squier to reassess the implications of her reading, based on a concept of marginality, in light of my own, based on a concept of excess.

In *Virginia Woolf and London,* Squier devotes an entire chapter to *Flush,* taking this canine text quite seriously. For her, *Flush* is anything but a joke; or if it is a joke, she says, it is so "only in the deep psychological sense, as unconscious truth-telling" (124). The serious subtext and the unconscious truth-telling come to the fore when this novel is read as "a serious critique of the values organizing London's social and political life" (122), in particular, its class and sex oppression. Squier flushes out the connections between the economic and moral systems of the upper-class Wimpole Street and the lower-class Whitechapel and discloses the mutual tyranny revealed by Elizabeth Barrett's imprisonment in one domain and Flush's imprisonment in the other. Wimpole Street and Whitechapel, she argues, are linked by "mutual economic dependence" (127).

Obviously, Squier's reading and my earlier reading have much in common, as do Squier's reading and the "popular" reading of the novel, but the difference lies in the point of each inquiry. Squier's point is to provide a consistent reading of *Flush* and to promote an alternative social order, one that is anything but consistent. "In order to move . . . from a world of uniformity, consistency, and authority into a world valuing creativity, spontaneity, and multiplicity," Squier says, "one must come to recognize and to renounce the values Wimpole Street embodies" (126). Certainly *Flush* helps us to recognize those values, but can we so easily renounce them? Is it simply a matter of renouncing the Wimpole Street bedroom for the Italian villa, patriarchal London for maternal Florence, insiders for outsiders, as Squier suggests (127)? I would draw a different conclusion from Squier's own reading. She points out that the significance of Woolf's portrait of the London slums is her recognition that the social system that produced the authority of Wimpole Street also produced the tyranny of Whitechapel, just as the economic system that produces the products at the docks also produces the marketplaces of Oxford Street, just as the literary economy that produces serious fiction also produces trash. What serves to perpetuate the system and to mask the economic complicity between Wimpole Street and Whitechapel, as Squier has argued so well, is the treatment of the slums as "another world" and its inhabitants as "a race apart" (129), much as the academy treats popular fiction as different in kind. By promoting one social order at the expense of another, by "separating off" the good values from the bad, Squier participates in the very kind of behavior that promotes the kind of economy she would renounce.

By contrast, the point of a noneconomical reading, or reading for the excess, is not to overthrow one order and put another in its place; it is, rather, a matter of responding differently to what is perceived to be an order, or a world apart, not rebelling (taking a firm position) but eluding (taking evasive action), much as joking can elude any semblance of authority. If Woolf reveals a change in Flush's value in moving from London to Florence, she may not be advocating one social order at the expense of another but acknowledging the importance of social contexts in the assessment, and the production, of aesthetic value. What we can learn from reading *Flush* is not what the right social order or the correct value system would be but the important insight that any order (social, literary, economic, moral) is always divided from itself. It is such self-division that Woolf brings to the fore in "The Docks of London" by attending to the excess of that economy; it is such self-division that the critic can bring to the fore by attending to the valuational history of *Flush* and to the excess of a canonical economy. As Shoshana Felman suggests, by our willingness to learn from the "least authoritative sources of information"—for example, jokes or silly fiction—we can give authority to knowledge that is never in complete possession of itself ("Psychoanalysis and Education" 40).[24] As a by-product, then, *Flush* may serve to validate silly fiction as an alternative form of knowledge or popular fiction as a different kind of investment, yielding a different kind of return.

What prevents Squier from making this different kind of investment, I argue, is that she reads *Flush* as representative experience. "Flush operates as a stand-in for the woman writer," Squier says, connecting "Woolf's comic biography of a cocker spaniel and her implicit, deeply serious portrait of a woman writer's development" (124, 128). Flush's social position parallels "the marginalization and oppression of [Elizabeth] Barrett (and, by implication, of all women)" (125). In support of this reading, Squier quotes the passage describing the initial meeting of Flush and Elizabeth Barrett:

> As they gazed at each other each felt: Here am I—and then each felt: But how different! Hers was the pale worn face of an invalid, cut off from air, light, freedom. His was the warm ruddy face of a young animal; instinct with health and energy. Broken asunder, yet made in the same mould, could it be that each completed what was dormant in the other? She might have been—all that; and he—But no. Between them lay the widest gulf that can separate one being from another. She spoke. He was dumb. She was woman; he was dog. Thus closely united, thus immensely divided, they gazed at each other. (F 23; Squier 124).

What Squier emphasizes in this and other passages is the "likeness between them" (Woolf's words), that is, similarity, resemblance, the repetition of an experience. What she downplays is the "gulf" between them, the very difference that will not allow us to equate canine and female marginality. She takes the narrator's question—"could it be that each completed what was dormant in the other?"—rhetorically, not literally. Thus, all difference is subordinated to the common features of a representative experience. This, of course, is the very gesture of canon making.[25]

What if we attend to that which, "by implication," is in excess of Squier's reading: other women? What if we consider the economic rather than the "mirror relation" (Squier 124) between Barrett and her dog? After all, Flush may resemble his mistress, not because their marginal social positions are similar, but because as personal property Flush *is* his mistress, belongs to her and thus takes on her characteristics and desires.[26] In this sense Flush resembles less the woman writer than the writer's servant, Wilson. Indeed, a six-page note on Wilson suggests many similarities between the servant and the spaniel. "Since she spoke almost as seldom as Flush," writes the biographer, "the outlines of her character are little known" (F 169), for biography had not yet "cast its searchlight so low" as to deal with ladies' maids or ladies' dogs (170). The biographer also notes the "extreme precariousness" of the servant's life, for Wilson, like Flush, is at the mercy of Elizabeth Barrett's whims. Just as Flush can be stolen if his mistress forgets his leash, so Wilson can be dismissed if she refuses to accompany her mistress to Whitechapel. And just as the biographer has

faced some difficulty in writing the life of Flush because she has no tradition on which to draw to record the "succession of smells" that was Flush's
life (130), so she cannot penetrate the thoughts of the aging Wilson, "for
[Wilson] was typical of the great army of her kind—the inscrutable, the
all-but-silent, the all-but-invisible servant maids of history" (174). Flush's
life may not stand in for the lives of women we know; rather, it may stand
as a testimony to the lives that will never be narrated, the inscrutable and
therefore unrepresentable, the discarded and therefore wasted.

I do not mean to suggest that Squier has not been sensitive to class
differences, for she certainly has.[27] Nor do I wish to replace Squier's representational reading with my own. Instead, I want to suggest that reading
*Flush* as a representation of a certain kind of experience (women's marginality) compels us to set up a choice between alternative social orders,
offering one as more highly valued than the other and thereby denying
the very diversity of values that the concept of marginality entails. For
however much we may associate marginality with multiplicity, by offering
it as an alternative to the dominant order, we must exclude certain forms
of diversity and thereby avoid "genuine evaluative conflict" (Smith, "Contingencies of Value" 13). Further, to produce a consistent reading, Squier
too ignores Woolf's changing and conflicting motives as she was writing
*Flush,* thereby elevating the book: it is "more than a joke" (137). Squier's
dismissal of the joke for the serious truth beneath unwittingly perpetuates
the very value system that has been used to trivialize many women's texts
and popular novels: what is obvious (on the surface for everyone to see)
is trivial ("only a joke"); what is hidden (to be extracted by an initiate)
is profound ("deeply serious"). Finally, to read *Flush* in terms of its representation of women's experience may be to perpetuate the modernist
tendency to gender popular literature and culture as female (see Huyssen,
chap. 3, esp. 47, 62).

In other words, by reducing complex differences to two absolutes—
patriarchal and matriarchal, upper class and lower class, authoritarian and
egalitarian—and then choosing between them, Squier's reading threatens to restore "a single hierarchy of value" that Radway associates with
the academic canon precisely because Squier reads for the representative
experience associated with a popular aesthetics. That is, *any* reader can
read canonically (or academically) when she or he seeks to promote a particular experience at the expense of another and to elevate a particular
text by producing a consistent reading. As Peter Rabinowitz (226) and
Smith ("Contingencies of Value" 30) point out, this tendency to impute
coherence or consistency to texts is what perpetuates canons.

My point, I hasten to add, is *not* to deny the value of Squier's reading
but to locate that value elsewhere: not in Squier's endorsement of an *alter-*

*native* value system but in her "acknowledgment of divergent systems of value" (Smith, "Contingencies of Value" 7); and it is this very diversity, Smith says, that undermines "established evaluative authority." Considered from the perspective of a popular aesthetics, what makes Squier's reading so valuable is that she reveals the different functions *Flush* can serve for a different set of readers with different needs and interests from those who have participated in *Flush*'s devaluation, whether through verbal abuse or benign neglect. In this way, Squier's reading does function as the BOMC's reading for use-value: it makes available a text and a way of reading it that can help some of us to survive in a world not predisposed to serve our interests (Smith, *Margins of Discourse* 85). However, to the extent that Squier presents her reading unself-consciously, neglecting its particular motivations and uses, and to the extent that she reads for the hidden subtext beneath the surface play, her reading resembles the kind associated with an academic aesthetics, the kind of reading a popular aesthetics, as well as postmodern criticism, would abjure.[28]

The conflict over how to read *Flush*—whether to take it seriously as more than a joke or to take it literally as a silly book—brings to the fore the novel's very function as the excess of a canonical economy. To read *Flush* as the excess, not the marginal, is to read it in terms of what Derrida calls the law of excess, that which corrupts distinctions between genres, or between popular and highbrow, mutt and pure-bred ("Genre" 210). While the *margin* marks the limit of what is desirable, the *excess* is part of the process of production, both a necessary component and a superfluous by-product. Reading popular fiction may have the effect of disclosing any art—whether high or low, modern or postmodern, male or female—as the arbitrary, contingent, and accidental construction that it is (cf. Bourdieu). Reading *Flush* can show us that readings, texts, and canons are always mixed, never pure, and that we give them the illusion of purity, permanence, and prestige by reading efficiently, separating off the excess that would expose this rather messy and conflicted system. In other words, reading from the perspective of popular fiction can reveal that our usual distinctions between academic and popular art, whether we maintain a "great divide" or dissolve boundaries, rely on the kind of thinking about literature and society bound up with a modernist aesthetics, in which art and life are assumed to be separate realms of experience, thus maintaining a false distinction between the formal qualities and the representational function of literature. If a popular aesthetics focuses on the various functions of literature, if a postmodern aesthetics implicates art in mass culture, then our evaluative activity must change in response to such productions. Conceiving art as function, not form, and as implicated in everyday life enables us to make more precise kinds of distinctions among these various kinds of writing and reading.

Where canonical criticism would either dismiss silly fiction for its silliness or dismiss its silliness for its serious subtext, I argue that the effect of popular fiction is to make literary criteria disposable and changeable in order to produce a noncanonical economy, or in Woolf's words, "a system that did not shut out" (Diary 4:127). This is not to say that we must value everything equally and refuse to discriminate but that we must evaluate contextually and refuse to discriminate absolutely. By means of her various writing projects, Woolf encourages us to suspend our economical reading, one that promotes a consistent approach and pays off with a firm position, one that excludes conflict, contradiction, equivocation, and excess. Instead of promoting a particular reading as attesting to the value of a text, we might begin by questioning how that text can be of value and then proceed to read with those particular uses foregrounded and with our own motives laid bare. When the payoff (what is to be gained by reading literature) is in dispute, as it is in our postmodern age, such a noneconomical reading becomes a valuable pursuit.

## NOTES

1. The original drafts of the *London Scene* essays are in the same holograph notebook as the first draft of *Flush* (Berg Collection, New York Public Library).

2. Many critics make no mention of *Flush* in their books on Woolf (e.g., Bowlby, DiBattista, Harper, Minow-Pinkney, Naremore); others pass over it in a sentence or a note (e.g., Marcus, Zwerdling, Transue) or dismiss it as simply a "relaxation," an exception to or escape from Woolf's typical writing (Nicolson, in Letters 4:xx). Interestingly, except for the first brief review, even the entries under *Flush* in Majumbar and McLaurin's *Virginia Woolf: The Critical Heritage* mention *Flush* only in passing, if they mention it at all. The notable exception to this critical neglect of *Flush* is Squier's book, which I discuss later in this chapter.

3. See my chapter 1 for a discussion of these modernist values.

4. Waugh comments that postmodernism is often considered an art of the marginal (*Feminine Fictions* 3), whether this means it takes up the cause of the marginal (e.g., women) or it incorporates marginal forms (e.g., popular art). But this marginal/central opposition may no longer hold in postmodern writing. By using the term *excess,* I suggest an alternative way of conceiving this relation.

5. Since readers of *Flush* are nearly nonexistent, I should explain that I am playing on Woolf's wording in a note on *Aurora Leigh,* in which she comments on how few people have read that poem. Woolf's note suggests one possible motive behind *Flush:* to (re)introduce Elizabeth Barrett Browning's poem to the canon (F 167–68).

6. Squier makes a similar argument, as we will see.

7. Said writes that it is "isolating and elevating the subject beyond his or her

time and society" that gives rise to the biographer's craft, as well as to canonical values, and produces "an exaggerated respect for single individuals," or single texts (150).

8. In turning to Woolf's personal writings, I may seem to forget my own advice at the end of the Introduction, where I caution critics against raiding Woolf's diaries and letters for proof of their readings of her literary texts. Yet my point is not to rule out such extratextual evidence (indeed, I rely on such evidence extensively throughout this book); rather, my point is to make us self-conscious about how we use such evidence. If I look to Woolf's personal writings for evidence of *Flush*'s value, I do so, in Barbara Johnson's words, to "seek in them not answers, causes, explanations, or origins, but new questions and new ways in which the literary and nonliterary texts [or the canonical and noncanonical texts] can be made to read and rework each other" (*World of Difference* 15).

9. Woolf comments, "I enjoy my freak of writing Flush— . . . to let my brain cool" (Diary 4:123). If *Flush* is discussed at all by critics, it is usually as a parody of Lytton Strachey's biographies. Even Woolf discusses Flush's death in terms of Queen Victoria's (Letters 5:232).

10. Writing on *Orlando,* Minow-Pinkney reminds us that "we should not confound a 'joke' with mere insignificance, even if the writer herself invites us to do so" (117), as Woolf does. Minow-Pinkney goes on to provide an explanation that Squier uses in writing on *Flush:* "Freud has demonstrated in *Jokes and Their Relation to the Unconscious* that in the jest and the relief gained from it there resides the truth of the unconscious" (117).

11. For dismissive reviews, see *The Nation,* October 18, 1933; *The Saturday Review of Literature,* October 7, 1933; and *Christian Century,* October 18, 1933.

12. For arguments linking the popular and the feminine, see Schor, Derrida ("Beehive"), and Levenson (esp. 30). Wexler discusses the relation of modernist writers to popular audiences, arguing that many modernist writers desired popularity, though they did believe it meant abandoning their principles and compromising their integrity as artists.

13. In "The Use of Poetry and the Use of Criticism," Eliot writes: "No honest poet can ever feel quite sure of the permanent value of what he has written: he may have wasted his time . . . for nothing" (*Selected Prose* 95).

14. Tanner offers an explanation for Pynchon's aversion to publicity that could pertain to Woolf's as well: "I think there is a dislike for publicity in the way that it can take over a writer's life and manipulate and exploit it, turning it into a saleable image, so that the 'life' and the works may become confused, or the life becomes the dominant 'fiction' to which the writer may succumb . . . to the detriment— or ignoring—of the imaginative 'life' contained in the work" (13). As recent feminist critics, such as Moi and Bowlby, have complained, Woolf's life often comes to dominate her fiction in Woolf criticism. Of course, a "saleable image" is exactly what Woolf and Pynchon have become, especially given the success of feminism and postmodernism in the academy.

15. Similarly, Woolf's diary entries while she was revising *Flush* and correcting the proofs reveal this conflict between the values of permanence and change: "There's no trifling with words—cannot be done: not when they're to stand 'for

ever'" (Diary 4:144); "I can't settle, & make up my story [*The Pargiters*], in which lies permanence" (151).

16. This comment suggests a change in Woolf's conception of the "common life" from that voiced in *A Room of One's Own* and quoted in chapter 1: "I am talking of the common life which is the real life and not of the little separate lives which we live as individuals" (117). From "common life" (ROO) to "separate people" (TG) suggests a shift in Woolf's concept of society, from a homogenous "common" life opposed to individual lives to a complex of many kinds of people. That is, as opposed to the emphasis on individualism that marks much realist and early modernist writing, Woolf valued the "common life"; yet if that life is conceived as homogeneous and unified, she advocated thinking in terms of "separate people," not mass culture. Thus, we cannot say simply that popular art appeals to the public, for how we conceive that public is crucial. In addition, the "common life," especially in the context of *A Room of One's Own*, draws attention to the role of history and tradition in artistic creation, while "separate people," in the context of the prewar society of *Three Guineas*, encourages a thinking at odds with the us-versus-them mentality then in vogue. Both concepts of the common life inform pragmatism, with which I am implicitly linking Woolf by means of postmodernism. As Cornel West writes: "for [C. S.] Peirce, *agathon* (the idea of the good) lies in convergence and coalescence, corporateness and oneness; for [William] James, in diversity and individuality, concreteness and plurality" (56). On the role of history and tradition in postmodern art, see Hutcheon (11).

17. Radway quotes from Jameson's *Political Unconscious* in this part of her discussion.

18. Woolf's label for *Flush*, a "silly book," may well serve to create a particular value for it and to promote a particular use of it. When Woolf lamented the novel's popular success—"Flush has been chosen by the American Book Society [the BOMC]. Lord!" (Diary 4:175)—she may have felt that the popular use of fiction was a silly use of *Flush*, or she may have feared that as popular fiction *Flush* would be inappropriately evaluated in the same way as her serious fiction—and it was.

19. In *Flush*, "Mrs. Woolf has avoided the complete immersion of her novels"; *Flush* is both "a real person and a real dog"; "*Flush* . . . is sheer pleasure"; "The flavour of the book is fresh"; *Flush* "awakens in the reader an acute delight in all the physical senses." All excerpts are from the *Book Review Digest*.

20. After her experience in Whitechapel, Elizabeth Barrett finds her inspiration as a writer in the lives of the common people, not the lives of the enshrined poets. She exclaims, "They [the faces in the street] stimulated her imagination as 'the divine marble presences,' the busts [of Homer, Chaucer, Shakespeare] on the bookcase, had never stimulated it" (F 96).

21. However much Woolf seems to share the values of a popular aesthetic, and however much *Flush* seems to be more concerned with social conduct and criticism than with language and technique, we can certainly find statements in Woolf's writings of this time that would support the art-for-art's-sake view. For example, in an early draft of *Flush* Woolf writes, "The wisest—& Flush was wise—leave the conduct of the world to others" (second holograph notebook, July 31, 1931,

p. 155, Berg Collection). In her essay on *Aurora Leigh* (also published in July 1931), Woolf writes that in Elizabeth Barrett Browning's poem, "life has impinged upon art more than life should" (SCR 185), admitting the difficulty of keeping the two apart. Woolf's own contradictory positions attest to the need for an alternative form of evaluation, not one that distinguishes between social engagement and aesthetic withdrawal, but *one that can relate social criticism to changing aesthetic practices and readers' changing expectations.*

A reading of Woolf's manuscripts suggests this kind of relation. Significantly, the opening paragraph of the 1932 holograph version of *Flush* shifts the focus of this novel from the problem of tracing the origin of Flush's family (as in the 1931 version) to the challenge of writing "the lives of the dumb . . . those who have left no love letters or documents . . . behind them." The nineteenth-century biographer would not have been able to write lives that left no written records, no memoirs, letters, or poems. But a change in aesthetic sensibility, not just more knowledge of such lives, allows for such an undertaking in the 1930s: "we to whom the flick [?] of a finger [?] speaks volumes, we to whom the turn of a head means a whole novel—how can we seek shelter under such an excuse [lack of information]? Dogs have tails; dogs have noses; tails wag, noses quiver—what more could we want?" (1932 holograph notebook, p. 5, Berg Collection). Woolf amusingly advocates writing the lives of the silent, not because it is the morally right thing to do, but because it is now aesthetically possible to do so.

22. See the Conclusion for a more detailed discussion of Gallop's essay.

23. In making this argument, I am drawing on Rorty's argument concerning Derrida's famous claim that there is nothing outside the text. The point of Derrida's statement, says Rorty, is to abandon "a certain framework of interconnected ideas," not to make a new claim about the "*real* nature" of either the text or the world (*Consequences of Pragmatism* 140).

24. Felman is discussing Freud's willingness to learn from literature, dreams, and his patients.

25. It is imperative that I point out here that Squier's reading is sanctioned by a remark Woolf makes in a letter to a delighted reader of her "silly book": "Yes, they are much alike, Mrs Browning and her dog" (Letters 5:234). That reader had obviously hit on a way to read *Flush* that resembles Squier's, and that pleased Woolf. Whether Woolf was confirming this way of reading or discovering it here, we cannot be sure. But in the 1932 holograph, Woolf's version of this passage seems to warn against the seductiveness of Squier's reading. Commenting on this similarity between Elizabeth Barrett and her dog, Woolf writes: "But there was also . . . — when [?] a likeness is infinitely more attractive, more powerful, more persuasive— a profound dissimilarity" (1932 holograph notebook, p. 43, Berg Collection). I quote this passage not as the "correct" reading but as a divergent reading.

26. For an interesting discussion of the master-servant relation, see Sedgwick (65–82).

27. Squier has anticipated my response here by insisting that class differences among women change "only the *nature*" of oppression, not "its existence" (131). She would not claim that all marginality is alike, only that all those who are marginalized are oppressed in some way, a point I would hardly contest. But it seems to

me that the "nature" of oppression—that is, its mode of functioning in a particular economy—is precisely what is at issue in this work.

28. Hutcheon remarks that, from the perspective of postmodernism, the point of criticism is no longer to disclose the hidden subtext or latent truth of the text, for postmodern fiction foregrounds its contradictions (211).

# 6

## Virginia Woolf as Critic: *Creating an Aesthetic, Self-reflexive Criticism*

> There must be some simpler, subtler, closer method of writing about books, as about people, could I hit upon it.
>
> —Virginia Woolf,
> Diary, 1931

> There *can* be masters on both sides of the board—great readers as well as great poets, matches for each other in the boldness and subtlety of their moves.
>
> —Barbara Herrnstein Smith,
> *On the Margins of Discourse*

Throughout this work, I have been stressing Virginia Woolf's increasing concern with the audience in her writing. Likewise, the most notable feature of her criticism is its concern with the reader, as the titles of the two critical collections published in her lifetime make apparent: *The Common Reader* (1925) and *The Second Common Reader* (1932). But the nature of her interest in the reader, and the nature of the reader herself, need further clarification, especially in light of the discussion in the previous chapter. If the value of the artwork for Woolf lies in its use by an audience, as I argue in chapter 1, then we must ask how readers use literature, and who is reading it and why. I began to address these questions in the previous chapter from the perspective of popular fiction. Here I take them up again from the perspective of criticism, for these are the questions underlying Woolf's critical essays. In her essays, as in her novels, Woolf advocates new ways of reading literature and new uses of criticism in an effort to create an audience for her own art and to make art responsive to a wider audience. This audience is frequently identified as the common reader. But before affirming the common reader as Woolf's unique contribution to the criticism of her day (and as the obvious connection to the criticism of our own), we should be sure we know what we mean, and what Woolf might have meant, by the "common reader." [1]

From a postmodern perspective, this concern with the reader is not surprising.[2] As Alain Robbe-Grillet writes of the new novel: "far from neglecting him, the author today proclaims his absolute need of the reader's cooperation, an active, conscious, *creative* assistance. What he asks of him is no longer to receive ready-made a world completed, full, closed upon itself, but on the contrary, to participate in a creation, to invent in his turn the work—and the world—and thus to learn to invent his own life" (*For a New Novel* 156). In a more recent essay on reader-response criticism, Christine Brooke-Rose says "the avowed purpose of the *nouveau roman*" is to make the reader "cooperate actively" in the textual production, and thereby to make her or him "hypercritical" ("Readerhood of Man" 134). Certainly, the creative assistance of the reader is evoked by Woolf's narrative techniques (see chap. 2), and the assumption that reading is a creative act informs her critical essays. A reader-oriented literature would seem to call for a reader-oriented criticism, and that is what has come about over the past two decades with the "confluence" of postmodernism and poststructuralism (Arac ix).[3] Susan Suleiman has identified the self-reflexive criticism of poststructuralism as a "homologue" of the self-reflexive turn in twentieth-century literature (44). Similarly, Mary Louise Pratt observes that reader-response criticism deals with the self-reflexiveness and indeterminacy that we find in much twentieth-century art. "Who would deny," she asks, "the mutually determining relationship between contemporary criticism and the *nouveau roman?*" (31). But is this relation between contemporary criticism and literature one of "homology"? The mutually determining relationship between Woolf's criticism and her fiction, which is often taken as a "given," is the very issue I want to explore in this chapter. Although Woolf's criticism is certainly self-reflexive, it is not just because her fiction is self-reflexive. There is more to be said about this relation.

Woolf's critical essays suggest a contemporary outlook in that they redefine several concepts: the literary canon as a fixed tradition of enduring works; the literary text as a discrete object of analysis; and the literary critic as an interpreter of the text. In doing so, Woolf comes to consider the reader's participation in and response to the text; her criticism is more concerned with description than with explication. The kinds of questions she asks—for example, What assumptions and connections shape this text? What is the nature of the transaction between text and reader?—give rise to her narrative critical style. She gives us, in Jonathan Culler's phrase, stories of reading. Thus, her criticism is aesthetic in its narrative quality as well as in its awareness of the "creative character" of reading ("Reading," CDB 169). It is self-reflexive in making explicit "the prejudices, the instincts, and the fallacies" grounding its own methods and conclusions ("An Essay in Criticism," GR 92).[4]

Many of these poststructuralist characteristics have been noted by others writing on Woolf's critical essays, and a few scholars have directly linked these traits to specific poststructuralist critics.[5] But without the underpinnings of a postmodern aesthetics, many of these critics cannot account for such features in terms of Woolf's aesthetic motives. Moreover, their assessment of her critical aims is often at odds with their assessment of her fictional ones. In this chapter, I argue that my approach to Woolf's novels and nonfiction essays, which I have been elaborating in terms of postmodernism in art, can provide us with a better understanding of Woolf's critical postulates and methods.

Rethinking the assumptions and practices of a largely humanistic and increasingly formalist tradition in criticism led Woolf to anticipate many contemporary critical issues. In separate essays she finds fault with Harold Williams and E. M. Forster because their criticism of the novel is not grounded in any aesthetic theory. That is, she objects to the very kind of impressionistic criticism often attributed to her own essays. In "The Art of Fiction," a review of Forster's *Aspects of the Novel,* Woolf says:

> To all this Mr. Forster would reply, presumably, that he lays down no laws; the novel somehow seems to him too soft a substance to be carved like other arts; he is merely telling us what moves him and what leaves him cold. Indeed, there is no other criterion. So then we are back in the old bog; nobody knows anything about the laws of fiction; or what its relation is to life; or to what effects it can lend itself. We can only trust to our instincts. (M 109–10)

His "humane as opposed to the esthetic view of fiction" treats fiction "as a parasite which draws its sustenance from life" and thereby ignores its very strategies and rhetoric: "Almost nothing is said about words," Woolf complains (M 109–11 passim). And yet, she objects as well to the kind of criticism that gives preference to the formal elements and structure of the book. In "The Anatomy of Fiction," she rejects Clayton Hamilton's effort to discriminate among fixed literary forms, such as realism and romanticism, by listing their distinctive traits. And writing on Percy Lubbock's *Craft of Fiction,* Woolf says:

> Here we have Mr. Lubbock telling us that the book itself is equivalent to its form, and seeking with admirable subtlety and lucidity to trace out those methods by which novelists build up the *final and enduring structure* of their books. The very patness with which the image comes to the pen makes us suspect that it fits a little loosely. (M 159; emphasis added)

In other words, she objected equally to criticism that measures the text against some static model "largely stuffed with straw" ("An Essay in Criticism," GR 88) and to criticism that evaluates the text in terms of life itself. When speaking out against such approaches in her own work on fiction, "Phases of Fiction" (1929), Woolf could be addressing Lubbock and Forster:

> But any such verdict must be based upon the supposition that 'the novel' has a certain character which is now fixed and cannot be altered, that 'life' has a certain limit which can be defined. And it is precisely this conclusion that the novels we have been reading tend to upset. (GR 144)[6]

And, I argue, it is precisely this conclusion that Woolf's own novels tend to upset. Only by relinquishing certain assumptions about the *nature* of art can we account for changes in the *function* of criticism.

However, the common readings of Woolf's fiction cannot take into account these criticisms by Woolf, for it is in terms of some essential concept of the novel or life that her fiction is so often evaluated. As long as we define the guiding motive of Woolf's novels as a quest for the essence of life itself, a desire to make something permanent, or a search for the right relation between art and life, we cannot explain her rejection of such critical criteria as Forster's or Lubbock's. The alternative to explaining her criticism in terms of her conception of art is either to look to precursors or successors for her ideas or to simply describe the features of her criticism as if her essays were mere "finger exercises" for her fiction (Schorer 377). Indeed, these are the common approaches to Woolf's critical essays.

A postmodern perspective enables us to avoid the weaknesses of these approaches to Woolf's criticism. On the one hand, we need not consider her critical style as an end in itself, as if by describing its features we have accounted for them. Such an approach stems from the uncritical acceptance of Woolf's critical statements and methods and can be seen in discussions by Joan Bennett, Vijay L. Sharma, and, to some extent, Barbara Currier Bell and Carol Ohmann. On the other hand, we can avoid the fallacy of post hoc, ergo propter hoc. Most books on Woolf's criticism, including two of the best by Perry Meisel (*The Absent Father*) and Mark Goldman (*The Reader's Art*), discuss Woolf's essays in terms of influences. But once we have traced an idea or method back to an earlier critic, or forward to a later one, we often find we have little else to say about it. And the positivistic gesture of singling out shared features among writers is one Woolf objected to in Williams's and Hamilton's criticism. The danger, as she saw it, lies in suppressing the differences within such categories by generalizing about texts apart from particular contexts, a danger she saw as well in Lubbock's emphasis on form.[7] But it is also, I argue, the danger potential in Woolf's and the poststructuralists' emphasis on the reader. That is, to offer the reader as our new critical value or standard without at the same time changing our model for literary discourse and our use of literary criticism is to risk repeating the same critical moves we intended to avoid. What we need in order to account for Woolf's objections to such critical approaches, as well as for her own alternative approach, is the very functional and relational concept of art I have been examining in terms of Woolf's postmodern strategies.

By reading Woolf's critical essays in terms of postmodernism, we are in a better position to explain her often cited, and frequently decried, definition of the artwork offered in opposition to Lubbock's "form": "the 'book itself' is not form which you see, but emotion which you feel" (M 160). Usually, this definition is taken literally, as if Woolf were giving preference to the reader's subjective responses. Unfortunately, Woolf's word choice suggests to the contemporary reader a kind of naive reader-response criticism. But read in the context of her narrative interests, and in comparison with her review of Forster's criticism, Woolf's definition neither reduces the novel to the individual reader's emotional response nor simply replaces one critical criterion (form) with another (emotion). Rather, it checks "the impulse to make museum pieces out of our reading" (SCR 7). "The question is not one of words only," Woolf writes. "It goes deeper than that, *into the very process of reading itself*" (M 158–59; emphasis added). This process of reading is necessarily bound up with the concept of the artwork, the very concept at issue in Woolf's essays, and in this book.

Woolf challenges Lubbock's concept of the novel by describing her reading of Flaubert's "Un Coeur Simple."[8] Whereas Lubbock explains how the skilled reader connects different elements of the text, responding "as the author intended" (M 158), Woolf shows how the casual reader connects different responses to the text, readjusting her or his sense of the whole as new information is acquired. Both emphasize the work as "a whole," but Lubbock's whole is located in the textual elements alone, whereas Woolf's lies in the reader's orderings of those elements. That is, Lubbock's "form" is static and author-oriented; Woolf's "emotion" is dynamic and reader-oriented.[9] In stressing the opposition between showing and telling in his discussion of Henry James's novels, Lubbock gives preference to showing: he approaches the novel as "form which you see" and he shows us how to delineate the form. Woolf prefers telling: she tells us the story of her own reading. But it is less the content of the reader's emotional response than the function of such responses that Woolf brings out in her reading. If the book is "emotion which you feel," then what you feel can only be communicated in the form of a story. Narrating, it seems, is the shared activity of writer and reader. And narrative for Woolf is not a matter of the right connection between things but of the different ways of forming connections (see chap. 1).

The whole debate between Lubbock's "form" and Woolf's "emotion" has typically been approached by means of the two-termed distinctions Woolf's fictional strategies confute. The question of what is in the text and what is supplied by the reader depends on a stable "inside" and "outside," and it is just such a distinction Woolf puts in question in her own novels, such as *Mrs. Dalloway*. The issue of "finding out" versus "making up" is ultimately elided by Woolf in that she adopts a functional conception of narrative discourse. Whether we posit a gap between or a fusion of text and reader, we are relying on the kind of dichotomous thinking that gives rise to the search for the essential or appropriate relation between the two. But Woolf's concern with the *point* of the narrative or the reading led her to examine the changing status of such relations, to look at different kinds of behavior and their consequences. Such an approach makes sense only if we concern ourselves with the function of art, not its nature.

My point is this: the focus on the reader rather than on the textual elements alone is not the key distinction to be made between Woolf's poststructuralist tendencies and the formalist criticism of her day. Rather, her focus on the reader changes the questions she asks as a critic, as well as her concept of the writing and reading process. Woolf does not turn her attention to the reader in order to solve the problem posed above, that is, whether to make the text or the world our standard for judgment. On the contrary, her focus on the reader complicates such a distinction and makes us reconsider the assumptions about literature and life on which it rests. In other words, the issue is not whether the critic should focus on the text (as Lubbock does), the world (as Forster does), or the reader (as poststructuralists do), but whether or not the critic understands the changing relations among the three.[10]

Woolf undertakes such an investigation in her proposed book on fiction, published as a series of articles entitled "Phases of Fiction" (in *Bookman*, April–June 1929; see also GR). Having rejected Hamilton's division of literature into types and Williams's into periods, she bases her own "phases" on different assumptions from those of the "positivist-minded critics," as Goldman (*Reader's Art*) calls them. She constructs her phases by distinguishing among the different purposes and effects of reading rather than the different traits and types of fiction. In this sense, "Phases of Fiction" is less a typology of narrative forms than a semiotics of reading.[11] Woolf's avowed purpose is "to record the impressions made upon the mind by reading a certain number of novels in succession" and thereby to explore "the nature of the interest and the pleasure" that we take in reading novels (GR 93). Because of her purpose, Woolf makes no attempt to summarize the novel in question, to analyze its theme, or to investigate the life and times of its author. Instead, she adopts a comparative approach, pitting different narratives against each other, looking at the differences within as well as among phases, and considering the kinds of beliefs and assumptions we agree to in different novels.[12] She is less concerned with the relation of fiction to the actual world of the writer or the reader than with the kinds of reality established through the fiction.

For example, the truth tellers like Defoe, who are interested in a character's relation to her or his social and physical environment, give us a world that is solid, substantial, and secure: "things are precisely as they say they are" (GR 95); "their actions are all in keeping with one another" (102). We experience the relief that comes from subjugating "all the mixed and ambiguous feelings of which we may be possessed at the moment" (95). Thus, when Moll Flanders abandons one child after another, we are invited not to probe the depths of her psychology but to consider her circumstances and to anticipate the next eventful scene (95). In such a world, Woolf says, "emphasis is laid upon the very facts that most re-assure us of stability in real life, upon money, furniture, food, until we seem wedged among solid objects in a solid universe" (95). The psychologists, conversely, give us a world "resting on no visible support" (121). Those "difficult and mixed emotions" subdued by the truth tellers are explored by the psychologists. As a result, we are "raised above the stress of circumstances" into a world like Proust's, "so porous, so pliable, so perfectly receptive" that "the commonest object" loses its familiar outlines and "the commonest actions" are no longer routine. The habitual becomes imbricated in "a whole series of thoughts, sensations, ideas, memories" (123–24). In the depths of the mind, "contradiction prevails," so instead of being reassured, we are induced to doubt, to question, even to despair (126, 130). In contrast, the character mongers like Austen detail personal relations and thus avoid the contradictory, the abstract and impersonal: "all suspicions and questions [are] laid at rest" (GR 115). We are neither reassured nor disturbed: "A world which so often ends in a suitable marriage is not a world to wring one's hands over. On the contrary, it is a world about which we can be sarcastic" (118). But as the psychologists raise us above the world of circumstance, the poets "let us pass beyond the range of personality" (135–36). Unconcerned with "the idiosyncrasy of character," the poets, such as Hardy and Emily Brontë, contemplate the relations of woman and man to the universe rather than to other women and men. They create a certain atmosphere rather than give us some sense of our physical, mental, or social existence.

As Woolf accounts for such changes in the reality conveyed and the effects produced by different phases of fiction, she stresses that such change comes from the variety of relations possible in fiction, not from the inevitable progression of life or the "development" of fiction. Her remark on

Austen could fit any of the authors she considers: "Thus, it is possible to ask not that her world shall be improved or altered (that our satisfaction forbids) but that another shall be struck off, whose constitution shall be different and shall allow of the other relations" (GR 118). Implicit in such an approach is the assumption that narrative consists of certain related activities in which we engage. The interactions between texts and readers, then, are controlled neither by the textual features alone nor by the individual reader's responses alone but by the system of literature itself from which both writers and readers extrapolate. Woolf's concept of "tradition" (if we use Eliot's terminology) or "intertextuality" (if we use poststructuralist terminology) enables her to account for new forms of literature in terms of their similarity to and difference from other forms.[13] In this way she avoids the extremes she notes in the criticism of others: setting up some normative or ideal standard for criticism on the one hand and reducing criticism to uncontrolled relativism on the other.

In her criticism of fiction, then, Woolf focuses on the kinds of commitments writers and readers make in certain narrative contexts. In doing so she investigates the use of narrative and the attitude toward reality that engender the common assumption that the novel represents life, not to reject representational fiction (as so often assumed), but to disclose the operations and the conventions that make it possible, and predominant. Her readings suggest that the life the novel represents is an *effect* of the kinds of agreements writers and readers enter into, and the kinds of activity they engage in as a result. In "Robinson Crusoe," Woolf presents this agreement in terms of a business transaction: "There is a piece of business to be transacted between writer and reader before any further dealings are possible" (SCR 43). And as we note the various ways writers "alter the relations of one thing to another . . . we see the whole world in perpetual transformation" (GR 141). Woolf's point here is much like Allen Thiher's in his chapter on Wittgenstein: "Reality only exists in function of the discourse that articulates it" (27). Reality, Woolf would show us, is *that which obtains between consenting adults in a particular discursive situation.*[14] Therefore, she asks what we are consenting to and how our consent is achieved. In this way we may come to find merit in a book that "outrages our sympathies, or describes a life which seems unreal to us" (GR 142). Woolf's goal was not simply to reject a type of fiction but to change a way of life. "For it is inevitable," Woolf tells us, "that the reader who is invited to live in novels as in life should go on feeling as he feels in life" (142). And Woolf, as we have seen, valued change.

At the end of "Phases of Fiction," Woolf asks a pragmatic question: what do we gain by such comparisons? One benefit is our awareness of the flexibility and the potentiality of fiction: "we have gained some sense of the vastness of fiction and the width of its range" (141). Another is our increased self-consciousness, which "is becoming far more alert and better trained. We are aware of relations and subtleties which have not yet been explored" (145). But most important in terms of a postmodern perspective is our awareness that the mimetic relation between life and text, where "novel and life are laid side by side" (142), is only one possible relation in fiction, not the defining one. Woolf demonstrates in "Phases of Fiction," as in other essays such as "Modern Fiction," what Robbe-Grillet points out in *For a New Novel*, Beckett in *Proust*, and Sarraute in *The Age of Suspicion:* our shared ways of talking about novels in terms of the art/life relation are based on a particular conception of art and life, one that imposes on us "the image of a stable, coherent, continuous, unequivocal, entirely decipherable universe" (Robbe-Grillet, *For a New Novel* 32). All these writers undermine the common assumption that the relation of art to life is the *essence* of the novel, and they question the concept of the world as *property*. To change our ways of talking about the novel is to change our ways of conceiving the world. And the "prime distinction" Woolf brings out in her different phases of fiction lies in "the changed attitude toward reality" (GR 132).[15]

Understanding Woolf's concern with different relations between art and life can help us assess her point in her famous essay "Modern Fiction." Woolf's most anthologized essay, it is one that is easily misunderstood apart from its context. In this *Common Reader* essay, Woolf does not advocate one kind of fiction (modernist) over another (traditionalist), as commonly assumed. Rather, she contrasts two approaches to fiction in order to offer another. "Modern Fiction," which opens with a reference to Woolf's previous essay on Austen, clarifies the point of her own comparative method: in comparing and contrasting past and present works, Woolf does not suggest that literature is evolving toward some better or ultimate form but that new forms of fiction can be conceived only in their similarity to and differences from other forms. When she goes on to contrast the materialists with the spiritualists, her essay on Austen helps us understand her argument. She is not condemning the materialists for portraying the daily life rather than the life of the mind, as the spiritualists do, for she has praised Austen for such a portrait. Rather, Woolf challenges the method of Bennett, Wells, and Galsworthy (those "materialists") that would mimic the outer world, and the method of Joyce and Richardson (those "spiritualists") that would confine us to a single mind because both concepts of fiction inhibit the creative power of the reader. The one is a slave to convention and, as such, allows us little room for choice and innovation; the other "never embraces or creates what is outside itself and beyond" and so restricts our access to the world (CR 156). The method

Woolf preferred is the method described in her Austen essay, one that calls forth the reader's own interpretive and creative powers.

Woolf uses the realism of Wells and Bennett as something with which to contrast, and thereby define, her concept of the novel: "So much of the enormous labour of proving the solidity, the likeness to life, of the story is not merely labour thrown away but labour misplaced to the extent of obscuring and blotting out *the light of the conception*" (CR 153; emphasis added). Her concern is with the conception of the work itself, not with the solid world it supposedly represents. The previous essay on Austen again helps us understand what this conception is. Woolf sensed in Austen's novels the suggestiveness of a modern prose method, for what endows Austen's novels with life is not her minute representation of daily existence but the way she induces the reader to participate in her novels: "[Austen] stimulates us to supply what is not there. What she offers is, apparently, a trifle, yet it is composed of something that expands in the reader's mind and endows with the most enduring form of life scenes which are outwardly trivial" (CR 142). It seems this conception is to be found not just in the author's mind but in the reader's activity as well. In his essay "Interaction between Text and Reader," Wolfgang Iser quotes this same passage from Woolf to illustrate his concept of "gap-filling" (111). His point is that such gap-filling forces the reader to modify her or his response to what is familiar in narrative (112). This is one goal of Woolf's criticism.

At the end of "Modern Fiction," Woolf celebrates the plurality of texts that her comparative method discloses rather than insisting on the superiority of one kind. Comparisons of fictions leave us "with a view of the infinite possibilities of the art and remind us that there is no limit to the horizon" (CR 158). Thus, Woolf's famous passage, "Let us trace the atoms as they fall," does not prescribe a method for fiction, as so many readers have assumed, but describes the particular method of Joyce and Richardson. And Woolf does not oust the materialists from her literary canon, as critics so often argue. What she does in this essay, as in her *Common Reader* collections as a whole, is open up the field of literature and make room for the reader in her literary tradition and in her concept of the text. Woolf presents a theory that shifts the locus of the text from the individual writer or reader to the interaction between the two, those interactions she explores in "Phases of Fiction."

The common misconception underlying critical discussions of "Modern Fiction," "Mr. Bennett and Mrs. Brown," and "Phases of Fiction" is that in them Woolf chooses between two kinds of fiction: materialist and spiritualist, modernist and conventional, representational and experimental. A better way to approach these essays is in terms of Woolf's interest in the different effects on readers produced by different narrative relations. Woolf distrusted fiction that makes readers comfortable with their view of the world, that conforms to their expectations of what fiction should be, and that confirms their biases and assumptions. For all her talk of the reader's cooperation with the writer, she was aware of the value of conflict as well, especially conflict within oneself. And it is such conflict and self-division that "good" literature, whether canonical or popular, produces.

As we saw in chapter 1, Woolf reverses the adage of Leslie Stephen and Henry James, that is, that good people make good writers because they can communicate moral values. For Woolf, good writers make good people, and their art matters even if, like Lily Briscoe's, it is neglected. But as I have argued, this statement makes sense only in terms of a change in the concept of the artist's work: from the creation of a lasting product to the commitment to a form of activity. Good writers are good people because, by inducing us to engage in a different form of activity, they challenge our comfortable perceptions of the world, thereby challenging us to create it over again. On reading the plays of the "lesser Elizabethans," Woolf writes:

> For we are apt to forget, reading, as we tend to do, only masterpieces of a bygone age how great a power the body of literature possesses to impose itself: how it will not suffer itself to be read passively, but takes us and reads us; flouts our preconceptions; questions principles which we had got into the habit of taking for granted, and, in fact, splits us into two parts as we read, making us, even as we enjoy, yield our ground or stick to our guns. (CR 49)

I return later to this idea that literature "reads us"; here, my point is to emphasize the conflictual model Woolf adopted at times for the reading process, one that depends on the conception of art as activity rather than property. It is not only the "lesser" or the "new" writers who disturb us but the "great writers":

> But the great writer—the Hardy or the Proust—goes on his way regardless of the rights of private property. . . . he inflicts his own perspective upon us so severely that as often as not we suffer agonies—our vanity is injured because our own order is upset; we are afraid because the old supports are being wrenched from us; and we are bored. . . . Yet from anger, fear, and boredom a rare and lasting delight is sometimes born. (SCR 44–45)

If both the lesser and the great novels produce such effects, if both non-canonical and canonical literature violate our property and our person, it would seem that the *body* of literature, as well as the *person* of the reader, needs to be redefined. Redefining the canon is an achievement often attributed to Woolf's criticism, but it is less the individual texts themselves that

Woolf has challenged than the concept of literature as body or property. After all, Woolf discusses mainly "canonical" works in "Phases of Fiction." Nonetheless, her approach undercuts the notion of the canon as an established or homogeneous tradition of valuable works.

From the two collections of essays Woolf compiled, *The Common Reader* and *The Second Common Reader,* it is easy to see why she is so often credited with changing the literary canon. Her essays discuss obscure writers, fragmentary works, and marginal genres. She writes as much about Chaucer's reader, John Paston, as she does about Chaucer himself. She devotes more time to discussing Austen's unfinished novel, *The Watsons,* and her childhood story "Love and Freindship" (*sic*) than she devotes to Austen's well-known works. She compares the memoirs of the obscure with the novels of the famous. And yet, to engage in literary criticism *is* to engage in debates about canon formation. More important than what texts Woolf reads is why she reads them. Establishing a countercanon is not the primary goal of her criticism but the *inevitable consequence* of her comparative method and aesthetic motives. In these two collections, Woolf shows us that the literary canon is continually remade by readers like herself, those who choose their reading not by discriminating between the great and the mediocre but, as I argue in chapter 5, by discriminating among various purposes for reading (CR 1–2). Referring to the "noncanonical" works she discusses in "How Should One Read a Book?" Woolf asks: "are we to refuse to read them because they are not 'art'? Or shall we read them, but read them in a different way, with a different aim?" (SCR 237). By juxtaposing classic works with obscure ones, established genres with popular ones, Woolf offers an alternative to the usual way of defining the canon: literary history is not created by the works we read but by the way we read. Woolf challenges the concept of a literary canon by defining literature not in terms of its ontological or formal status (i.e., its essence or nature) but in terms of its functional status: certain works are treated as literature by certain readers for certain purposes.[16] Far from establishing a countercanon, Woolf shows us how any canon is already divided from itself, traversed by a mixture of motives and methods. Of primary importance, then, is the point or aim of the reading. As we see in "Phases of Fiction," Woolf's literary canon is a construct fashioned for her particular use: to investigate and illuminate the act of narrating in its multifold relations to the act of reading.

If the literary canon is determined by the way we read, then the question naturally arises, how should one read a book? Although the question of reading is one Woolf poses throughout her essays, it is one she never answers, at least not definitively. Instead, she raises other questions in response to this one: What book? Who's reading? For what end? In what context? Compared with what? [17] Because she asks a variety of questions and explores a variety of relations, Woolf tests out a variety of reading responses. Sometimes she sounds like Lubbock: the reader arranges the elements of the novel "at the novelist's bidding" (GR 143). Sometimes she sounds like Wayne Booth: the reader's primary task is to master the implied author's perspective and to grasp "how the novelist orders his world" (SCR 43). Sometimes she sounds like Roland Barthes: the pleasure in reading comes first and is, "by its nature, removed from analysis" (GR 116). And quite often she sounds like Iser: the whole of the book "expands in the reader's mind" as she "[supplies] what is not there" (CR 142). Woolf cannot recommend any one method of reading or any one countercanon, not just because books change (though they do) or because readers change (though they do too) but because she would have to stabilize the relations she has been investigating. This is not to say that we can read any way we like. The issue is not control or no control but where to locate control. Woolf does not center it in any one place (author, text, reader); rather, she disperses it through a system of literary discourse. In other words, she does not deny any "ground" to our critical activity but grounds that activity differently: in changing purposes and shared activity, not enduring standards and values. Woolf makes her criticism speculative and self-conscious in order to explore the possibilities and the limitations of any one approach. She discloses her aims and her methods to remind us that the knowledge we gain and the pleasure we take in reading are bound up with our motives, methods and interests.

For example, in three essays on very different writers—"Robinson Crusoe" (SCR), "Jane Eyre and Wuthering Heights" (CR), and "Notes on D. H. Lawrence" (M)—Woolf reveals the initial assumptions that determined her "angle of approach" to each work: Defoe's book considers the nature of humankind and society; Charlotte Brontë's world is "antiquated"; Lawrence is cryptic and crude. In each case Woolf narrates her reading experience to show how she was "rudely contradicted on every page" (SCR 45). As a result, she tells us, we must "alter our attitude" and "alter our proportions" as we read these texts; and in doing so, we can better discover "the connections which things in themselves different have had for the writer" (CR 163): "Finally, that is to say, we are forced to drop our own preconceptions and to accept what [the writer] wishes to give us" (SCR 46). Thus we learn that Defoe's middle-class viewpoint is concerned with common objects and practical explanations, not philosophical speculation; Brontë's world is "steeped through and through with . . . the indignation of Charlotte Brontë" (160–61), not with the curiosities of a past era; and Lawrence's novel emerges "with astonishing vividness," not with the "more mazy and more mystic" images we might expect given his reputation as a prophet (M 94). We read these novelists, then, for the different kinds of relations their fiction gives us: Defoe for the factual, Brontë for the poetic, Lawrence for the physical. By narrating her changing responses, Woolf focuses on the interactive experience of reading. She begins by announcing her own biases to show that no reading is totally objective and value free (GR 93) and that reading alters our "attitude toward reality" (132). Granted, the assumptions with which Woolf says she initially approached these novels may well be "fictitious" in that they are articulated only after her reading of each text and after she has decided to write an essay about how her assumptions changed in the course of her reading. But the *point* of these essays lies in the stories of reading she tells, not in her "real" state of mind at the time of her reading.[18]

Usually, the self-reflexiveness of Woolf's criticism is praised as a more open and honest approach than other criticisms. Woolf's own remarks endorse such a view. In "An Essay in Criticism," for example, she announces her intention to "pull down the imposing curtain which hides the critical process until it is complete" (GR 86). But such openness does not in itself attest to the value of the criticism.[19] We should be wary of valuing self-reflexiveness in itself, since self-reflexive criticism may not always function in the same way and since it may not always be used for the same ends. Again, a postmodern viewpoint can serve us well in understanding Woolf's statement. If the artwork is an autonomous object containing some meaning that the critic conveys to us, then the critic's disclosure of her or his methods would seem to be an unnecessary courtesy to the reader. But if the artwork is in part shaped by the literary system itself and by the reader's expectations, then what the critic compares it to, and what assumptions the critic begins with, would seem to make all the difference. Woolf realized that she was evaluating the "thing itself," not as it is, but as it comes to be apprehended. In "Phases of Fiction," she writes that we compare texts to something else because "all the mind can do is to make a likeness of the thing, and, by giving it another shape, cherish the illusion that it is explaining it, whereas it is, in fact, only looking at it afresh" (GR 116–17). In other words, if we retain certain modernist assumptions about the artwork (i.e., a belief in its wholeness, its autonomy, its permanence) in connection with Woolf's fiction, then we can only attribute her self-reflexive strategies to her openness about her method. Such a conclusion tells us little, however, about the usefulness of her method.

Rather than being a "homologue" of her fiction, Woolf's self-reflexive criticism is a function of her understanding of literary language as a "pragmatic force" (as Barthes calls it) acting *in* the world, not a structure bearing some relation *to* the world. Although Woolf acknowledges in "The Narrow Bridge of Art" that one of the critic's duties is to prepare us for literary forms to come, the purpose of her own criticism is not only to teach us how to read her fiction (though her critical essays may well have this effect). More importantly, Woolf's aim is to change our expectations of what fiction and criticism do and thereby increase our options in reading and our tolerance for differences. The critic should help us determine the reasons for which we read and the audiences for which we write. We might reconsider, therefore, Patricia Waugh's assumption about such self-reflexive criticism: "To be *successfully decoded,* then, experimental fiction of any variety requires an audience which is itself self-conscious about its linguistic practices" (*Metafiction* 64; emphasis added). I agree that Woolf's writings, both critical and fictional, make us self-conscious about how we use language, but it is not our ability to successfully decode the work that concerned Woolf—if, that is, the concept of "decoding" is taken to mean "making intelligible."[20] The concept of the text as a message to be deciphered or as a structure with a hidden depth to be revealed rests on the very assumptions about art and criticism that Woolf has called into question.

My point here is that the relation to be considered is not between new fiction and new criticism but between the ways in which changes in the one effect our expectations about the other; that is, the extent to which new narrative interests and new critical interests modify our thinking about literature in general.[21] When Waugh refers to our improved ability to decode the text (*Metafiction*), when David Lodge denies any alternative to playing the "about game" in criticism, that is, asking what the text is about (*Modes of Modern Writing*), and when Brooke-Rose raises the question of what is in the text and what is put there by the reader ("Readerhood of Man"), they confine new fiction and new criticism to old frameworks. They return to the concept of literature as something we make, not something we do. If the strategies of postmodern fiction confuse us, outrage us, or bore us, it is not just because the "old supports are being wrenched from us" (SCR 45) but because we insist on reappropriating such strategies into the old supports, as if such conflict and confusion were problems to be cleared up. As a result, we fail to challenge our assumptions about our own behavior. This is not to say that we must choose between two kinds of reading (e.g., modern and postmodern, academic and popular) but to stress that we must be cognizant of the effects different texts produce. Woolf's concern as a critic is with our ability to adapt to a variety of linguistic practices with an increased awareness of what is at stake in each. The skilled reader is one who masters a variety of language games, not one who masters the individual text.

What makes Woolf a particularly skilled reader, less personal than Forster and less impressionistic than Walter Pater, is her awareness that she reads, in Culler's words, "with the hypothesis of a reader" (*On Deconstruction* 67). She gives us not her own subjective readings but stories of reading as a Woolfian reader. The Woolfian reader judges not impressionistically or systematically but pragmatically. She understands reading as a constructed and learned activity, not something we all just naturally do (without thinking about it and without needing to think about it): "nobody reads simply by chance or without a definite scale of values" (GR 93); "Each has read differently, with the insight and the blindness of his own generation" (SCR 32). Reading "brings to light" the designs and values by which we read so that they can be noticed, and changed. Woolf was conscious of reading as both a culturally acquired activity developed from the texts we read (as revealed in *The Pargiters*) and as personal activity directed by our own fantasies, desires, and interests (as shown in essays like "Reading"). That is, Woolf was aware of the reader as an individual and as a function of various discursive systems. Reading becomes part of the process of forming an identity as the reader performs various textual functions.[22] Thus, in Woolf's fiction, as in the fiction of Beckett, Kafka, and many postmodern writers, which does not always maintain a consistent point of view or give a consistent set of directions, the reader must assume various and even contradictory roles. The profusion of narrative perspectives in a novel like *Jacob's Room* undermines any single mediator between the text and the reader. Determining the author's meaning or worldview in such fiction is not a matter of precise interpretation or successful decoding; rather, it is a matter of tenacious pursuit.

The reader thus becomes a function of the text, not just an identity in relation to it. Walter Benn Michaels expresses a similar view, connecting the poststructuralist notion of the self with Peirce's pragmatism. He says that in attacking the Cartesian concept of the self, Peirce argues against its primacy and shows that the self is "already embedded in a context, the community of interpretation or system of signs"; it is "always committed" (194). Thus, in Jane Tompkins's words, "Michaels presents the self as a function of its interpretative strategies" (xxiv). Put another way, the reader, like Orlando, learns how to adapt to changing situations and changing relations.

We are now in a position to reconsider what is the most important concept to come out of Woolf's criticism: the common reader. The concept of the common reader has been oversimplified by many critics who see only one aspect of its nature as a critical concept for Woolf. As with other terms, Woolf is not always consistent in her use of the "common reader" from essay to essay. At times it suggests the casual reader ("The Common Reader"); at others, the Woolfian reader ("How Should One Read a Book?"); at still others, the contemporary reader ("The Patron and the Crocus"); and even a transhistorical, generalized reader ("The Reader"). Still, the concept of the common reader is an important critical tool for Woolf, not just a "mask" she adopted in her *Common Reader* volumes and abandoned in her other essays (Manuel 29).

The usual interpretation of Woolf's "common reader" presents this figure as the average or literate reader, the one Woolf supposedly substitutes for the critic or academician as the arbiter of literary tastes and the role she supposedly assumes in her own essays. Undoubtedly, Woolf denies any authoritative role for herself in her critical essays, insisting that she does not prescribe any one method or set of rules: "I do not want to attribute to the world at large the opinions of one solitary, ill-informed, and misguided individual" ("Mr. Bennett and Mrs. Brown," CDB 95). While such apologies tend to support the common reading of the common reader, this interpretation raises some disturbing questions. In identifying Woolf as the average reader, not the critic or theoretician of literature, do we not risk depreciating her essays? Do we not tend to see them as only illuminations of her own reading process and her own responses and tastes, and therefore of little value generally? Seeing her as a common reader, we risk reducing her essays to mere drawing room chitchat, delightfully entertaining but of little use for critical inquiry. And, we might well ask, is Woolf so common a reader? Would the average reader peruse a copy of *Poems and Fancies* by the Duchess of Newcastle? Has the average reader written a novel like *Jacob's Room*? Finally, in substituting "common reader" for "critic," do we not risk replacing one authority (well educated, analytic) with another (literate, intuitive), or risk denying any kind of standard and saying there are only individual readings?

Woolf's concept of the common reader does suggest the average reader reading a particular text at a particular time; further, the common reader suggests a *female* reader given that the casual reader, in contrast to the critic, has often been feminized in literary history. In this sense the concept contains a political value that I do not deny. But it is most useful as a *critical* construct when it presents a concept of the reader as a function of literature: that is, as a community of readers and as a reader-in-the-text. Such a concept has political implications as well. As I mentioned earlier, Woolf presents the interaction between text and reader as controlled neither by the individual author nor by the individual reader but by some tradition from which we extrapolate. This sense of community, which Woolf develops in terms of Anon and the Reader in her late essays by those names, represents the interaction between author and audience, the interpersonal over the personal or impersonal.

In "Anon" Woolf discusses literature as a "common product," "written by one hand, but so moulded in transition that the author [has] no sense of *property* in it" (A 395; emphasis added). Like Barthes, Woolf considered it an unfortunate "blow" to literature when "the author[']s name is attached to a book" (A 385) and we therefore read "through the life of the author" (SCR 42), for such a perspective distracts us from "the book itself." If, however, we conceive of literature as a common activity and the writer and reader as functions of literature, then "no one tries to stamp his own name, to discover his own experience" in a particular work (A 385). We read to change our perspective of the world, not to reinforce our own views (SCR 44). This is the point of reading in "Phases of Fiction," in which Woolf's reader is embedded in literary history. In this sense the common reader differs from the critic, not in the extent of her literary knowledge or level of critical skills, not even in her openness or objectivity, but in the nature of her interest in reading. Where the critic stands apart from the text to investigate the author's life, the text's message, or the formal structure, the common reader is situated within the textual process, observing her own responses and noting how the text functions in relation to other texts and other readings. In other words, the common reader does not take literature as *"a matter of course,"* assuming "that a writer writes quite simply *to express himself"* (Barthes, *Critical Essays* 250). The common reader questions why writers write and why readers read. What we discover in "Phases of Fiction" is that the novel changes in response to the changing interests and needs of the reading public. This means not only that we must enlarge the reading public if we are to diversify literary forms but also that we must question, as Janice Radway does, the functions of literature for any reading public before evaluating the form of literature (see chap. 5).

My argument is that Woolf's "common reader" is no more a unique or special individual or type than is her artist figure, and therein lies the very strength of this concept. To relinquish the notion of the artist's uniqueness and originality while retaining the notion of the reader's uniqueness and originality would be to distort the kind of relational and interpersonal model Woolf develops in her fiction. Contemporary critics did not suddenly come to recognize that readers differ, whereas the New Critics were ignorant of this fact; rather, contemporary critics must grant more authority to the reader because of their relational model of the literary work, a model that owes much to the insights of structuralist and poststructuralist theorists, such as Saussure and Barthes. If the artwork is, as Woolf mockingly suggests, "a broken jar . . . to be stood in a cabinet behind glass doors" (CR 101), then who handles the jar makes little difference, as long as that person has access to the cabinet. But if the text is a transaction that we grasp through the stories of reading we tell, as Woolf shows us, then who is telling the stories makes a world of difference (cf. Tompkins xxv). And yet, as Woolf's own narrative critical style reveals, reading is a shared activity, not a private one. To exalt any one type of reader would be to limit that difference and to make our stories homogeneous. To exalt the individual reader would be to neglect Woolf's concept of reading as a learned activity and her concept of the self as that which is formed through relationships.[23] This is not to deny the argument that Woolf's desire is to remove literature from the hands of the specialists and turn it over to the populace. Rather, I want to point out that such an argument must be preceded by a change in thinking about art, and further, that it is not an argument for making art or criticism more authentic or natural. For the audience as well as the artist is embroiled in the "economy of discourses" (Foucault's phrase) making up the literary event. To argue for the importance of the common reader while retaining a belief in art's autonomy, authenticity, or truth-value would not make much sense.

Those who affirm the common reader as a more natural, free, or unbiased reader retain a notion of language and self that Woolf came to relinquish. We can see this change by looking at two essays on language, "On Not Knowing Greek" (1918) and Woolf's BBC broadcast, "Craftsmanship" (1937). In the earlier essay, Woolf envies the ancient Greek writers for the freshness and originality of their language which gave them a natural relation to language that modern writers, in their extreme self-consciousness over words, lack. Because Greek language was free of ambiguity, Woolf says, Greek writers could express the essence of things. But as Woolf experimented with different narrative relations over the years, she came to consider some kinds of ambiguity of value. In the later essay, Woolf values words not for their univocal nature but for their multivalence. Because words "mean" in relation to other words, they cannot represent any one thing. From probing the essence that words express, Woolf turns to questioning "the proper use of words" (DM 201): "How can we combine the old words in new orders *so that they survive,* so that they create beauty, so that they tell the truth? That is the question" (DM 204; emphasis added). This truth is constructed in relationships, not confirmed by returning to a more pristine language or a more natural self.

Woolf does recognize differences among readers, even stresses the differences in her essays as well as in her fiction: "It seems that a profound, impartial, and absolutely just opinion . . . is utterly unknown. Either we are men, or we are women. Either we are cold, or we are sentimental. Either we are young, or growing old" (JR 71–72). And she does want to make reading and writing common activities, in the sense of communal activities. However, the primacy she grants relations, motives, and contexts, whether in the formation of the self or of the artwork, prevents her from reducing differences to relativisim or enshrining differences in distinct categories. As I note in chapter 5, the distinction between a trained reader and an untrained one is ultimately a false one *in terms of Woolf's relational thinking,* much as the distinction between a serious use of language and a nonserious or fictional use is ultimately a false one in terms of Wittgenstein's linguistic philosophy, as Stanley Fish argues.[24] Only the assumption of an essential self existing apart from systems of discourse would enable us to affirm the common reader as a more natural, unbiased individual. But the "new novel" or postmodern fiction is not built on stable or essentialist concepts of self and world. The common reading of Woolf's fiction as a quest for truth or essence, or as the search for an appropriate form for women's writing, encourages such readings of the common reader as the ideal reader or as the liberated individual. The common reader, though, is not merely affirmed; rather, she is constructed through the very stories she reads and the stories she tells. In this sense literature, as Woolf says, reads us. It splits us in that we, like the artist, are a part of and apart from the work we are creating. Like Clarissa Dalloway, we organize and observe our own activity. We read both to change our culture and to preserve it (Tompkins xxv).[25]

While this emphasis on reading literature as a means of preserving our culture seems to echo Woolf's adversary F. R. Leavis, and while Woolf's comparative method and her attention to literary tradition bring to mind T. S. Eliot, the important difference lies in their different concepts of culture. And this difference comes to the fore in Woolf's postmodern assumptions and strategies. Where Eliot's and Leavis's culture is (ideally) organic, Woolf's is dynamic. The one is self-contained; the other, self-divided. The one is at peace with itself; the other is never at rest. Although Eliot's tradition makes room for and adjusts to new members, those members often confirm rather than challenge that tradition, a point Terry Eagleton also argues (*Literary Theory* 39). In other words, Eliot's tradition is more homogeneous than heterogeneous. Leavis in particular lamented the loss of an organic relation between high and popular culture. He deprecated urban sophistication, suburban pretensions, commercialism, and advertising jargon—all forces, in his view, that corrupt natural language and natural values and induce a split in society.[26]

Woolf, by contrast, accepts such changes in social organization as giving a different view and providing a different pleasure. What Woolf wants to preserve is the plurality of discourses making up any one society; she does not seek to reinstate some organic relation through increased homogenization. What is needed, on the contrary, is increased diversification.[27] For this reason Woolf opposed the elevation of criticism into a specialized activity, as seen in Lubbock's *Craft of Fiction,* and the teaching of literature as a separate discipline, as fostered by Leavis's Cambridge curriculum. Because Woolf's own writing is often seen as promoting a more just and free society, as harmonizing or unifying society, her difference from these critics is attributed solely to differences in gender or background. For example, Goldman argues that Woolf's Bloomsbury individualism and her feminist sensitivity to her own lack of a university education led Woolf to reject prescriptive and positivist-minded criticism ("Woolf and the Critic" 165). Certainly, Woolf rejected such criticism, but the reason she did so can be found in her own concept of art and its corresponding concept of culture. Culture, like art, is never complete but is continually produced. It is not monologic but dialogic. It consists of both the impulse toward order and the pull against stasis. It is no one group's private ground but a field of competing interests and perspectives.

Whereas Pound's slogan, "Make it new," was an effort to keep art at the vanguard of culture and in the hands of an elite, Woolf's expedient, "Break the rhythm" (*Between the Acts*), is conjoined with an increasing concern for the democratization of art (as expressed most clearly in "The Leaning Tower"). Hers was an effort to assimilate art into mass culture as a way of assuring the survival of art by keeping it out of the control of the few. That control is what had proven so disastrous not only for women writers but for the leaning-tower poets and for the war-torn society analyzed in *Three Guineas*. Woolf's goal as a reader and writer of literature was to provide new ways of reading our texts, ourselves, and our world in order to give reading a new function and value in society (compare my argument on pp. 56–57). In this sense the common reader is less an individual type than a strategy for survival. To entrust the survival of art to any one group is the very threat Woolf's changing strategies were meant to subvert.

What makes Woolf such a subtle and skillful reader, a match for the variety of authors she engages in her criticism, is the very resiliency of her comparative, speculative, and narrative critical approach. Her functional conception of literature keeps her criticism open to change. And her different stories of reading keep her, and keep us, from adopting any one authority (whether critic, system, or school), thereby throwing us back on our own questions. After all, it is our own questions and our own responses that we must test against the readings of other critics. As Woolf tells us, the critics "are only able to help us if we come to them laden with questions and suggestions won honestly in the course of our own reading. They can do nothing for us if we herd ourselves under their authority and lie down like sheep in the shade of a hedge. We can only understand their ruling when it comes in conflict with our own and vanquishes it" (SCR 244).

NOTES

1. One thing I do not mean by the "common reader" is what Radway means by the "general reader" (see chap. 5). I use the term here to designate a critical construct, not just the audience of popular or nonacademic fiction.

2. Frankly, from a modernist perspective, this concern with the reader is not unusual either. For instance, in "The Use of Poetry and the Use of Criticism," Eliot proclaims that "what a poem means is as much what it means to others as what it means to the author"; later in that same essay he writes, "The poet is much more vitally concerned with the social 'uses' of poetry and with his own place in society" (88, 92). I quote Eliot not to claim his views are the same as Woolf's (though the work from which I quote contains statements very much like those in Woolf's essays of the late 1920s, such as "The Narrow Bridge of Art," "Impassioned Prose," and "Phases of Fiction"), and not to claim his views are like the postmodernists, but to stress the need to clarify what we mean when we claim as *new* a concern with the reader or with the social function of art.

3. This confluence of the creative and the critical reveals the extent to which writing a novel is itself a critical act. As Waugh writes of self-reflexive novels, they "explore a *theory* of fiction through the *practice* of writing fiction" (*Metafiction* 2).

4. Suleiman defines self-reflexive criticism similarly in her introduction to *The Reader in the Text* (4). Iser uses the term *aesthetic* to refer to the reader's realization of the text, that is, the creative actualization of the text she or he reads ("Interaction between Text and Reader" 106).

5. For example, Bell and Ohmann list several distinguishing features of Woolf's critical method, including her nonauthoritarian tone, her narrative style, and her new subject matter, specifically, her choice of works outside "the standard canon of English literature" (364–69). Richter (244) and DiBattista ("Joyce, Woolf, and the Modern Mind" 112) both note how Woolf anticipated later critical trends, mentioning Robbe-Grillet and Barthes, respectively. Minow-Pinkney traces the connections between Woolf and Kristeva, though she focuses on Woolf's fiction more than on her criticism. And Moi points out in her introduction to *Sexual/Textual Politics* that Meisel's book on Woolf and Pater suggests affinities between Woolf and the deconstructionists (17–18).

6. As Martin notes, Lubbock and Forster represent two prominent and opposing critical position of the 1920s and 1930s (*Recent Theories of Narrative* 20).

7. In "Caution and Criticism," Woolf objects to Williams's reliance on literary periods: "the Victorianism of the Victorian age . . . was not of one texture, nor disappeared all at once. . . . nothing so dramatic as a fresh age could immediately succeed it. It was replaced gradually by a patchwork of influences" (CW 18). In "The Anatomy of Fiction," she challenges Hamilton's distinct types: "But learning from books is a capricious business at best, and the teaching so vague and changeable that in the end, far from calling books either 'romantic' or 'realistic,' you will be more inclined to think them, as you think people, very mixed, very distinct, very unlike one another" (GR 54). The method Woolf adopted to write about books that are "very mixed" and periods that are "not of one texture" is similar to the one she adopted in her fiction to deal with characters and history: that is, she tested out and compared various perspectives and relations.

8. Woolf often narrates her own reading of a work in her criticism of it, as in her reading of Mary Carmichael's novel in *A Room of One's Own* and her reading of Bennett's *Hilda Lessways* in "Mr. Bennett and Mrs. Brown."

9. Barthes writes that emotion "contradicts the general rule that would assign bliss [or the text] a fixed form" (*Pleasure of the Text* 25). Such an awareness leads to the concept of the text as function, not form. Thus, for Barthes as for Woolf, the writer becomes a function of the text, not necessarily the origin of its meaning. We see this idea in *The Waves,* where Woolf retains some control over the text but does not necessarily have the first word (chap. 1). Barthes' concept of the "death of the author" has frequently been misunderstood apart from its context. He does not deny that the author plays a role but that the author's "biographical person" is our concern (27). Woolf, too, has objected to criticism that focuses on "the institution" of the author ("Phases of Fiction," GR; "Robinson Crusoe," SCR).

10. Compare Hutcheon's comment on postmodern criticism, namely, that postmodern critics are concerned not just with the author or the text or the reader but with the "enunciating act" itself (78).

11. Culler describes a semiotics of reading: "Instead of attempting to legislate solutions to interpretive disagreements, one might attempt to analyze the interpretive operations that produce these disagreements. . . . Such a program falls under the aegis of semiotics, which seeks to identify the conventions and operations by which any signifying practice (such as literature) produces its observable effects of meaning" (*Pursuit of Signs* 48).

12. I am aware that Woolf read Eliot's "Tradition and the Individual Talent" in which he advocates a comparative approach to criticism. However, I am looking not for the influences on but for the implications of Woolf's critical assumptions. We need only read Eliot's essay in conjunction with any of Woolf's to note the telling differences, especially in tone and tropes. Eliot's tone is authoritative; Woolf's is conversational and speculative. Eliot's favored trope is metaphor; Woolf's is apostrophe and personification. She addresses the dead author or the hypothesized reader, and she attributes human qualities to the text itself. And where Eliot's concept of tradition is impersonal, Woolf's is interpersonal. Both views, though, suggest the structuralist notion that, as Scholes puts it, "the fundamental external conditioner of any work of literature is the literary tradition itself" (112). But, of course, it is the concept of tradition that is at issue.

13. Thiher writes: "Perhaps the key postmodern understanding of writing is that every text, consciously or not, is penetrated with and composed of traces of other texts. Such an understanding of writing further entails the belief that the ultimate locus of meaning is never one text, centered upon itself, but all the other texts that inhabit writing in a free play of *différance*" (90). Intertextuality, as Hutcheon notes, "replaces the challenged author-text relation with one between reader and text, one that situates the locus of textual meaning within the history of discourse itself" (126). Although Eliot's tradition and Kristeva's intertextuality have in common a concern with the literary system over the individual writer, they differ, as we will see, in the kind of system each values. See also note 27.

14. This is not to say that language constitutes the world or that there is nothing outside the text. Rather, it is to say that we can engage with and negotiate our world only by means of a particular discourse. As Cornel West explains this prag-

matic position: "the claim is that evolving descriptions and ever-changing versions of . . . the world issue forth from various communities as responses to certain problems, as attempts to overcome specific situations, and as means to satisfy particular needs and interests" (201).

15. If we do not conceive of the world or the novel as property, then we can consider, in Smith's words, "the multiple functions and contextually variable identity" of any narrative (*Margins of Discourse* xiii). Smith mentions the novels of Beckett, Robbe-Grillet, and Sarraute in particular as narrative structures that cannot be described in terms of a two-termed structure (185). These writers reconsider, as Woolf does in "Phases of Fiction," the assumptions behind a belief in "property" and the relation of narrative to various forms of discourse.

16. This idea of the canon as construct is discussed by Eagleton in *Literary Theory* (11). A functional definition of literature is proposed by Ellis (chap. 2) and by Smith (*Margins of Discourse* 44–46).

17. Johnson asks many of these same questions in her discussion of an essay by Zora Neale Hurston (*World of Difference* 178). Her point is to show that differences are "always a function of a specific interlocutionary situation." More gratifying than finding other critics reaching the same conclusions is finding other critics asking the same questions.

18. For different discussion of Woolf's "Robinson Crusoe," see Kennard's "Ourself behind Ourself." She emphasizes not just Woolf's identification with the writer but, more importantly, her affirmation of her own values and viewpoints through her confrontation with another's (74). As I argue, however, reading is part of the process of forming an identity, not affirming one.

19. However open Woolf may have been about her motives in this essay, I have trouble accepting her criticism of Hemingway's use of dialogue. Woolf's criterion is simply that too much dialogue is not good, but we can say of the story she uses to support her view, "Hills Like White Elephants," that too much dialogue is precisely the point. After reading Woolf's reviews of other American writers, I must wonder if she does indeed reveal all her biases in "An Essay in Criticism"—not that one ever could.

20. By "decoding," though, Waugh may well mean to emphasize *reading* as opposed to *hermeneutics* (interpretation), or in Schor's words, "something that is done *in* fiction" rather than "something that is done *to* fiction" (*Reading in Detail* 121).

21. My point here is much like one Quigley makes in the *The Modern Stage and Other Worlds:* "criticism needs to keep pace with the speed at which [writers] and audiences adapt to and make use of successive changes" (xi). Discussions of Woolf's critical and fictional writings and of postmodern and poststructuralist writings tend to draw one-to-one correspondences between the criticism and the fiction instead of exploring the various implications of such changes.

22. Tompkins points out this view in the reader-response criticism of Walker Gibson (xi). It is also the view expressed in criticism of postmodern fiction in particular. See, for example, Robbe-Grillet's *For a New Novel* and Mistacco's "Theory and Practice of Reading Nouveaux Romans."

23. Woolf's relational sense of self is discussed at length by Waugh in *Feminine Fictions*.

24. In "How To Do Things with Austin and Searle," Fish argues that the distinction between serious and fictional discourse has nothing to do with their relationship to the real world but has everything to do with their relationship to their users. He continues: "In large part, my argument follows from Wittgenstein's notion of a 'language game' in which words are responsible not to what is real but to what has been laid down as real . . . by a set of constitutive rules" (241).

25. Woolf values change, but change must be seen in relation to continuity, a point Hassan makes in "The Question of Postmodernism" and Quigley reiterates in *The Modern Stage and Other Worlds*. The importance of tradition or continuity for Woolf can be seen in her criticism of Lawrence: "one feels that he echoes nobody, continues no tradition, is unaware of the past, of the present save as it affects the future. As a writer, this lack of tradition affects him immensely" (M 97). The effect is that Lawrence, in Woolf's opinion, was not interested in "literature as literature" but only as a forum for his own theories.

26. This point is expressed in Leavis's essay "Literature and Society" and is discussed by Annan in "Bloomsbury and the Leavises" (31–32). What strikes us now is how much Leavis's comments in this essay sound like the complaints against postmodern literature and society raised by critics such as Graff, Newman, and Jameson.

27. Johnson explains the difference between the conventional notion of literary tradition and the poststructuralist notion of intertextuality in terms of property: the former speaks of a "transfer of property," the latter of "violations of property." That is, intertextuality "designates the multitude of ways a text has of not being self-contained" (*World of Difference* 116).

# Conclusion:
## *Issuing*

I will go on adventuring, changing, opening my mind and my eyes, refusing to be stamped & stereotyped.

—Virginia Woolf,
Diary, 1933

Now I know how to go on!

—Ludwig Wittgenstein,
*Philosophical Investigations*

Throughout this work, I have returned again and again to the same critical impasse, that is, the necessity of choosing between or reconciling two alternatives, engendered by the application of dualistic distinctions (e.g., fact/fiction, surface/depth, form/content, art/politics) to the works of Virginia Woolf. I have sought to offer alternatives to a choice between two alternatives by pointing out the changing contexts in which certain distinctions can function and the changing conceptions of language and narrative in Woolf's writings that work against these dualistic approaches. Stressing the conceptual differences generated by motival and rhetorical differences in Woolf's works, I have noted the different kinds of relations possible in different kinds of texts and contexts, and thus the different kinds of conclusions we can reach in each particular case. My purpose has been to enact a way of thinking about and responding to narrative discourse that considers different ways of relating things rather than the distinction between two things. But in relying on postmodern assumptions and strategies to make my point, am I not in danger of falling back into the same kind of critical practice I take issue with, namely, setting up an opposition between two types of writing, modernism and postmodernism? Do I not risk replacing a modernist or feminist referential with a postmodernist one, thereby making the same kind of move for which I have criticized some feminist critics in the Introduction? For all my talk of refusing to choose and resisting right readings, do I not offer postmodernism as the right choice after all?

I must say that I have worried over these questions from time to time while writing this book. How can I take issue with others for their certainty, their oppositional stances, and their new right readings without being just as certain, oppositional, and right? And I have found comfort in the realization that I am not alone in asking such questions, in wondering if my resistance to right readings is a new right reading. Linda Hutcheon asks of her own (and anyone else's) attempt to theorize postmodernism, "From what position can one 'theorize' (even self-consciously) a disparate, contradictory, multivalent, current cultural phenomenon?" (13). More pointedly, throughout *The Daughter's Seduction*, Jane Gallop returns to the question of whether or not she is offering her own position as the right one. By setting up exchanges between seemingly opposing positions within and between psychoanalysis and feminism, and by changing her own position within these exchanges, Gallop attempts to defy "the fallacies of integrity and closure" (xiii) that shore up disputes between mutually exclusive, defensive, and suspicious positions. She refuses to be pinned down and sees such flexibility as a strength, yet she worries that she might be offering her own refusal to choose as the right choice, the desired or desirable position for the feminist critic (e.g., 103).

But Gallop worries needlessly. For we have a choice here, we face this dilemma, only if we try to define a feminist practice as Elaine Showalter does in *The New Feminist Criticism*, that is, in terms of its distinctive subject (women's writing) or method (gynocriticism). Gallop is doing something else, however, as her essay "The Problem of Definition," a review of Showalter's book, makes apparent. Gallop's concept of a "double discourse," which she finds useful for a feminist practice, differs from Showalter's "double-voiced discourse" in that Gallop's does not depend on the definitive distinction between two things (e.g., between a dominant [male] discourse and a muted [female] one) but on the contextual, functional, and rhetorical distinctions between things. By reading texts against each other, Gallop notes the theoretical and rhetorical commitments writers make in particular discursive exchanges and the consequences of those commitments—the possibilites they allow for, the impasses they face, the limitations they impose. She does not *define* a practice but *enacts* a way of proceeding. Where Showalter's goal is to define a "genuinely woman centered, independent, and intellectually coherent" critical practice, possessing "its own subject, its own system, its own theory, and its own voice" (247), Gallop's point is to violate and thereby disturb the boundaries of such definitions and to raise questions about what else feminist criticism might do.[1] Thus, Gallop's enactment and Showalter's definition of a double discourse are not two versions of the same thing. Although their terms are similar, the terms of their discussion are not. Like modernism and postmodernism, they differ in logic, in motive, in rhetoric. They cannot be compared on the same terms for they are meant to do different things.[2]

I offer this digression as a way of answering, not avoiding, the questions I raise. To the extent that I have offered postmodernist concepts of language and narrative as more useful than modernist ones in describing Woolf's changing textual practice and in assessing the feminist implications of her writing, I could be seen to present the correct reading of Woolf and the correct position for feminist critics. But to the extent that I resist generalizing from reading Woolf in terms of postmodernism to concluding that she *is* postmodernist, and to the extent that I argue not that my postmodernist reading is always more appropriate than a modernist one but more appropriate in terms of the particular relations we are trying to account for, my approach is not "normative" (arguing for right readings) but "corrective" (arguing for better ways of reading in light of different concepts of language and literature).[3] Gerald Graff might well accuse me of "redeeming a bad situation by redescribing it" (45), and in drawing on Wittgenstein's theorizing about language, this is precisely my strategy. But such behavior is irresponsible or futile, as Graff implies, only if we believe not so much that there is something outside our descriptions (for, of course, there is) but that there is some *thing* outside our descriptions (i.e., our modes of inquiry) against which we can measure them. As Brian McHale points out, arguments against postmodernism, such as Graff's, come from measuring postmodernism against a norm for fictional behavior, the norm of realism, even though that norm as been revealed to be a set of conventions (220).

Such arguments also come, I argue, from accepting a certain norm for critical behavior, one that is largely governed by modernist motives and that leads us to suspect that the refusal to choose may be, as Graff seems to fear, a way of diffusing opposition and maintaining the status quo. Yet if postmodern literature seems to be against literature itself, it may well be due more to our habitual ways of thinking about and responding to literature than to anything intrinsic to the fiction. If taken seriously, in the sense of attending to the implications of its strategies, not reading through them, postmodern writing may not defeat literature, but it may make a certain way of talking about and valuing literature no longer tenable. Graff criticizes attacks on the correspondence theory of truth made by postmodernists, arguing that the problem is not in the theory itself but in a particular correspondence (89). That is, one can argue not that the correspondence theory is untenable but that a particular ideology "fails to correspond to reality" and then offer an alternative that "corresponds more closely" (89). This is exactly what many of the feminist critics I have discussed attempt to do. But it is just such an alternative (a more highly valued choice) that those Graff calls "textualists" and those I call "postmodernists" do not want to set up. For an "ideology of common agreement" functions by exclusion, by drawing boundaries around distinct domains. Postmodern writing functions by exposing the aporias of such domains and by acknowledging that we draw boundaries for certain purposes, and there would be no need to draw boundaries if we did not anticipate that they would be crossed (cf. Wittgenstein, *Philosophical Investigations* #69, #499).

As Gallop's writing reveals, the refusal to choose can become the right choice only when the motive of our investigations is to describe the subject in question (whether postmodernism, Virginia Woolf, or women's writing) or the mode of inquiry (whether modernist, feminist, or postmodernist) in terms of its distinctive features or appropriate form; only when our goal is to establish a common ground, to codify a coherent practice, or to reach some kind of consensus. That is, when our goal is to replace an outmoded or suspect literary or critical form with another, more appropriate one. But postmodernism differs from modernism in just these goals. As Ihab Hassan argues, postmodernism marks a change in motivation: where modernism attempts to replace a lost ground, belief, or center, postmodernism attempts to comply with such a loss (*Postmodern Turn* 44–45); or, as Alice Jardine puts it, to affirm and assume such a loss (*Gynesis* 68). Therefore, we should reconsider what we mean when we speak of postmodernism's refusal to choose.

This refusal to choose is commonly attributed to postmodern texts. Hassan, for example, defines postmodernism as defying either/or choices, as a persistent oscillation (*Postmodern Turn* 89); McHale discusses postmodernism in terms of its hesitation or oscillation between the literal and the metaphorical (134); and Jardine talks in terms of its uncertainty and undecidability (*Gynesis* 25). While such terms (hesitation, oscillation, undecidability) get at the different motivating structures of postmodern texts, they designate not the shared traits of such writing but the similar effects of a writing that can no longer be adequately described in terms of modernist discourse. After all, a refusal to choose may be a gesture of resignation (Why bother?), a gesture of resistance (I refuse to choose!), or a gesture of negotiation (What else could we do?). Such undecidability, that is, may function differently in different texts and may depend on our behavior with respect to different contexts. In other words, postmodernism may not be indecisive by nature; rather, our ways of describing its behavior may at times be inadequate. Our ways of defining may produce undecidability as an effect. As I have argued throughout this book, we need another way of talking about these texts so that we refrain from focusing only on what they *do not* do.[4]

In keeping with my gesture of discussing a particular text, I turn now to David Lodge's *Modes of Modern Writing* to show how a certain way of talking about literature and a certain conception of our tasks as critics leads to certain kinds of conclusions. I choose Lodge as my example because he too characterizes postmodernism by its refusal to choose and because he applies his concept of writing to Woolf's canon.

In *The Modes of Modern Writing,* Lodge wants to resist a totalizing historicist position that suppresses certain traits in the writing of a period to argue the inevitability of others. In this he is joined by Woolf, who also refused to see historical periods as coherent and self-contained, as most evident in *Orlando*. In her late essay "The Leaning Tower," Woolf writes: "Directly we speak of tendencies or movements we commit ourselves to the belief that there is some force, influence, outer pressure which is strong enough to stamp itself upon a whole group of different writers so that all their writing has a certain common likeness" (M 129–30). As she has argued in so many essays (e.g., "Caution and Criticism," "The Anatomy of Fiction," "The Art of Fiction," "The Narrow Bridge of Art"), our narrative theories and critical purposes create categories of novels, not shared traits "stamped" on writers by some social or historical force. This is not to deny the effect of social factors and historical variables, only to recognize that they are neither determinant nor monolithic. We need a methodology, not just a chronology, to group novels into types.[5] When planning "Phases of Fiction," Woolf wrote in her diary, "I think I will find some theory of fiction." She continues: "I don't think it is a matter of 'development' but something to do with prose & poetry, in novels. For instance Defoe at one end: E. Brontë at the other. Reality something they put at different distances" (Diary 3:50).

Woolf's theory of fiction seems at first to be much like Lodge's, only where Woolf uses prose and poetry as ways of mapping the phases of fiction, Lodge offers "a way of mapping the literary history of the modern period" by situating all writing between two modes of discourse, the metaphoric and the metonymic: "there is nowhere for discourse to go except between these two poles" (*Modes of Modern Writing* 220).[6] His model relies on a representational concept of narrative that gives us two options: the metaphoric text offers a "model of reality" in general; the metonymic text gives us "a representative *bit* of reality" (109). Reading fiction in relation to life, Lodge asks, "What is the text *about?*" For "there is no alternative to the 'about game,'" he tells us, "unless we are to sit before works of literature in dumb silence" (110), the way many sit before postmodern novels.

But there is an alternative, of course. We can change the rules of the game by changing what counts as a legitimate move. Lodge's model, which at first seems so much like Woolf's, privileges the semantic relation between text and world, whereas Woolf considers the pragmatic relation between text and reader. In "Phases of Fiction," Woolf stresses the changing motives, interests, and desires of readers; for Lodge, however, "there is no alternative to the 'about game.'" But as we have seen in the preceding chapters, an alternative is to rephrase our question, from What is the text about? (to what does it refer or correspond) to How does the text come about? or What does the text bring about? (what are its functions and effects).

Because he plays the "about game," Lodge has trouble placing postmodern novels either on the side of the metonymic antimodernist narratives or on the side of the metaphoric modernist ones: "it would seem that we can best define the formal character of postmodernist writing by examining its efforts . . . to defy (*even if such defiance is ultimately vain*) the *obligation* to choose between these two principles" (228; emphasis added). Thus, Lodge's model presents postmodern texts as defiant, irresponsible, or self-defeating. What his discussion of postmodern novels reveals, however, is not how these novels "defy the obligation to choose" between two modes but how they defy the concept of a choice between two modes and the concept on which such a choice is based, namely, that literature bears some relation to life, represents something, is about something. To Lodge, postmodern novels are "absurd" because they resist this kind of reading. On the contrary, postmodern novels are absurd because we persist in this kind of reading, reading them as representations, as referring to a world beyond, as one thing as opposed to another. Postmodern narratives expose and exploit our tendency to read this way, to play the "about game." Their humor and playfulness, as well as their absurdity, come from mistaking one function of narrative for another (e.g., the performative for the referential) or one level of discourse for another (e.g., the rhetorical for the logical). That is, their gesture may not be a refusal to take a position but a refusal to ground a position, for what makes their game possible is the absence of that very "norm" that controls Lodge's language game.[7] Rather than thrusting a choice on them, then, we might do better to learn how to play their game.

Let's look at the effects of the "about game" by noting what happens when Lodge applies his model to the writings of Virginia Woolf. According to Lodge, Woolf's novels develop from the metonymic realism of *The Voyage Out* and *Jacob's Room* to the metaphoric modernism of *To the Lighthouse* and *The Waves*, with *Mrs. Dalloway* as the "transition" between these two modes. Coincidentally, this happens to be the order in which Woolf wrote these novels, suggesting a natural or inevitable evolution of her writing toward some "logical terminous" (181), as Lodge refers to *The Waves*. This normative conception of narrative development is quite common and quite compelling. For instance, McHale, who draws on Lodge in his own work, argues that Pynchon's novels develop from the modernism of *V.* to the late modernism of *The Crying of Lot 49* to the postmodernism of *Gravity's Rainbow*. There is nothing wrong with this scenario, it just isn't normative, as becomes most apparent when Jardine reads *V.* as an example of postmodern writing, or when we notice what has been left out of this particular story.[8] That is, this kind of development Lodge notes in Woolf's texts, like the development McHale notes in Pynchon's, comes from playing the "about game"; the justification for this development is to be found in Lodge's critical motives, not in the structure and strategies of the texts themselves. Thus, after asking, What is the text about? the question remains, What is the questioner about (up to) in reading the text as one thing rather than another?

In Woolf's case, Lodge's scenario leads him to dismiss half of Woolf's novels, and all of her comedies, as aberrations. Eliminating the anomalies, or reappropriating and legitimizing them, are the two strategies used in Woolf criticism to smooth out the wrinkles in her writing. Thus Lodge dismisses Woolf's comedies as aberrations, even as Susan Squier assures us that they are really "deeply serious" (*Virginia Woolf and London*). But these "anomalies" may just mark the moment when Woolf shifts to another order of discourse, another conception of language, another language game. Ironically, many of the novels that Lodge dismisses as "deviations" from the norm of Woolf's narrative development (such as *Orlando, Flush, The Years,* and *Between the Acts*) can be characterized, as we have seen, by the "refusal to choose" that Lodge attributes to postmodern novels. What this suggests is not that Woolf's novels *really* develop from modernism to postmodernism but that Lodge's normative concept of narrative is unable to account for writing that reconceives the concept of narrative such that the norm/deviation model no longer applies. That is, Lodge's map does not cover the entire territory, as he implies it does. His two poles may certainly help us make comparisons "at the same level" within particular works, as he says, but they hardly succeed as a general principle for categorizing types of narratives or for explaining literary development, because the "about game" on which they depend traps us, in Henry Staten's words, "in a discursive space within which we are condemned to bounce back and forth among a set of answers whose form is constrained by the form of the question" ("Intricate Evasions of 'Is'" 287): in this case, What is this text about?[9] Postmodern texts do not refuse to play this game; rather, they expose the game for what it is.

A reading of *The Voyage Out* suggests the limitations of Lodge's two modes of modern writing. We could easily challenge his theory of evolution in Woolf's works by revealing the metaphoric functioning of Woolf's first novel, *The Voyage Out* (e.g., in its many similarities to *The Waves*, in its heavy reliance on similes, in its controlling metaphor of the voyage) and by considering, as Lodge does not, a late novel like *The Years*, which displays the more metonymic structure of realism. That is, we could argue that Woolf's novels develop from the metaphoric modern novel (*The Voyage Out, Mrs. Dalloway, The Waves*) to the more metonymic postmodern novel (*Orlando, The Years, Between the Acts*). But whether we put the cart before the horse or the horse before the cart, we still have a cart and a horse. It might be more useful to question the dualism on which Lodge's reading of Woolf's novels, like most readings of them, is based.

Critical discussions of *The Voyage Out* tend to emphasize its structure of oppositions. James Naremore reads it in terms of the surface (English civilization) and depth (South American jungle) of life, the unity beneath individuation, and the masculine world of reason and the feminine world of feeling. Harvena Richter traces the journey from the outer world of physical existence to the inner world of emotions; Madeline Moore as a voyage from words to silence ("Short Season").[10] What is significant in *The Voyage Out*, though, is not the way it is structured by meaningful oppositions but the ways in which the meanings of oppositions vary contextually. The position of the observer and the point of her or his inquiry into the relations among oppositions is stressed, not the oppositions themselves.

The emphasis throughout *The Voyage Out* on perspectives and distances, on the multiple and shifting relationships in space and in time among objects, people, and places, complicates any assertion of *two* worlds or principles. From the first paragraph, the narrative calls attention to perspectives in the tall eccentric figures of the Ambroses walking among the "small agitated figures" on the London street. Over and over again, people change size. At times they are small, insignificant figures; at others, large, imposing presences. Our attention is drawn to "reality . . . at different distances" (Diary 3:50): from the distant view of the land from the sea or the ship from the shore to the close-up view of people espied through a window; from the history of a people and a continent to the biography of an individual; from the interpersonal perspective of particular though unspecified people (VO 31) to the individual's perspective. We see that putting reality at different distances does not refer to one kind of relation only, that is, to the representational function only. The distances between individual and reality, and between different individuals, are not only temporal (as in the recurring references to Elizabethan and prehistoric times) and spatial (as in the vast perspectives of towns seen from mountains) but also sexual, social, and educational (e.g., 170, 296). All distances are relative to the specific comparison being made: "The time of Elizabeth was only distant from the present time by a moment of space compared with the ages which had passed since the water had run between those banks" (264). In other words, the narrative draws attention to the particular distinctions being made in particular scenes and particular circumstances. Any attempt to set up an opposition between two things will be futile unless we know what relationships are at stake and what distinctions are being made in each case.

There are implications here for narrative theory in general. It does little good, for example, to set up an opposition between traditional and modern novels in terms of the individual as central (nineteenth-century realism) and the individual as decentered (twentieth-century postmodernism), for as *The Voyage Out* shows, the individual is of great importance to some activities (falling in love, telling a story) and less so to others (translating Greek, writing a parody). The status of the individual changes in different contexts. Likewise, it does little good to set up a general definition of postmodernism in terms of its refusal to choose (Lodge) or a general definition of feminism in terms of its both/and vision (DuPlessis) unless we first specify the particular options being considered and the particular stakes in choosing or not choosing.

What the constantly shifting relations in *The Voyage Out* should caution us against is talking of a single distinction between two things, between male and female worlds, for example, as the critics of this novel so often do. For the various oppositions posited—between change and continuity, individual and type, male and female, civilization and jungle—function in different ways. And oppositions so important to some are not even acknowledged by others:

> "It's dreadful," said Mrs. Dalloway. . . . "When I'm with artists I feel so intensely the delights of shutting oneself up in a little world of one's own, with pictures and music and everything beautiful, and then I go out into the streets and the first child I meet with its poor, hungry, dirty little face makes me turn round and say, 'No, I *can't* shut myself up—I *won't* live in a world of my own. I should like to stop all the painting and writing and music until this kind of thing exists no longer.' Don't you feel," she wound up, addressing Helen, "that life's a perpetual conflict?"
> Helen considered for a moment. "No," she said. "I don't think I do." (45)

Helen refuses to concede to such an opposition between the political and the aesthetic, the public and the private realm. It is not that she refuses to choose but that she refuses to succumb to the illusion that there is a choice to be made here. Bonds established between people or between texts, classifications established for people or for texts, conventions established in society or in narrative are always being forged and broken

(215–16). It is the possibility of a bond being broken, a boundary being crossed, a convention being changed that makes them genuine, not some essential nature: "Slight [the ties that bind people] may be, but vivid and genuine, merely because the power to break them is within the grasp of each" (195). Their survival depends on their adaptability, not their authenticity. The fact that the pompous and conventional Richard Dalloway pays tribute to the continuity of the British culture, sees the world as a whole, and believes in "unity of aim, of dominion, of progress" (64) is enough to remind us that unity, wholeness, continuity, and progress are not valuable or meaningful in themselves. The kind of thinking that conceives of the world as a smooth-running machine (Sir Isaac Newton or Richard Dalloway) or as a dualism, a perpetual conflict (René Descartes or Clarissa Dalloway) is the kind associated with positivism, not pragmatism; with modernist literature, not postmodernist.

The effect of Woolf's method can be seen in one of the most perplexing scenes in *The Voyage Out,* the supposed sexual encounter between Rachel and Terence in the jungle interior (282–84). Because the scene defies easy summary, I quote it here at some length. Leaving the boat and the other members of their party behind, Terence and Rachel walk off together into the jungle:

> Voices crying behind them never reached through the waters in which they were now sunk. The repetition of Hewet's name in short, dissevered syllables was to them the crack of a dry branch or the laughter of a bird. The grasses and breezes sounding and murmuring all round them, they never noticed that the swishing of the grasses grew louder and louder, and did not cease with the lapse of the breeze. A hand dropped abrupt as iron on Rachel's shoulder; it might have been a bolt from heaven. She fell beneath it, and the grass whipped across her eyes and filled her mouth and ears. Through the waving stems she saw a figure, large and shapeless against the sky. Helen was upon her. Rolled this way and that, now seeing only forests of green, and now the high blue heaven, she was speechless and almost without sense. At last she lay still, all the grasses shaken round her and before her by her panting. Over her loomed two great heads, the heads of a man and a woman, of Terence and Helen.
>
> Both were flushed, both laughing, and the lips were moving; they came together and kissed in the air above her. Broken fragments of speech came down to her on the ground. She thought she heard them speak of love and then of marriage. Raising herself and sitting up, she too realised Helen's soft body, the strong and hospitable arms, and happiness swelling and breaking in one vast wave. When this fell away, and the grasses once more lay low, and the sky became horizontal, and the earth rolled out flat on each side, and the trees stood upright, she was the first to perceive a little row of human figures standing patiently in the distance. For the moment she could not remember who they were. (283–84)

The shifting perspectives, the instability of the pronouns, and the presence of Helen account for the disturbing quality of this scene (from which I have quoted only a part). Usually this scene is explained symbolically in terms of Rachel's (and Woolf's) sexual repression (e.g., Moore, "Some Female Versions of Pastoral") or is faulted for its indirection and ambiguity (e.g., Naremore). Both readings, though, depend on some necessary or presupposed connection between the figurative and the literal rather than looking at the place and function of this scene in this novel. In a Sarraute novel, with its precarious pronouns and inexplicit perspectives, the passage would not be nearly so obtrusive, for example; but in this novel, it calls attention to our desires and our expectations in reading. The reader recognizes the conventions of a love scene (a man and a woman walking off together, in an exotic setting, saying "I love you") and yet faces elements that cannot be accounted for in terms of this convention (a third person rolling on top of the woman and kissing the man). In a scene that should certainly rely on a difference between two entities, a man and a woman, Woolf complicates the polarity by introducing a third person. In doing so she keeps the readers, not just the characters, from being satisfied, *and it is this lack of satisfaction that keeps the disturbing force of sexuality vibrating through the novel.* The disturbing quality of the scene is its point, not some obscurity to be cleared up or dismissed. The disturbing quality, then, is not located in the content and form but in the context and function of the scene. The effect of this passage may not be due to Woolf's failings as a writer or as a woman but to our own reading conventions based on a reference theory of meaning and on a heterosexual concept of love. This love scene recalls those other scenes of sexual encounters in this novel where our desire to know, our desire for consummation and confirmation, remains unsatisfied (Arthur and Susan, 157; Rachel and Terence, 270) and those odd scenes where pronouns and nouns falter, undermining identification and representation: for example, in a passage clearly describing the emaciated Hirst, the name Hewet appears (115); and the engagement dance begins with the old man bowing the fiddle and his daughter playing the piano (150) and ends with the daughter packing up the fiddle and the old man sitting at the piano (165).[11]

If we attend to the *effects* of Woolf's narrative strategies, we may well learn to read differently by resisting the urge to interpret a scene or a text in terms of Woolf's personal life (her own sexuality) or in terms of some prior standards for narrative (direct, unambiguous). By blurring the distinctions between different characters, as discussed in chapter 2, Woolf frustrates our attempt to draw one-to-one correspondences or to see "meaning" as that to which a statement or action refers. She directs our attention to the language of the discourse and to the textual strategies themselves. Paying attention to these strategies, not merely reading through them, leads us to ask different questions and to note different relations rather than to seek the fundamental meaning of the work. It is this search for fundamental meanings that a postmodern perspective calls into question and can call attention to in modernist and feminist readings of Woolf.

My point in ending with Woolf's first novel is twofold. First, I want to dispel any lingering belief that my purpose has been to classify Woolf's writing as postmodernist; rather, my purpose has been to explore the possibilities of reading Woolf in the afterglow (or aftermath, depending on one's point of view) of postmodern writing. By ending with her first novel, I want to emphasize that the postmodern novel is not a form her novels evolve into but a possible way of categorizing them from the beginning.[12] In making this argument, I agree with David Lodge and John Ellis that new features in fiction do not signal a radical break with the past but derive from, in Ellis's words, "a range of possibilities that has always been and will continue to be available" in literary history (219).[13] But I also argue for the need to change our conceptual models and critical methods in response to new practices in fiction. When we apply the same conceptual models of language and narrative to so-called new novels, as Lodge does, we make their newness, what Woolf calls their most "superficial" quality (SCR 242), the most significant aspect, as if changing narrative techniques were an end in itself, as if newness were simply technical innovation and not a change in our thinking about the function of art. In "An Essay in Criticism," Woolf challenges Hemingway's status as a modernist by arguing that his supposed modernity rests on the newness of his subject matter and his treatment of it alone, not on "any fundamental novelty in his conception of the art of fiction" (GR 87). New emphases in narrative theory (e.g., on process over product, contradictions over coherency, indeterminacy over determinacy) do not always or necessarily involve a new conception of narrative discourse, and thus our behavior as readers is not radically altered despite claims for the radically different nature of the texts read. As a result, in our treatment of new fiction we assume the narrative elements themselves change, but not our ways of treating them. Thus, the common belief that postmodern fiction reflects a postmodern world, or that postmodern fiction reflects only itself, is so compelling because of our habit of reference-theory thinking that encourages us to see the relation of narrative to the world as *the defining relation* of the novel.

My second reason for ending with a reading of *The Voyage Out* is the awkwardness I feel when facing an ending, a conclusion that, by definition, must sum up the whole or provide a coherent theory. After all my examples of ways to read Woolf in terms of postmodern motives and strategies,

my conclusion cannot codify a new method or present the right reading
without falling back into the kind of practice I began by challenging. At
best, my conclusion can provide yet another example, as I have done by
reading *The Voyage Out*. In taking issue with specific positions throughout,
I have also dissented from taking a final position here, for as the Preface
and Introduction make clear, it is the point and context of my readings,
the problems they respond to and the confusions they are meant to clear
up, that matter. In trying to get us unstuck from certain habitual ways of
thinking, I would hope my concluding insight is not, "Now I have gotten
it right!" but Wittgenstein's, "Now I know how to go on!" (*Philosophical
Investigations* #154). Hence the title of this chapter. "Issuing" is meant to
suggest our emergence from the structure of debates that has entrapped
us in certain kinds of arguments and, as a result, the opening up of new
questions to pursue.

If we value open-endedness, difference, ambiguity, equivocation, and,
above all, the freedom to change, then as postmodernist and feminist critics it would seem we must, like Woolf, "go on adventuring, changing . . .
refusing to be stamped & stereotyped" (Diary 4:187). And if we refuse to
be "stamped," then our new readings can be no more universal, enduring,
or true than those they seek to replace. To prevent such corrective readings from becoming normative, we need a mode of inquiry that allows for
doubt, equivocation, contradiction, and change, that affirms the tenuous
and provisional status of the artwork as well as the tentative and partial (in
both senses of the word) status of our own critical metaphors. If we are to
learn the lessons of postmodernism, we must learn, as Jane Flax says, "to
tolerate and interpret ambivalence, ambiguity, and multiplicity as well as
to expose the roots of our needs for imposing order and structure" (643).
Austin Quigley makes a similar point in discussing the significance of Wittgenstein's philosophizing for literary theorizing: "To restore mobility and
multiplicity to literary theory is to maintain in the means of inquiry features that are indispensable when that which is being inquired into is itself
mobile, multiple, and elusive" ("Wittgenstein's Philosophizing" 232).

For this reason I have demonstrated many instances of a postmodern
reading of Woolf rather than defining such a practice in advance. For this
reason, too, I have resisted seeking the "internal coherence" (as Jardine
does) or the "fundamental ground" (as McHale does) of postmodernism
but seek instead its "functional continuity." The desire to get to the bottom
of things works against postmodernism's attention to surfaces, and the
effort to supply a general definition of postmodernism may well neglect
its local effects. To provide a coherent story of postmodernism would be
to assume that diversity, difference, ambiguity, and lack of consensus are
obstacles to be overcome in our critical readings rather than indications of

the relational and changeable nature of the thing we are describing.[14] The reason we desire such a story, I argue, is that our critical practice, whether as feminists or postmodernists, is still largely based on modernist assumptions and values. My point in bringing postmodernism to bear on feminist as well as modernist readings of Woolf is to bring to the fore those unacknowledged assumptions and values that keep our critical practices as well as our fictional works locked within the same options. It is to show us, as Bernard comes to see, the thin places in our stories (TW 230).

A successful reading of Woolf (or women's writing or postmodern novels) need not provide us with a new privileged definition or codify a new practice or distinguish one kind of writing from another. Instead, it can enable us to see the various kinds of relations possible in a discourse and the ways in which we can move from one kind of investigation to another. A successful reading can provide what Quigley says Wittgenstein's philosophy provides, namely, "principles of access" (and, I might add, principles of egress): "the appropriate feeling is not that we have arrived but that we have learned how to go on" ("Wittgenstein's Philosophizing" 233). A postmodern reading based on pragmatic motives does not seek to resolve conflict or to reach consensus but to discover how to go on in the face of conflict and in the absence of consensus. It seeks to remove the impasses in our arguments by showing how our descriptions, not just the thing in question, create those impasses, thereby enabling us to change our critical game and thus our responses to different texts and contexts.[15]

If we are ever to resist repeating the same moves and offering the same choices in narrative theory, it will not be by professing *new* narrative techniques or by advocating *one* mode of reading. Rather, it will be by enacting a different understanding of narrative discourse, one that relies on nothing essential in human nature or in literary history but on ever-renewed, ever-varied performances. What postmodernism has shown us is, to borrow Peggy Kamuf's words, "the necessity of replacing this discourse with another and of finding always another place from which to begin again" ("Replacing Feminist Criticism" 47). By beginning to read Woolf again from the place of postmodernism, I have attempted to show that her narrative project was both more and less radical than we have thought: less radical in that Woolf's point was not to forge a new social order, a feminist claim (and if we alter society, Woolf asks, what then?), or to forge a new narrative order, a modernist claim (for we have only to alter, not to recast, the standards of the past, Woolf says, to accommodate the new fiction of the present); more radical in that, by staying on the surface, so to speak, Woolf revealed how much narrative and social behavior is bound by various conventions, and enacted a different way of thinking by means of which we can free ourselves, not from all conventions, but from our unawareness of some conventions and thus from the inevitable repetition of the same. What Woolf's narratives show us is that a change in narrative behavior is easy to bring about (even Hemingway, Woolf admits, employed modernist techniques); what is more difficult is changing our conceptual paradigms and our understanding of how literature and language function. As Wittgenstein points out, such a change in our language game would mean a change in our form of life (*Philosophical Investigations* #19, #23).

When it comes to assessing the implications of Woolf's writing for feminist criticism, and when it comes to assessing the implications of my own postmodern reading for Woolf criticism, I like to think that Wittgenstein's comment on his own work voices Woolf's sentiment as well and serves as a fitting conclusion to this book: "I am by no means sure I should prefer a continuation of my work by others to a change in the way people live which would make all these questions superfluous" (*Culture and Value* 61e).

## NOTES

1. In *Reading Lacan* Gallop asks, "what would be a feminist criticism that neither read women's texts nor read for the representation of women?" (18).

2. A similar confusion over different uses of the "same" term can be seen in Hirsch's *Mother/Daughter Plot*. Discussing the "double consciousness" of Woolf's writing, Hirsch cites Mary Jacobus along with Sandra Gilbert, Elaine Showalter, and Rachel DuPlessis as critics who have participated in the creation of this double consciousness as "a paradigm for the discussion of women's writing" (95). Yet the fact that Jacobus takes on Gilbert's and Showalter's concepts of gender and identity might caution us against talking about their uses of "double" in the same way. Gilbert and Showalter use "double consciousness" to turn undecidable or shifting positions into the "very fixities" that Jacobus's reading challenges (*Reading as a Woman* 6–14).

3. Quigley assesses Wittgenstein's writings in similar terms, as offering not the correct position but corrections to positions readily adopted ("Wittgenstein's Philosophizing" 213). Thus, Wittgenstein's reliance on particular examples over general assertions is a way to prevent, in Quigley's words, "seeing something in terms of X" from degenerating into "seeing something as X" (228). Staten also confronts the possibility that Wittgenstein offers the "correct" position, noting that Wittgenstein faces a self-contradiction in "turning normative" at times, "insofar as Wittgenstein tries to show that the classical philosophical views of language and mind are wrong and should be abandoned" ("Wittgenstein's Boundaries" 314). However, Staten explains, that classical view is not one view among others but one that "underlies philosophy itself" and thus threatens to turn Wittgenstein's own practice into a method against itself (the allusion to Graff's title is intentional). What Wittgenstein's method shows us, though, is the way out of this impasse of

method/antimethod, literature/antiliterature, modernism/antimodernism, for as Staten points out, Wittgenstein's method pays attention to "the form of the question" and shows us other ways of forming the questions and thus other possible responses ("Intricate Evasions of 'Is'" 286–87).

4. Mistacco is one critic who stresses postmodernism's constructive, not just its subversive, activity. Because postmodernism is based on a different "logic" and different conventions than modernism, she argues, it cannot be read only in terms of modernist fiction (371–72, 398–99). Alcoff objects to Kristeva's poststructuralist critique of subjectivity by arguing that "you cannot mobilize a movement [i.e., feminism] that is only and always against: you must have a positive alternative" (418–19). While this sounds much like my claim in the Preface, that postmodernism and feminism should no longer be defined primarily as *against* something else, Alcoff and I differ on the implications of refusing a final position. Alcoff fears that poststructuralist undecidability "undercuts our ability to oppose the dominant trend . . . in mainstream Western intellectual thought, that is, the insistence on a universal, neutral, perspectiveless epistemology, metaphysics, and ethics" (420). On the contrary. Postmodern thought, I argue, prevents us from setting up a simple opposition between the dominant and the marginal, as if what we called the "dominant" were the same everywhere, and from offering a new "universal, neutral, perspectiveless epistemology, metaphysics, and ethics" in place of the old dominant.

5. Quigley notes that the continuity of the field of modern drama is methodological, not chronological (*Modern Stage* xiii). Arac remarks that postmodernism is not "straightforwardly chronological," for *boundary 2* has uncovered "an ever-receding history of postmodernism" (x-xi), not because postmodern features inform earlier works, but because these *boundary 2* writers have learned to read in new ways.

6. These are, of course, Jakobson's terms for the two axes of language: the axis of selection and the axis of combination ("Two Aspects of Language"). Lodge makes this argument as well in "Historicism and Literary History" (68–75).

7. Lodge concludes *The Modes of Modern Writing* by stating that if postmodernism succeeded in its refusal to choose, if it expelled "the idea of order (whether expressed in metonymic or metaphoric form) from modern writing, then it would truly abolish itself, by destroying the norms against which we perceive its deviations" (245). As I have argued throughout this book, to the extent that we accept some norm for narrative, this is so; but what postmodern writing does is expose such norms as provisional and contingent constructs. Thus, it is not just postmodern art that is self-abolishing; rather, from the perspective of postmodernism, all art is.

8. At this point I should comment on my own selection of writers. Throughout this work I have referred to Kafka, Beckett, Robbe-Grillet, and Sarraute as postmodernists, along with contemporary writers and artists such as Acker, Barthelme, Pynchon, Calvino, García Márquez, Cage, and Warhol. Not all postmodern theorists would sanction my use of those earlier writers. Hutcheon, for one, would not since she considers the *nouveau roman* to be late modernist. But she acknowledges that our theories of postmodernism (like our theories of modernism and femi-

nism) will differ depending on the texts we read, and, I would add, the way we read. While Hutcheon narrows postmodernism to historiographic metafiction in order to introduce some consistency into our use of the term, I use postmodernism without a fixed meaning, agreeing with Wittgenstein that "inexact" does not mean "unusable" (*Philosophical Investigations* #79, #88).

9. Staten says that asking what a poem means (what it is about) traps us in such a space ("Intricate Evasions of 'Is'" 287). See also Brooke-Rose's discussion of *The Modes of Modern Writing* in her *Rhetoric of the Unreal* (354–63). She points out that Jakobson "never suggested that one or the other pole [the metonymic or the metaphoric] should ever apply *collectively*" to groups of texts (355).

10. Guiguet, Blackstone, and Daiches (*Virginia Woolf*) also read this novel in terms of oppositions. All references to *The Voyage Out* are to the 1920 American edition (copyrighted by George Doran), revised by Woolf from the 1915 British edition.

11. If these are mistakes (and they may well be), they are ones that Woolf did not correct for the American edition.

12. Smith's remarks on the difference between poetic and nonpoetic language hold for the point I make here about my use of *postmodernism:* "To observe that the term *poetry* cannot be usefully defined, or that there is a constantly shifting and dissolving borderline between what we usually call *poetry* and all the other things from which we might like to distinguish it, does not oblige us to deny the possibility of any relevant distinction between classes of verbal composition. It merely suggests that the distinctiveness of those classes is not reflected in the consistency of our labels for them. Their distinctiveness may, however, be reflected in something else at least as significant, namely, the distinctiveness of our actual behavior and experiences with respect to them" (*Margins of Discourse* 44). Smith also writes that "one's perception of and/or response to an event not only determine but are determined *by* how one classifies it: what we 'see,' and how we subsequently behave toward it, will depend on what we see something *as*" (48). As Wittgenstein says, "naming," such as calling a text *postmodern*, "is a preparation for description" (*Philosophical Investigations* #49), not a correct or incorrect identification of the object.

13. Lodge writes, "What looks like innovation . . . is therefore also in some sense a reversion to the principles and procedures of an earlier phase" (*Modes of Modern Writing* 220).

14. Quigley makes this argument in terms of literary theory in general ("Wittgenstein's Philosophizing" 227–28), Flax in terms of feminist theory in particular (638; quoted earlier).

15. More and more feminist and postmodernist theorists—such as Catharine Stimpson, Nancy Fraser and Linda Nicholson, Jane Flax, and Ihab Hassan—are discovering that a pragmatic perspective seems best suited to our postmodern age. I find the pragmatic philosophy of the later Wittgenstein, the postaxiological theory of Smith, and the social theory of Lyotard more conducive to a postmodern concept of literature and society than the kinds of approaches I have taken issue with throughout this book.

# Selected Bibliography

## NOVELS

Acker, Kathy. *Don Quixote, Which Was a Dream*. New York: Grove, 1986.
———. *Great Expectations*. New York: Grove, 1983.
Allende, Isabelle. *The House of the Spirits*. New York: Bantam, 1986.
Barnes, Djuna. *Nightwood*. New York: Harcourt Brace Jovanovich, 1937.
Barth, John. *The End of the Road*. Garden City, N.Y.: Doubleday, 1958.
———. *Giles Goat-Boy*. Garden City, N.Y.: Doubleday, 1966.
———. *Lost in the Funhouse*. New York: Doubleday, 1968.
Barthelme, Donald. *City Life*. New York: Farrar, Straus & Giroux, 1970.
———. *Snow White*. New York: Atheneum, 1986.
Beckett, Samuel. *How It Is*. New York: Grove, 1964.
———. *Stories and Texts for Nothing*. New York: Grove, 1967.
———. *Three Novels: "Molloy," "Malone Dies," "The Unnamable."* Trans. Patrick Bowles, with the author. New York: Grove, 1955, 1956, 1958.
Bernhard, Thomas. *Concrete*. Trans. David McLintock. New York: Knopf, 1984.
———. *Wittgenstein's Nephew: A Friendship*. Trans. Ewald Osers. London: Quartet Books, 1986.
Borges, Jorge Luis. *Ficciones*. Ed. Anthony Kerrigan. Trans. Emecé Editores. New York: Grove, 1962.
Calvino, Italo. *The Castle of Crossed Destinies*. Trans. William Weaver. New York: Harcourt Brace Jovanovich, 1977.
———. *Cosmicomics*. Trans. William Weaver. New York: Harcourt Brace Jovanovich, 1968.
———. *If on a Winter's Night a Traveler*. Trans. William Weaver. New York: Harcourt Brace Jovanovich, 1977.
Carter, Angela. *Nights at the Circus*. London: Chatto, 1984.
Cliff, Michelle. *No Telephone to Heaven*. New York: Random House, 1987.
Drabble, Margaret. *The Waterfall*. New York: Knopf, 1969.
Duras, Marguerite. *The Lover*. Trans. Barbara Bray. New York: Harper & Row, 1986.
Ford, Ford Madox. *The Good Soldier*. New York: Random House, 1951.
Fowles, John. *The French Lieutenant's Woman*. New York: Signet, 1970.
Fuentes, Carlos. *The Old Gringo*. Trans. Margaret Sayers Peden, with the author. New York: Harper & Row, 1985.

García Márquez, Gabriel. *The Autumn of the Patriarch*. Trans. Gregory Rabassa. New York: Avon, 1976.

———. *One Hundred Years of Solitude*. Trans. Gregory Rabassa. New York: Avon, 1971.

Hardy, Thomas. *Far from the Madding Crowd*. New York: Signet, 1960.

Harris, Bertha. *Lover*. Planfield, Vt.: Daughters, 1976.

Joyce, James. *Finnegans Wake*. New York: Viking, 1959.

———. *Ulysses*. New York: Vintage Books, 1961.

Kafka, Franz. *The Castle*. Trans. Willa Muir and Edwin Muir. New York: Schocken Books, 1974.

———. *The Complete Stories*. Ed. Nahum N. Glatzer. New York: Schocken Books, 1946.

———. *The Trial*. Trans. Willa Muir and Edwin Muir. New York: Schocken Books, 1968.

Kingston, Maxine Hong. *The Woman Warrior*. New York: Vintage Books, 1977.

Lessing, Doris. *The Golden Notebook*. St. Albans: Panther, 1973.

Lispector, Clarice. *Family Ties*. Trans. Giovanni Pontiero. Austin: University of Texas Press, 1960.

Nabokov, Vladimir. *Lolita*. New York: Putnam, 1955.

———. *Pale Fire*. New York: Putnam, 1962.

Pynchon, Thomas. *The Crying of Lot 49*. Rpt. New York: Harper & Row, 1986.

———. *Gravity's Rainbow*. New York: Bantam, 1973.

———. *V*. New York: Harper & Row, 1963.

Reed, Ishmael. *Mumbo Jumbo*. New York: Atheneum, 1988.

Robbe-Grillet, Alain. *The Erasers*. Trans. Richard Howard. New York: Grove, 1964.

———. *Jealousy*. Trans. Richard Howard. New York: Grove, 1959.

———. *In the Labyrinth*. Trans. Richard Howard. New York: Grove, 1960.

———. *The Voyeur*. Trans. Richard Howard. New York: Grove, 1958.

Sarraute, Nathalie. *Between Life and Death*. Trans. Maria Jolas. New York: George Braziller, 1969.

———. *Childhood*. Trans. Barbara Wright, with the author. New York: George Braziller, 1984.

———. *The Golden Fruits*. Trans. Maria Jolas. London: John Calder, 1964.

———. *Tropisms*. Trans. Maria Jolas. New York: George Braziller, 1963.

———. *The Use of Speech*. Trans. Barbara Wright, with the author. New York: George Braziller, 1983.

Sukenick, Ronald. *Blown Away*. Los Angeles: Sun and Moon, 1986.

Wittig, Monique. *Across the Acheron*. Trans. David Le Vay, with Margaret Crosland. London: Peter Owen, 1987.

———. *Les Guerilleres*. Trans. David Le Vay. Boston: Beacon Press, 1985.

Wolf, Christa. *Cassandra*. Trans. Jan Van Heurck. New York: Farrar, Straus & Giroux, 1984.

———. *A Model Childhood*. Trans. Ursule Molinaro and Hedwig Rappolt. New York: Farrar, Straus & Giroux, 1980.

———. *The Quest for Christa T.* Trans. Christopher Middleton. New York: Farrar, Straus & Giroux, 1979.


## CRITICISM AND THEORY

Abel, Elizabeth, " 'Cam the Wicked': Woolf's Portrait of the Artist as Her Father's Daughter." In Marcus, *Woolf and Bloomsbury* 170–94.

———, ed. *Writing and Sexual Difference*. Brighton, U.K.: Harvester, 1982.

Albright, Daniel. *Personality and Impersonality: Lawrence, Woolf, and Mann*. Chicago: University of Chicago Press, 1978.

Alcoff, Linda. "Cultural Feminism versus Post-Structuralism: The Identity Crisis in Feminist Theory." *Signs* 13.3 (Spring 1988): 405–36.

Annan, Noel. "Bloomsbury and the Leavises." In Marcus, *Woolf and Bloomsbury* 23–38.

Arac, Jonathan, ed. *Postmodernism and Politics*. Minneapolis: University of Minnesota Press, 1986.

Aronowitz, Stanley. "Going Public." *Village Voice Literary Supplement* October 1988: 26.

Auden, W. H. "A Consciousness of Reality." *New Yorker* 6 March 1954: 111–16.

Auerbach, Erich. *Mimesis: The Representation of Reality in Western Literature*. Trans. Willard Trask. Princeton: Princeton University Press, 1955.

Austin, J. L. *How to Do Things with Words*. London: Oxford University Press, 1962.

Baker, G. P., and P. M. S. Hacker. *Wittgenstein: Meaning and Understanding*. Chicago: University of Chicago Press, 1980.

Bakhtin, Mikhail. *The Dialogic Imagination*. Ed. Michael Holquist. Trans. Caryl Emerson and Michael Holquist. Austin: University of Texas Press, 1981.

———. *Rabelais and His World*. Trans. Helene Iswolsky. Bloomington: Indiana University Press, 1984.

Barth, John. "The Literature of Exhaustion." *Atlantic Monthly* August 1967: 98–114.

———. "The Literature of Replenishment: Postmodern Fiction." *Atlantic Monthly* January 1980: 65–71.

Barthes, Roland. *Critical Essays*. Trans. Richard Howard. Evanston: Northwestern University Press, 1972.

———. *Elements of Semiology*. Trans. Annette Lavers and Colin Smith. 1968. New York: Hill & Wang, 1979.

———. *The Pleasure of the Text*. Trans. Richard Miller. New York: Hill & Wang, 1975.

———. *S/Z: An Essay*. Trans. Richard Miller. New York: Hill & Wang, 1974.

———. *Writing Degree Zero*. Trans. Annette Lavers and Colin Smith. 1967. New York: Hill & Wang, 1979.

Batchelor, J. B. "Feminism in Virginia Woolf." *English* 17 (Spring 1968): 1–7.

Bateson, Gregory. *Mind and Nature*. New York: Bantam, 1979.

Baym, Nina. "The Madwoman and Her Languages: Why I Don't Do Feminist Literary Theory." In Benstock 45–61.

Bazin, Nancy Topping. *Virginia Woolf and the Androgynous Vision*. New Brunswick: Rutgers University Press, 1973.

——. "Virginia Woolf's Quest for Equilibrium." *Modern Language Quarterly* 32 (1971): 305–19.

Beckett, Samuel. *Proust*. New York: Grove, 1931.

Beebe, Maurice. "What Modernism Was." *Journal of Modern Literature* 3 (July 1974): 1065–84.

Beja, Morris, ed. *Critical Essays on Virginia Woolf*. Boston: G. K. Hall, 1985.

——, ed. *Virginia Woolf, "To the Lighthouse": A Casebook*. London: MacMillan, 1970.

Bell, Barbara Currier, and Carol Ohmann. "Virginia Woolf's Criticism: A Polemical Preface." *Critical Inquiry* 1 (December 1974): 361–71.

Bell, Quentin. *Bloomsbury*. New York: Basic Books, 1968.

——. *Virginia Woolf: A Biography*. New York: Harcourt Brace Jovanovich, 1972.

Bell-Villada, Gene H. "Pronoun Shifters, Virginia Woolf, Bela Bartok, Plebian Forms, Real-Life Tyrants, and the Shaping of García Márquez's *Patriarch*." *Contemporary Literature* 28 (1987): 461–82.

Bennett, Arnold. "Is the Novel Decaying?" In Majumdar and McLaurin 112–14.

Bennett, Joan. *Virginia Woolf: Her Art as a Novelist*. 2d ed. Cambridge: Cambridge University Press, 1964.

Benstock, Shari, ed. *Feminist Issues in Literary Scholarship*. Bloomington: Indiana University Press, 1987.

Black, Naomi. "Virginia Woolf and the Women's Movement." In Marcus, *Feminist Slant* 180–97.

Blackstone, Bernard. *Virginia Woolf: A Commentary*. New York: Harcourt Brace Jovanovich, 1949.

Blain, Virginia. "Narrative Voice and the Female Perspective." In Clements and Grundy 115–36.

Bloom, Harold, ed. *Modern Critical Views: Virginia Woolf*. New York: Chelsea House, 1986.

Bourdieu, Pierre. "The Field of Cultural Production; or, The Economic World Reversed." *Poetics* 12 (November 1983): 311–56.

Bowlby, Rachel. *Virginia Woolf: Feminist Destinations*. Oxford: Basil Blackwell, 1988.

Boyers, Robert. *F. R. Leavis: Judgment and the Discipline of Thought*. Columbia: University of Missouri Press, 1978.

Brombert, Victor. "Flaubert and the Status of the Subject." In Schor and Majewski 100–115.

Brooke-Rose, Christine. "The Readerhood of Man." In Suleiman and Crosman 120–48.

——. *The Rhetoric of the Unreal: Studies in Narrative and Structure, Especially of the Fantastic*. Cambridge: Cambridge University Press, 1981.

Brownstein, Marilyn L. "Postmodern Language and the Perpetuation of Desire." *Twentieth-Century Literature* 31 (1985): 73–88.

Burke, Kenneth. *The Philosophy of Literary Form*. Baton Rouge: Louisiana State University Press, 1941.

Burt, John. "Irreconcilable Habits of Thought in *A Room of One's Own* and *To the Lighthouse*." In Bloom 191–206.

Calinescu, Matei. *Faces of Modernity*. Bloomington: Indiana University Press, 1977.

Cannon, JoAnn. *Italo Calvino: Writer and Critic*. Ravenna, Italy: Longo Editore, 1981.

Caramagno, Thomas C. "Manic-Depressive Psychosis and Critical Approaches to Virginia Woolf's Life and Work." *PMLA* 103 (January 1988): 10–23.

Carroll, David. *The Subject in Question: The Languages of Theory and the Strategies of Fiction*. Chicago: University of Chicago Press, 1982.

Cassirer, Ernst. *An Essay on Man*. New Haven: Yale University Press, 1945.

Chabot, C. Barry. "The Problem of the Postmodern." *New Literary History* 20 (Autumn 1988): 1–20.

Chatman, Seymour. *Story and Discourse: Narrative Structure in Fiction and Film*. Ithaca: Cornell University Press, 1978.

Cixous, Hélène. "The Laugh of the Medusa." In Marks and de Courtivron 245–64.

———. "Reaching the Point of Wheat; or, A Portrait of the Artist as a Maturing Woman." *New Literary History* 19.1 (Autumn 1987): 1–23.

Clements, Patricia, and Isabel Grundy, eds. *Virginia Woolf: New Critical Essays*. New York: Barnes & Noble, 1983.

Cohn, Ruby. "Art in *To the Lighthouse*." *Modern Fiction Studies* 8 (Summer 1962): 127–36.

Comstock, Margaret. "'The Current Answers Don't Do': The Comic Form of *Night and Day*." *Women's Studies* 4 (1977): 153–71.

———. "The Loudspeaker and the Human Voice: Politics and the Form of *The Years*." *Bulletin of the New York Public Library* 80 (Winter 1977): 252–75.

Creed, Barbara. "From Here to Modernity: Feminism and Postmodernism." *Screen* 28 (1987): 47–67.

Culler, Jonathan. *On Deconstruction: Theory and Criticism after Structuralism*. Ithaca: Cornell University Press, 1982.

———. *The Pursuit of Signs: Semiotics, Literature, Deconstruction*. Ithaca: Cornell University Press, 1981.

———. *Structuralist Poetics: Structuralism, Linguistics, and the Study of Literature*. Ithaca: Cornell University Press, 1975.

Daiches, David. *The New Criticism*. Isle of Skye, Scotland: Aquila, 1982.

———. *The Novel and the Modern World*. Chicago: University of Chicago Press, 1939.

———. *Virginia Woolf*. Norfolk, Conn.: New Directions, 1942.

De George, Richard T., and Fernande M. De George, eds. *The Structuralists: From Marx to Lévi-Strauss*. New York: Anchor Books, 1972.

De Quincey, Thomas. *Selected Essays on Rhetoric*. Ed. Frederick Burwick. Carbondale: Southern Illinois University Press, 1967.

Derrida, Jacques. "Devant la Loi." Trans. Avital Ronell. In Udoff 128–49.

———. "The Law of Genre." *Glyph* 7 (Spring 1980): 202–32.

————. "Women in the Beehive: A Seminar with Jacques Derrida." In Jardine and Smith 189–203.

DeSalvo, Louise. "Shakespeare's *Other* Sister." In Marcus, *New Feminist Essays* 61–81.

————. *Virginia Woolf's First Voyage: A Novel in the Making.* Totowa, N.J.: Rowman & Littlefield, 1980.

————. "Virginia Woolf's Revisions for the 1920 American and English Editions of *The Voyage Out.*" *Bulletin of Research in the Humanities,* Woolf Issue 2 (Autumn 1979): 338–66.

DiBattista, Maria. "Joyce, Woolf, and the Modern Mind." In Clements and Grundy 96–114.

————. *Virginia Woolf's Major Novels: The Fables of Anon.* New Haven: Yale University Press, 1980.

Dick, Susan. "The Tunnelling Process: Some Aspects of Virginia Woolf's Use of Memory and the Past." In Clements and Grundy 176–99.

DuPlessis, Rachel Blau. "For the Etruscans." In Showalter, *New Feminist Criticism* 271–91.

————. *Writing Beyond the Ending.* Bloomington: Indiana University Press, 1985.

Eagleton, Terry. "Brecht and Rhetoric." *New Literary History* 16 (Spring 1985): 633–38.

————. *Literary Theory: An Introduction.* Minneapolis: University of Minnesota Press, 1983.

Edel, Leon. *Bloomsbury: A House of Lions.* New York: Lippincott, 1979.

————. "The Novel as Poem." In *The Modern Psychological Novel.* Rev. ed. New York: Grosset & Dunlap, 1964. 183–204.

Eisenberg, Nora. "Virginia Woolf's Last Words on Words: *Between the Acts* and 'Anon.'" In Marcus, *New Feminist Essays* 253–66.

Eliot, T. S. "The Use of Poetry and the Use of Criticism." In *Selected Prose of T. S. Eliot.* Ed. with an Introduction by Frank Kermode. New York: Farrar, Straus & Giroux, 1975. 79–98.

Ellis, John M. *The Theory of Literary Criticism: A Logical Analysis.* Berkeley: University of California Press, 1974.

Evans, Martha. *Masks of Tradition: Women and the Politics of Writing in Twentieth-Century France.* Ithaca: Cornell University Press, 1987.

Felman, Shoshana. *The Literary Speech Act.* Trans. Catharine Porter. Ithaca: Cornell University Press, 1983.

————. "Psychoanalysis and Education: Teaching Terminable and Interminable." In B. Johnson 21–44.

————. "Rereading Femininity." *Yale French Studies* 62 (1981): 19–44.

Fish, Stanley. *Is There a Text in This Class? The Authority of Interpretive Communities.* Cambridge: Harvard University Press, 1980.

Flax, Jane. "Postmodernism and Gender Relations in Feminist Theory." *Signs* 12.4 (Summer 1987): 621–43.

Fleishman, Avrom. *Virginia Woolf: A Critical Reading.* Baltimore: Johns Hopkins University Press, 1975.

Flynn, Elizabeth A., and Patrocinio Schweickart, eds. *Gender and Reading: Essays on Readers, Texts, and Contexts*. Baltimore: Johns Hopkins University Press, 1986.

Forster, E. M. *Anonymity: An Enquiry*. London: Folcroft Press, 1970.

———. *Aspects of the Novel*. New York: Harcourt Brace & Co., 1927.

———. *Virginia Woolf*. New York: Harcourt Brace & Co., 1942.

Foster, Hal, ed. *The Anti-Aesthetic: Essays on Postmodern Culture*. Port Townsend, Wash.: Bay Press, 1983.

Foucault, Michel. *The History of Sexuality*. Vol 1: *An Introduction*. Trans. Robert Hurley. New York: Pantheon, 1978.

Fox, Stephen. "The Fish Pond as Symbolic Center in *Between the Acts*." *Modern Fiction Studies* 18 (Autumn 1972): 467–73.

Fox-Genovese, Elizabeth. "The Claims of a Common Culture: Gender, Race, Class, and the Canon." *Salmagundi* 72 (Fall 1986): 131–43.

Fraser, Nancy. "On the Political and the Symbolic: Against the Metaphysics of Textuality." *boundary 2* 14 (1985/86): 195–209.

Fraser, Nancy, and Linda Nicholson. "Social Criticism without Philosophy: An Encounter between Feminism and Postmodernism." In Ross 83–104.

Freedman, Ralph. "Kafka's Obscurity: The Illusion of Logic in Narrative." *Modern Fiction Studies* 8 (1962): 61–74.

———. *The Lyrical Novel: Studies in Hermann Hesse, André Gide, and Virginia Woolf*. Princeton: Princeton University Press, 1963.

———, ed. *Virginia Woolf: Revaluation and Continuity*. Berkeley: University of California Press, 1980.

Friedman, Ellen G., and Miriam Fuchs, eds. *Breaking the Sequence: Women's Experimental Fiction*. Princeton: Princeton University Press, 1989.

Friedman, Melvin, and John Vickery. *The Shaken Realist*. Baton Rouge: Louisiana State University Press, 1970.

Friedman, Norman. "The Waters of Annihilation: Double Vision in *To the Lighthouse*." *ELH* 22 (1955): 61–79.

Froula, Christine. "Rewriting Genesis: Gender and Culture in Twentieth-Century Texts." *Tulsa Studies in Women's Literature* 7 (Fall 1988): 197–220.

———. "When Eve Reads Milton: Undoing the Canonical Economy." *Critical Inquiry* 10 (December 1983): 321–47.

Frye, Northrop. *Anatomy of Criticism*. Princeton: Princeton University Press, 1951.

Fussell, B. H. "Woolf's Peculiar Comic World: *Between the Acts*." In Freedman, *Virginia Woolf* 263–83.

Gallop, Jane. *The Daughter's Seduction: Feminism and Psychoanalysis*. Ithaca: Cornell University Press, 1982.

———. "The Problem of Definition." *Genre* 20 (Summer 1987): 111–32.

———. *Reading Lacan*. Ithaca: Cornell University Press, 1985.

Gilbert, Sandra. "Costumes of the Mind: Transvestism as Metaphor in Modern Literature." *Critical Inquiry* 7 (Winter 1980): 391–417.

———. "Woman's Sentence, Man's Sentencing: Linguistic Fantasies in Woolf and Joyce." In Marcus, *Woolf and Bloomsbury* 208–24.

Gilbert, Sandra, and Susan Gubar. *No Man's Land: The Place of the Woman Writer in the Twentieth Century.* New Haven: Yale University Press, 1988.

————. "Sexual Linguistics: Gender, Language, Sexuality." *New Literary History* 16 (Spring 1985): 515–43.

Gillespie, Diane Filby. "Political Aesthetics: Virginia Woolf and Dorothy Richardson." In Marcus, *Feminist Slant* 132–51.

Goffman, Erving. *Frame Analysis.* Cambridge: Harvard University Press, 1974.

Goldman, Mark. *The Reader's Art: Virginia Woolf as Literary Critic.* Paris: Mouton, 1976.

————. "Virginia Woolf and the Critic as Reader." In Sprague 155–68.

Gordon, Lyndall. "Our Secret Life: Virginia Woolf and T. S. Eliot." In Clements and Grundy 77–95.

————. *Virginia Woolf: A Writer's Life.* New York: Oxford University Press, 1984.

Gorsky, Susan. "'The Central Shadow': Characterization in *The Waves.*" *Modern Fiction Studies* 18 (Autumn 1972): 449–66.

Graff, Gerald. *Literature against Itself: Literary Ideas in Modern Society.* Chicago: University of Chicago Press, 1979.

Graham, J. W. "Point of View in *The Waves:* Some Services of Style." In Lewis 94–112.

Gravin, Harry R., ed. *Romanticism, Modernism, Postmodernism.* Lewisburg: Bucknell University Press, 1980.

Grossberg, Lawrence. "Putting the Pop Back into Postmodernism." In Ross 167–90.

Guiguet, Jean. *Virginia Woolf and Her Works.* Trans. Jean Stewart. New York: Harcourt, Brace & World, 1966.

Hafley, James. "The Creative Modulation of Perspective." In Beja, *Casebook* 133–48.

————. *The Glass Roof: Virginia Woolf as Novelist.* Berkeley: University of California Press, 1954.

Harper, Howard. *Between Language and Silence: The Novels of Virginia Woolf.* Baton Rouge: Louisiana State University Press, 1982.

Hartman, Geoffrey. *Beyond Formalism.* New Haven: Yale University Press, 1970.

Hassan, Ihab. *The Dismemberment of Orpheus: Toward a Post-Modern Literature.* New York: Oxford University Press, 1971.

————. "Joyce, Beckett, and the Postmodern Imagination." *Tri Quarterly* 34 (Fall 1975): 170–200.

————, ed. *Liberations: New Essays on the Humanities in Revolution.* Middleton: Wesleyan University Press, 1971.

————. "Making Sense: The Trials of Postmodern Discourse." *New Literary History* 18 (Winter 1987): 437–59.

————. "POSTmodernISM." *New Literary History* 3 (Autumn 1971): 5–30.

————. *The Postmodern Turn: Essays in Postmodern Theory and Culture.* Columbus: Ohio State University Press, 1987.

————. "The Question of Postmodernism." In Gravin 117–26.

Heath, Stephen. *The Nouveau Roman.* London: Elek London, 1972.

Heilbrun, Carolyn. *Toward a Recognition of Androgyny.* New York: Knopf, 1973.

————. "Virginia Woolf in Her Fifties." In Marcus, *Feminist Slant* 236–53.

Heine, Elizabeth. "The Earlier *The Voyage Out:* Virginia Woolf's First Novel." *Bulletin of Research in the Humanities,* Woolf Issue 2 (Autumn 1979): 294–316.

Henke, Suzette. *"Mrs. Dalloway:* The Communion of Saints." In Marcus, *New Feminist Essays* 125–47.

Hirsch, Marianne. *The Mother/Daughter Plot: Narrative, Psychoanalysis, Feminism.* Bloomington: Indiana University Press, 1989.

Hoffman, Charles C. "From Short Story to Novel: The Manuscript Revision of Virginia Woolf's *Mrs. Dalloway." Modern Fiction Studies* 14 (1968): 171–86.

Howe, Irving, ed. *The Idea of the Modern in Literature and the Arts.* New York: Horizon, 1968.

Hutcheon, Linda. *A Poetics of Postmodernism: History, Theory, Fiction.* New York: Routledge, 1988.

Huyssen, Andreas. *After the Great Divide: Modernism, Mass Culture, Postmodernism.* Bloomington: Indiana University Press, 1986.

Hynes, Samuel. "The Whole Contention between Mr. Bennett and Mrs. Woolf." In Spilka 179–89.

Iser, Wolfgang. *The Implied Reader: Patterns of Communication in Prose Fiction from Bunyan to Beckett.* Baltimore: Johns Hopkins University Press, 1974.

———. "Interaction between Text and Reader." In Suleiman and Crosman 106–19.

Jacobus, Mary. *Reading Woman: Essays in Feminist Criticism.* New York: Columbia University Press, 1986.

Jakobson, Roman. "Linguistics and Poetics." In De George and De George 85–122.

———. "Two Aspects of Language and Two Types of Aphasia Disturbances." Part 2 of *Fundamentals of Language,* by Roman Jakobson and Morris Halle. 2d rev. ed. Paris: Mouton, 1971.

James, Henry. "The Art of Fiction." In *"The Art of Fiction" and Other Essays.* New York: Oxford University Press, 1948.

———. *The Art of the Novel: Critical Prefaces.* New York: Scribner, 1962.

Jameson, Fredric. "Flaubert's Libidinal Historicism." In Schor and Majewski 76–83.

———. Foreword. In Lyotard vii–xxi.

———. "Postmodernism and Consumer Society." In Foster 111–25.

———. *The Prison-House of Language.* Princeton: Princeton University Press, 1972.

Jardine, Alice. "Gynesis." *Diacritics* 12 (Summer 1982): 54–65.

———. *Gynesis: Configurations of Woman and Modernity.* Ithaca: Cornell University Press, 1985.

Jardine, Alice, and Paul Smith, eds. *Men in Feminism.* New York: Methuen, 1987.

Jensen, Emily. "Clarissa Dalloway's Respectable Suicide." In Marcus, *Feminist Slant* 162–79.

Johnson, Barbara. *The Critical Difference.* Baltimore: Johns Hopkins University Press, 1980.

———, ed. "The Pedagogical Imperative." Special issue of *Yale French Studies* 63 (1982).

————. *A World of Difference*. Baltimore: Johns Hopkins University Press, 1987.

Johnston, Judith. "The Remediable Flaw: Revisioning Cultural History in *Between the Acts*." In Marcus, *Woolf and Bloomsbury* 253–77.

Johnstone, J. K. *The Bloomsbury Group: A Study of E. M. Forster, Lytton Strachey, Virginia Woolf, and Their Circle*. New York: Noonday Press, 1954.

Kamuf, Peggy. "Penelope at Work: Interruptions in *A Room of One's Own*." *Novel* 16 (Fall 1982): 5–18.

————. "Replacing Feminist Criticism." *Diacritics* 12 (Summer 1982): 42–47.

————. "Writing Like a Woman." In McConnell-Ginet, Borker, and Furman 284–99.

Kaplan, E. Ann. "Feminism/Oedipus/Postmodernism: The Case of MTV." In *Postmodernism and Its Discontents* 30–44.

————, ed. *Postmodernism and Its Discontents: Theories, Practice*. London: Verso, 1988.

Kelley, Alice Van Buren. *The Novels of Virginia Woolf: Fact and Vision*. Chicago: University of Chicago Press, 1973.

Kennard, Jean E. "Ourself behind Ourself: A Theory for Lesbian Readers." In Flynn and Schweickart 63–80.

Kermode, Frank. *The Art of Telling: Essays on Fiction*. Cambridge: Harvard University Press, 1983.

————. *The Sense of an Ending*. New York: Oxford University Press, 1967.

Kiely, Robert, ed. *Modernism Reconsidered*. Cambridge: Harvard University Press, 1983.

King, Merton. "*The Waves* and the Androgynous Mind." *University Review* 30 (December 1963): 128–34.

Kipnis, Laura. "Feminism: The Political Conscience of Post-modernism?" In Ross 149–66.

Kirkpatrick, B. J. *A Bibliography of Virginia Woolf*. 3d ed. Oxford: Clarendon, 1980.

Knopp, Sherron E. "'If I Saw You Would You Kiss Me?': Sapphism and the Subversiveness of Virginia Woolf's *Orlando*." *PMLA* 103.1 (January 1988): 24–34.

Kristeva, Julia. *Desire in Language: A Semiotic Approach to Literature and Art*. Ed. Leon S. Roudiez. Trans. Thomas Gora, Alice Jardine, and Leon S. Roudiez. New York: Columbia University Press, 1980.

————. "Oscillation between Power and Denial." In Marks and de Courtivron 165–67.

————. "Postmodernism?" In Gravin 136–41.

————. *Revolution in Poetic Language*. Trans. Margaret Waller. New York: Columbia University Press, 1984.

Kuhn, Thomas S. *The Structure of Scientific Revolutions*. 2d ed. Chicago: University of Chicago Press, 1970.

Laing, D. A. "An Addendum to the Virginia Woolf Bibliography." *Notes and Queries* 49 (September 1972): 338.

Lanham, Richard. *Literacy and the Survival of Humanism*. New Haven: Yale University Press, 1983.

Leaska, Mitchell. "The Death of Rachel Vinrace." *Bulletin of Research in the Humanities*, Woolf Issue 2 (Autumn 1979): 328–37.

——. *Virginia Woolf's Lighthouse: A Study in Critical Method*. New York: Columbia University Press, 1970.

——. "Virginia Woolf, the Pargeter: A Reading of *The Years*." *Bulletin of the New York Public Library* 80 (Winter 1977): 172–210.

Leavis, F. R. "After *To the Lighthouse*." *Scrutiny* 10 (January 1942): 295–98.

——. "Literature and Society." In *The Norton Anthology of English Literature*. Eds. M. H. Abrams, et al. 4th ed. 2 vols. New York: Norton, 1979. 2:2350–60.

Leavis, Q. D. "Caterpillars of the Commonwealth Unite!" *Scrutiny* 7 (September 1938): 203–14.

Lee, Hermione. *The Novels of Virginia Woolf*. London: Methuen, 1977.

Levenson, Michael. *A Genealogy of Modernism: A Study of English Literary Doctrine, 1908–1922*. Cambridge: Cambridge University Press, 1984.

Levin, Harry. "What Was Modernism?" *Refractions: Essays in Comparative Literature*. New York: Oxford University Press, 1966.

Lewis, Thomas S. W., ed. *Virginia Woolf: A Collection of Criticism*. New York: McGraw-Hill, 1975.

Lilienfeld, Jane. "Where the Spear Plants Grew: The Ramsays' Marriage in *To the Lighthouse*." In Marcus, *New Feminist Essays* 148–69.

Little, Judy. *Comedy and the Woman Writer*. Lincoln: University of Nebraska Press, 1983.

——. "*Jacob's Room* as Comedy: Woolf's Parodic *Bildungsroman*." In Marcus, *New Feminist Essays* 105–24.

Lodge, David. "Historicism and Literary History." In *Working with Structuralism* 68–75.

——. *The Modes of Modern Writing: Metaphor, Metonymy, and the Typology of Modern Literature*. Ithaca: Cornell University Press, 1977.

——. "*The Novelist at the Crossroads*" *and Other Essays on Fiction and Criticism*. Ithaca: Cornell University Press, 1971.

——. *Working with Structuralism: Essays and Reviews on Nineteenth- and Twentieth-Century Literature*. Boston: Routledge & Kegan Paul, 1981.

Love, Jean O. *Worlds in Consciousness: Mythopoetic Thought in the Novels of Virginia Woolf*. Berkeley: University of California Press, 1970.

Lubbock, Percy. *The Craft of Fiction*. New York: J. Cape and H. Smith, 1929.

Lyotard, Jean-François. *The Postmodern Condition: A Report on Knowledge*. Trans. Geoff Bennington and Brian Massumi. Minneapolis: University of Minnesota Press, 1984.

McCaffery, Larry, ed. *Postmodern Fiction: A Bio-Bibliographical Guide*. New York: Greenwood, 1986.

McCallum, Pamela. *Literature and Method: Towards a Critique of I. A. Richards, T. S. Eliot, and F. R. Leavis*. Dublin: Gill and MacMillan, 1983.

McConnell, Frank D. "'Death among the Apple Trees': *The Waves* and the World of Things." In Sprague 117–29.

McConnell-Ginet, Sally, Ruth Borker, and Nelly Furman, eds. *Woman and Language in Literature and Society*. New York: Praeger, 1980.

McGrath, F. D. *The Sensible Spirit: Walter Pater and the Modernist Paradigm*. Tampa: University of South Florida Press, 1986.

McHale, Brian. *Postmodernist Fiction*. New York: Methuen, 1987.

McLaurin, Allen. *Virginia Woolf: The Echoes Enslaved*. Cambridge: Cambridge University Press, 1973.

Majumdar, Robin, and Allen McLaurin, eds. *Virginia Woolf: The Critical Heritage*. London: Routledge & Kegan Paul, 1975.

Manuel, M. "Virginia Woolf as the Common Reader." *Literary Criterion* 7 (Summer 1966): 28–32.

Marcus, Jane. "Enchanted Organs, Magic Bells: *Night and Day* as Comic Opera." In Freedman, *Virginia Woolf* 97–122.

———, ed. *New Feminist Essays on Virginia Woolf*. Lincoln: University of Nebraska Press, 1981.

———. " 'No More Horses': Virginia Woolf on Art and Propaganda." *Women's Studies* 4 (1977): 265–90.

———. "Reappraisal of *The Years*" and "*The Years* as Greek Drama, Domestic Novel, and *Gotterdammerung*." *Bulletin of the New York Public Library* 80 (Winter 1977): 137–39, 276–301.

———. "Still Practice: A/Wrested Alphabet: Toward a Feminist Aesthetic." In Benstock 79–97.

———. "Thinking Back through Our Mothers." In *New Feminist Essays* 1–30.

———, ed. *Virginia Woolf: A Feminist Slant*. Lincoln: University of Nebraska Press, 1983.

———, ed. *Virginia Woolf and Bloomsbury: A Centenary Celebration*. Bloomington: Indiana University Press, 1987.

———. *Virginia Woolf and the Languages of Patriarchy*. Bloomington: Indiana University Press, 1987.

Marder, Herbert. *Feminism and Art: A Study of Virginia Woolf*. Chicago: University of Chicago Press, 1968.

———. "Virginia Woolf's 'System That Did Not Shut Out.' " *Papers on Language and Literature* 4 (1968): 106–11.

Marks, Elaine, and Isabelle de Courtivron, eds. *New French Feminisms*. New York: Schocken Books, 1981.

Martin, Wallace. "Postmodernism: Ultima Thule or Seim Anew?" In Gravin 143–55.

———. *Recent Theories of Narrative*. Ithaca: Cornell University Press, 1986.

May, Keith. "The Symbol of 'Painting' in Virginia Woolf's *To the Lighthouse*." *Review of English Literature* 8 (April 1967): 91–98.

Meisel, Perry. *The Absent Father: Virginia Woolf and Walter Pater*. New Haven: Yale University Press, 1980.

———. *The Myth of the Modern: A Study in British Literature and Criticism after 1850*. New Haven: Yale University Press, 1987.

Mellor, Anne. *English Romantic Irony*. Cambridge: Harvard University Press, 1980.

Mepham, John. "Mourning and Modernism." In Clements and Grundy 137–56.

Messer-Davidow, Ellen. "The Philosophical Bases of Feminist Literary Criticism." *New Literary History* 19 (Autumn 1987): 63–103.

Meyerowitz, Selma. "What Is to Console Us?: The Politics of Deception in Woolf's Short Stories." In Marcus, *New Feminist Essays* 238–52.

Michaels, Walter Benn. "The Interpreter's Self: Peirce on the Cartesian Subject." In Tompkins 185–200.

Middleton, Victoria S. "*The Years:* 'A Deliberate Failure.'" *Bulletin of the New York Public Library* 80 (Winter 1977): 158–71.

Miller, J. Hillis. *Fiction and Repetition.* Cambridge: Harvard University Press, 1982.

———. "The Rhythm of Creativity in *To the Lighthouse.*" In Kiely 167–89.

———. "Virginia Woolf's All Souls' Day: The Omniscient Narrator in *Mrs. Dalloway.*" In Friedman and Vickery 100–127.

Miller, Nancy K. "Emphasis Added: Plots and Plausibilities in Women's Fiction." In Showalter, *New Feminist Criticism* 339–60.

Minow-Pinkney, Makiko. *Virginia Woolf and the Problem of the Subject.* Brighton, U.K.: Harvester, 1987.

Mistacco, Vicki. "The Theory and Practice of Reading *Nouveaux Romans:* Robbe-Grillet's *Topologie d'une cité fantome.*" In Suleiman and Crosman 371–400.

Moers, Ellen. *Literary Women.* New York: Anchor, 1977.

Moi, Toril, ed. *The Kristeva Reader.* New York: Columbia University Press, 1986.

———. *Sexual/Textual Politics: Feminist Literary Theory.* London: Methuen, 1985.

Moore, Madeline. *The Short Season between Two Silences: The Mystical and the Political in the Novels of Virginia Woolf.* Boston: George Allen & Unwin, 1984.

———. "Some Female Versions of Pastoral: *The Voyage Out* and Matriarchal Mythologies." In Marcus, *New Feminist Essays* 82–104.

———. "Virginia Woolf's *The Years* and Years of Adverse Male Reviewers." *Women's Studies* 4 (1977): 247–63.

Morgenstern, Barry S. "The Self-conscious Narrator in *Jacob's Room.*" *Modern Fiction Studies* 18 (Autumn 1972): 351–61.

Mulhern, Francis. *The Moment of 'Scrutiny'.* London: NLB, 1979.

Naremore, James. "Nature and History in *The Years.*" In Freedman, *Virginia Woolf* 241–62.

———. *The World without a Self: Virginia Woolf and the Novel.* New Haven: Yale University Press, 1973.

Newman, Charles. *The Post-modern Aura: The Act of Fiction in an Age of Inflation.* Evanston: Northwestern University Press, 1985.

Noel, Roger. "Nathalie Sarraute's Criticism of Virginia Woolf." *Revue des langues vivantes* 36 (1970): 266–71.

Norris, Christopher. *The Deconstructive Turn: Essays in the Rhetoric of Philosophy.* London: Methuen, 1983.

Novak, Jane. *The Razor Edge of Balance: A Study of Virginia Woolf.* Coral Gables: University of Miami Press, 1978.

Ortega y Gasset, José. *The Dehumanization of Art and Notes on the Novel.* New York: Doubleday, 1948.

Parkes, H. B. "The Tendencies of Bergsonism." *Scrutiny* 4 (March 1936): 407–24.

Pechter, Edward. "The New Historicism and Its Discontents: Politicizing Renaissance Drama." *PMLA* 102 (May 1987): 292–303.

Pederson, Glenn. "Vision in *To the Lighthouse.*" *PMLA* 73 (December 1958): 585–600.

Pratt, Annis. "Sexual Imagery in *To the Lighthouse:* A New Feminist Approach." *Modern Fiction Studies* 18 (Autumn 1972): 417–32.

Pratt, Mary Louise. "Interpretive Strategies/Strategic Interpretations: On Anglo-American Reader-Response Criticism." In Arac 26–54.

Quigley, Austin E. *The Modern Stage and Other Worlds*. New York: Methuen, 1985.
———. *The Pinter Problem*. Princeton: Princeton University Press, 1975.
———. "Wittgenstein's Philosophizing and Literary Theorizing." *New Literary History* 19.2 (Winter 1988): 209–37.
Rabinowitz, Peter. *Before Reading: Narrative Conventions and the Politics of Interpretation*. Ithaca: Cornell University Press, 1987.
Radin, Grace. *Virginia Woolf's "The Years": The Evolution of a Novel*. Knoxville: University of Tennessee Press, 1981.
Radway, Janice. "The Book-of-the-Month Club and the General Reader: On the Uses of 'Serious' Fiction." *Critical Inquiry* 14 (Spring 1988): 516–38.
Raval, Suresh. *Metacriticism*. Athens: University of Georgia Press, 1981.
Richardson, Robert. "Point of View in Virginia Woolf's *The Waves*." *Texas Studies in Language and Literature* 14 (Winter 1973): 691–709.
Richter, Harvena. *Virginia Woolf: The Inward Voyage*. Princeton: Princeton University Press, 1970.
Rigney, Barbara Hill. "Objects of Vision: Women as Art in the Novels of Virginia Woolf." In Beja, *Critical Essays* 239–48.
Robbe-Grillet, Alain. *For a New Novel: Essays on Fiction*. Trans. Richard Howard. New York: Grove, 1965.
Roberts, John. "Vision and Design in Virginia Woolf." *PMLA* 61 (September 1946): 835–47.
Robertson, P. J. M. *The Leavises on Fiction: An Historic Partnership*. New York: St. Martin's, 1981.
Rorty, Richard. *The Consequences of Pragmatism*. Minneapolis: University of Minnesota Press, 1982.
Rose, Phyllis. *Woman of Letters: A Life of Virginia Woolf*. New York: Oxford University Press, 1978.
Rosenbaum, S. P. "The Philosophical Realism of Virginia Woolf." *English Literature and British Philosophy*. Chicago: University of Chicago Press, 1971.
Ross, Andrew, ed. *Universal Abandon? The Politics of Postmodernism*. Minneapolis: University of Minnesota Press, 1988.
Ruddick, Sara. "Private Brother, Public World." In Marcus, *New Feminist Essays* 185–215.
Ruthven, K. K. *Feminist Literary Studies: An Introduction*. Cambridge: Cambridge University Press, 1985.
Said, Edward W. "Opponents, Audiences, Constituencies and Community." In Foster 135–59.
Samuelson, Ralph. "More Than One Room of Her Own: Virginia Woolf's Critical Dilemmas." *Western Humanities Review* 19 (Summer 1965): 249–56.
Sarraute, Nathalie. *The Age of Suspicion*. Trans. Maria Jolas. New York: George Braziller, 1963.
Schlack, Beverly Ann. "Fathers in General: The Patriarchy in Virginia Woolf's Fiction." In Marcus, *Feminist Slant* 52–77.
———. "The Novelist's Voyage from Manuscript to Text: Revisions of Literary Allusions in *The Voyage Out*." *Bulletin of Research in the Humanities*, Woolf Issue 2 (Autumn 1979): 317–27.

———. "Virginia Woolf's Strategy of Scorn in *The Years* and *Three Guineas.*" *Bulletin of the New York Public Library* 80 (Winter 1977): 146–50.

Scholes, Robert. "An Approach through Genre." In Spilka 41–51.

Scholes, Robert, and Robert Kellogg. *The Nature of Narrative.* New York: Oxford University Press, 1966.

Schor, Naomi. "Fiction as Interpretation/Interpretation as Fiction." In Suleiman and Crosman 165–82.

———. *Reading in Detail: Aesthetics and the Feminine.* New York: Methuen, 1987.

Schor, Naomi, and Henry F. Majewski, eds. *Flaubert and Postmodernism.* Lincoln: University of Nebraska Press, 1984.

Schorer, Mark. "New Books in Review." *Yale Review* 32 (December 1941): 377–81.

Schug, Charles. *The Romantic Genesis of the Modern Novel.* Pittsburgh: University of Pittsburgh Press, 1979.

Schweickart, Patrocinio P. "Reading Ourselves: Toward a Feminist Theory of Reading." In Flynn and Schweickart 31–62.

Scott, Bonnie Kime. *Joyce and Feminism.* Bloomington: Indiana University Press; Brighton, U.K.: Harvester, 1984.

Sears, Sallie. "Notes on Sexuality: *The Years* and *Three Guineas.*" *Bulletin of the New York Public Library* 80 (Winter 1977): 211–20.

———. "Theater of War: Virginia Woolf's *Between the Acts.*" In Marcus, *Feminist Slant* 212–35.

Sedgwick, Eve Kosofsky. *Between Men: English Literature and Male Homosocial Desire.* New York: Columbia University Press, 1985.

Sharma, Vijay L. *Virginia Woolf as Literary Critic: A Revaluation.* New Delhi: Arnold-Heinemann, 1977.

Showalter, Elaine. *A Literature of Their Own.* Princeton: Princeton University Press, 1977.

———, ed. *The New Feminist Criticism: Essays on Women, Literature, and Theory.* New York: Pantheon, 1985.

Silver, Brenda, ed. "'Anon' and 'The Reader': Virginia Woolf's Last Essays." *Twentieth-Century Literature* 25 (1979): 356–441.

———. "Virginia Woolf and the Concept of Community: The Elizabethan Playhouse." *Women's Studies* 4 (1977): 291–98.

———, ed. *Virginia Woolf's Reading Notebooks.* Princeton: Princeton University Press, 1983.

Smith, Barbara Herrnstein. "Contingencies of Value." *Critical Inquiry* 10 (Autumn 1983): 1–35.

———. *Contingencies of Value: Alternative Perspectives for Critical Theory.* Cambridge: Harvard University Press, 1988.

———. "Narrative Versions, Narrative Theory." *Critical Inquiry* 7 (Autumn 1980): 213–36.

———. *On the Margins of Discourse: The Relation of Literature to Language.* Chicago: University of Chicago Press, 1978.

Solomon-Godeau, Abigail. "Living with Contradictions: Critical Practices in the Age of Supply-Side Aesthetics." In Ross 191–213.

Sontag, Susan. *"Against Interpretation" and Other Essays*. New York: Farrar, Straus & Giroux, 1966.

Spacks, Patricia Meyer. *The Female Imagination*. New York: Knopf, 1975.

Spilka, Mark, ed. *Towards a Poetics of Fiction*. Bloomington: Indiana University Press, 1977.

Spivak, Gayatri. "Unmaking and Making in *To the Lighthouse*." In McConnell-Ginet, Borker, and Furman 310–27.

Sprague, Clair, ed. *Virginia Woolf: A Collection of Critical Essays*. Englewood Cliffs, N.J.: Prentice Hall, 1971.

Squier, Susan M. "The Politics of City Space in *The Years*." In Marcus, *New Feminist Essays* 216–37.

———. "A Track of Our Own: Typescript Drafts of *The Years*." In Marcus, *Feminist Slant* 198–210.

———. *Virginia Woolf and London: The Sexual Politics of the City*. Chapel Hill: University of North Carolina Press, 1985.

Staten, Henry. *Wittgenstein and Derrida*. Lincoln: University of Nebraska Press, 1984.

———. "Wittgenstein and the Intricate Evasions of 'Is.'" *New Literary History* 19 (Winter 1988): 281–300.

———. "Wittgenstein's Boundaries." *New Literary History* 19 (Winter 1988): 309–18.

Steiner, George. *Language and Silence*. New York: Atheneum, 1967.

Stewart, Jack. "Existence and Symbol in *The Waves*." *Modern Fiction Studies* 18 (Autumn 1972): 433–47.

Stimpson, Catharine. "Nancy Reagan Wears a Hat: Feminism and Its Cultural Consensus." *Critical Inquiry* 14 (Winter 1988): 223–43.

———. *Where the Meanings Are: Feminism and Cultural Spaces*. New York: Methuen, 1988.

Suleiman, Susan R. "Introduction: Varieties of Audience-oriented Criticism. In Suleiman and Crosman 3–45.

Suleiman, Susan R., and Inge Crosman, ed. *The Reader in the Text: Essays on Audience and Interpretation*. Princeton: Princeton University Press, 1980.

Summerhayes, Don. "Society, Morality, Analogy: Virginia Woolf's World between the Acts." *Modern Fiction Studies* 9 (Winter 1963–64): 329–37.

Swingle, L. J. "Virginia Woolf and Romantic Prometheanism." In Gravin 88–105.

Tanner, Tony. *Thomas Pynchon*. London: Methuen, 1982.

Thrall, William Flint, and Addison Hibbard. *A Handbook to Literature*. Rev. and enl. by C. Hugh Holman. New York: Odyssey Press, 1960.

Thiher, Allen. *Words in Reflection: Modern Language Theory and Postmodern Fiction*. Chicago: University of Chicago Press, 1984.

Tompkins, Jane P., ed. *Reader-Response Criticism: From Formalism to Post-Structuralism*. Baltimore: Johns Hopkins University Press, 1980.

Transue, Pamela J. *Virginia Woolf and the Politics of Style*. New York: State University of New York Press, 1986.

Udoff, Alan, ed. *Kafka and the Contemporary Critical Performance: Centenary Readings*. Bloomington: Indiana University Press, 1987.

Walker, Cynthia. "Virginia Woolf's *The Voyage Out:* A Prelude of Images." *Virginia Woolf Quarterly* 3 (1978): 222–29.

Wasson, Richard. "From Priest to Prometheus: Culture and Criticism in the Postmodern Period." *Journal of Modern Literature* 3 (July 1974): 1188–1202.

———. "Notes on a New Sensibility." *Partisan Review* 36 (1969): 460–77.

Waugh, Patricia. *Feminine Fictions: Revisiting the Postmodern.* London: Routledge, 1989.

———. *Metafiction: The Theory and Practice of Self-conscious Fiction.* New York: Methuen, 1984.

West, Cornel. *The American Evasion of Philosophy: A Genealogy of Pragmatism.* Madison: University of Wisconsin Press, 1989.

West, Paul. "Enigmas of Imagination: *Orlando* through the Looking Glass." In Bloom 83–100.

Wexler, Joyce. "Modernist Writers and Publishers." *Studies in the Novel* 17 (Fall 1985): 286–95.

White, Hayden. "The Culture of Criticism." In Hassan, *Liberations* 55–69.

Whitehead, Lee M. "The Shawl and the Skull: Virginia Woolf's 'Magic Mountain.'" *Modern Fiction Studies* 18 (Autumn 1972): 401–16.

Wilkinson, Ann Y. "A Principle of Unity in *Between the Acts.*" In Sprague 145–54.

Wilson, J. J. "Why Is *Orlando* Difficult?" In Marcus, *New Feminist Essays* 170–84.

Wittgenstein, Ludwig. *The Blue and Brown Books.* New York: Harper & Row, 1965.

———. *Culture and Value.* Ed. G. H. Von Wright and Heikki Nyman. Trans. Peter Winch. Chicago: University of Chicago Press, 1980.

———. *On Certainty.* Ed. G. E. M. Anscombe and G. H. Von Wright. Trans. Denis Paul and G. E. M. Anscombe. New York: J & J Harper, 1969.

———. *Philosophical Investigations.* Trans. G. E. M. Anscombe. New York: Macmillan, 1953.

Zimmerman, Bonnie. "Feminist Fiction and the Postmodern Challenge." In McCaffery 175–88.

Zwerdling, Alex. *Virginia Woolf and the Real World.* Berkeley: University of California Press, 1986.

# Index

Page numbers in **boldface** indicate detailed
discussion of individual works.

# A Note on the Author

PAMELA L. CAUGHIE received her Ph.D. in 1988 from the University of Virginia and is a member of the English department faculty at Loyola University of Chicago. Her essays on Virginia Woolf have appeared in two collections, *Discontented Discourses: Feminism/Textual Intervention/Psychoanalysis* and *Writing the Woman Artist,* and in *Women's Studies* and *Tulsa Studies in Women's Literature.*